P9-AGS-422

Gotcha Again for Guys!

Gotcha Again for Guys!

More Nonfiction Books to Get Boys Excited about Reading

**Kathleen A. Baxter and
Marcia Agness Kochel**

LIBRARIES UNLIMITED

AN IMPRINT OF ABC-CLIO, LLC
Santa Barbara, California • Denver, Colorado • Oxford, England

Library of Congress Cataloging-in-Publication Data

Baxter, Kathleen A.
  Gotcha again for guys! : more nonfiction books to get boys excited about reading /
Kathleen A. Baxter and Marcia Agness Kochel.
    p. cm.
  Includes bibliographical references and indexes.
  ISBN 978-1-59884-376-7 (pbk. : acid-free paper) — ISBN 978-1-59884-377-4 (ebook)
 1. Boys—Books and reading—United States. 2. Children's literature, American—Bibliography.
 3. Book talks—United States. I. Kochel, Marcia Agness. II. Title.
 Z1039.B67B38 2010
 028.5'5—dc22   2010036577

ISBN: 978-1-59884-376-7
EISBN: 978-1-59884-377-4

14 13 12 11 10   1 2 3 4 5

This book is also available on the World Wide Web as an eBook.
Visit www.abc-clio.com for details.

Libraries Unlimited
An Imprint of ABC-CLIO, LLC

ABC-CLIO, LLC
130 Cremona Drive, P.O. Box 1911
Santa Barbara, California 93116-1911

This book is printed on acid-free paper ∞
Manufactured in the United States of America

Contents

List of Figures

Introduction

We are back again with booktalks and booklists of nonfiction with guy appeal. It's a hot topic right now, and thank heaven for that. Many experts are warning us that our educational system is often failing boys. The library profession and elementary schools are populated mostly by women—and a lot of women seem to have a problem with the topics that interest many boys.

Women need to get over the "ick" factor. Let's face it, adult men do not often read the same books that adult women read. Boys will grow up into men who read different things than a typical woman might read. There's a big difference, and we need to acknowledge and respect that difference. Let us make sure our classroom and library collections have plenty of guy appeal—and make sure that boys know that we have high-interest materials.

I've been giving seminars on boys and reading for years and have accumulated a few tips that I'd like to share:

- Book clubs are all the rage, as we know, and that's good news. How about starting one about gross and disgusting books? Think outside the box to see if you can attract a nontraditional audience. Also consider a "Bookclub in a Bag" program like the one at the Mid-Hudson Library System (http://midhudson.org/program/BCB/staff.htm). Their kits include ten books and a discussion guide.

- Consider making a PowerPoint slideshow on CD or DVD that will highlight new titles available in your library or media center. We know we will never be able to place every appealing book face out on the shelves. Think of how cool it would be to sit down in front of a computer with a slideshow, all books numbered to make requesting them easier, and note that the library has books on all sorts of intriguing topics. Make copies and give them to every classroom. This is a great volunteer project. Publishers do not at all object to our use of book covers for in-house promotion. Better yet, use a digital picture frame at the checkout desk to show off those book covers.

- Contact local reenactor groups at historic sites in your area. Many of these people would be delighted to do programs, frequently for nothing. For example, have a Civil War program in which the reenactor tells stories, drills the audience of kids, and talks about the Civil War—or any other historical events in your area. You surely will have a supply of books to display and booktalks that go along with your topic.

- Take a look at storytubes—the YouTube of kids promoting books to other kids (www.storytubes.info/drupal).

- Initiate a program to teach older kids, including babysitters, to read to younger ones. Schools can do kids a great favor by recruiting older boys to read to younger boys.

- Public librarians: Find out which schools in your area have Title I programs. Contact the coordinator. The schools must do evening programs that include parents and families of their students. I have done a lot of these. You get to read a story, booktalk some books that will get them excited about checking out books, and promote the heck out of the library. Be dramatic and bring out your wild side. If you are good, they will ask you back and tell every other Title I program to invite you. Just like us, they want free programs. Nobody has any money.

- Ditto for school and classroom visits. Offer to visit classes to promote books and the library. Again, be dramatic and exciting. They will beg you to come at least every year. A young Canadian librarian told me she tells teachers she will bring books that she *guarantees* boys will want to read. She is stunned at how well books on "boy topics" work in not only getting them excited in the classroom, but straight into the public library.

- Set up a program to teach adults about reading to groups of kids. Grandpas often have free time, and boys are in dire need of male reading models. As we all know from bitter experience, bombing while reading to children is not fun. Start a program in which you model reading aloud and they practice in front of each other. Pick a selection of surefire read-aloud winners. Call the schools and alert them to the availability of trained people in the community to read to kids, or ask the readers to volunteer to read in the library.

- Public libraries: Promote a "good book" consultation service. Most people need help in finding books their children will really enjoy. Make sure the staff who are working on the desk know the collection well. Make a sign that says, "Children's Book Expert Available to Help You Pick Out Books You Will Enjoy!"

- Traditional programs, author visits, storytimes, and summer reading programs have always worked well and continue to do so. So many programs for children require adults to transport them. I feel one of the best things we can do is reach out to adults. Ask to speak to any women's or church groups in your area about some of the wonderful children's books in the library.

- Children need to see that reading is an important part of life. If an adult is seen reading regularly, then it is! If not, it must not be. Read. Talk about what you read. Kids need to know that we consider reading fun. A lot of them today consider reading only for work.

- With boys in the 'tween years, the highest quality book is not the issue. The issue is finding books they will actually read.

- Never tell a boy in any way, verbally or in body language, that the books he likes are bad and that the books girls like are good.

- Kids need our permission to read easy books. Include plenty of easier books in your booktalks.

- In a recent study, reluctant readers indicated that they only liked to read when they got to pick whatever they want to read. *Let them choose!* Encourage everyone to let that happen.

- Studies show that reading comprehension is related to a reader's interest in the topic. Interested readers can comprehend materials normally considered to be beyond their reading level.

- Boys are less likely to talk about or overtly respond to their reading than girls are. But they *love* information that exports readily to conversation—that they can repeat to other people. This is one reason that nonfiction works well.

- Leonard Saxe recommends that you recommend books to a boy conversationally, side by side, standing next to each other, rather than confrontationally, face to face. "And look at *this* picture!"

- Keep a list in a prominent place of the most popular books in your library or media center. Create buzz so you get a waiting list. Hey, that's a goal!

- If you are a school librarian, take over the teachers' suggestions and recommendations for summer reading for their classes. Tell them you will remove any books that are outdated, out of print for ages, and no longer available. The resulting list, which can be consolidated, of course, will be a lot more viable than a list that includes mostly out-of-print books. Include an extra statement: If nothing on this list looks good to you, ask at your library or bookstore for a book you might like. Wouldn't it be great if the public library sent out a list of high-interest books that they have available to add to the school list?

We wish you well in your continuing efforts to get those guys reading, and we hope this book will be helpful.

Kathleen A. Baxter

Chapter 1

Sports

It's a given that many boys play sports, watch sports, and want to know more about sports. As teachers and librarians we want to take that natural interest and use it to motivate them to read for information and enjoyment. So how do we get them to read about sports? Fill the shelves with up-to-date information about the sports they like best. Take a look at the titles in this chapter. It's full of books about contemporary sports stars and teams as well as some unexpected titles about horse racing, rodeos, ninjas, and more. Use it as a guide for locating well-reviewed titles that boys will love.

BOOKTALKS

Cook, Sally, and James Charlton. *Hey Batta Batta Swing! The Wild Old Days of Baseball.* Illustrated by Ross MacDonald. Margaret K. McElderry Books, 2007. ISBN 141691207X. 48 p. Grades 3–5.

They say that baseball is the great American pastime, and although it has been around for well over 100 years, it was not always the same as it is today. This book is a really fun look at the way baseball used to be. Here are some examples:

- In an early rule, any runner who was not on a base could be put out immediately by being hit with a ball. The thrower could just throw the ball straight at him. You can get hurt that way!

- In early games, the teams all wore the same color clothes. You could not tell which side was which. By 1883 the team owners had decided that the colors of the teams' stockings would be chosen by the baseball Leagues. In Boston the team had to wear red stockings, and in Chicago they had to wear white socks. Does anyone know what that still means today? (Their names became the Red Sox and the White Sox.)

- Originally, players did not have numbers on their uniforms. In fact, when the owners started putting numbers on the uniforms, they players said they felt like convicts!

- The 1928 New York Yankees were sometimes called "Murderer's Row"—partly because they had great players like Babe Ruth and Lou Gehrig on the team.

- The Brooklyn Dodgers got their name because their fans had to dodge trolleys on the streets to get to the games. Their fans were called "Trolley Dodgers." When they needed a name for the team, there it was.

This is a great book, with funny and colorful illustrations.

Crowe, Ellie. *Surfer of the Century: The Life of Duke Kahanamoku*. Illustrations by Richard Waldrep. Lee & Low Books, 2007. ISBN 9781584302766. Unpaged. Grades 3–6.

Duke Kahanamoku had a lot of strikes against him. He was born in Hawaii in 1890, and he was Hawaiian. His skin was dark. That meant a lot of people didn't think too much of him—he could not possibly be as good as they thought they were.

Duke did not do well in school, but in the ocean he was amazing. He had big hands and big feet and he could swim impossibly fast. In 1911 a Honolulu attorney who liked swimming offered to coach Duke. Duke took him up on it and began to show the world what he could do. He qualified for the Olympic tryouts. He broke world records! But getting to those tryouts posed another problem. Duke's family was poor, and he could not afford the expensive trip to the mainland.

But others could help him to get there, and they did—and he proved to them that their faith in him was more than justified. Duke officially became the fastest swimmer in the world when he won the Gold Medal.

And of course he also was one of the main athletes who popularized surfing. He was a gifted man with a wonderful story. You will enjoy reading about him.

Lewin, Ted. *At Gleason's Gym* (Neal Porter Books). Roaring Brook Press, 2007. ISBN 9781596432314. Unpaged. Grades 1–4.

Gleason's gym in Brooklyn, New York, is the most famous boxing gym in the world. Boxers such as Muhammad Ali have trained there. But not everyone who trains there is a famous boxer or wrestler. Some are kids, ordinary kids, boys and girls both, who are learning to fight.

This book focuses on one of them, a real kid named Sugar Boy Younan, who starts coming to the gym when he is two years old. He trains hard, six days a week, with his dad, who is a professional fighter and his coach.

Sugar Boy is good—really good. At the end of the book we learn that he became the National Silver Gloves Champion, 110-Pound Bantam Weight Division, in 2006.

If you like boxing, and you like gyms and reading about the people who work out there—plus great pictures—you will enjoy this book.

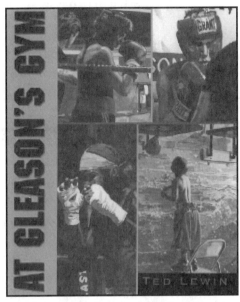

At Gleason's Gym by Ted Lewin. Jacket shown with permission from Roaring Brook Press.

Nelson, Kadir. *We Are the Ship: The Story of Negro Leagues Baseball*. Words and paintings by Kadir Nelson. Foreword by Hank Aaron. Jump at the Sun/Hyperion, 2008. ISBN 9780786808328. 88 p. Grades 5–up.

Wow! This is a wonderful book!

Have you ever heard of the Negro Leagues? Did you know that African Americans were pretty much not welcome at all in major Leagues sports before Jackie Robinson broke through the color barrier and joined the Brooklyn Dodgers in 1947? Do you know why?

Some of the African Americans who never played in the major Leagues may have been better than the best. They had to play in their own Leagues, the Negro Leagues, where the pay was a lot lower; they had to play multiple games in a day with smaller teams; and they often did not get to sleep in a bed, but rather crowded in a car or a beater of a bus. But they got to play. And almost every Negro Leagues player loved to play.

This book tells the story of how those Leagues got started, how they worked, and also some of the famous players.

"We played a different brand of baseball from the majors. Negro baseball was fast! Flashy! Daring! Sometimes it was even funny. But always very exciting to watch. People would come early to the ballpark just to see us practice. We would whip that ball around the infield with such precision, they'd applaud" (page 17).

Negro Leagues teams had many firsts—including the first night game, played with lights. Not very good lights, but, still, they played at night!

They had Satchel Paige, who may be the greatest baseball player of all time. He was a pitcher who could strike out almost anyone. They had Cool Papa Bell, who was the fastest man in baseball. He could circle the bases in twelve or thirteen seconds. Try that sometime!

You will have so much fun reading about these incredible people who had so much against them—and who managed to succeed in spite of it all.

Author Profile: Kadir Nelson

Kadir Nelson knew he wanted to be an artist from a very young age but didn't consider book illustration until actress and dancer Debbie Allen asked him to illustrate her book, *Dancing in the Wings*. Since then he has illustrated numerous award-winning children's books. He made his debut as an author with *We Are the Ship: The Story of Negro Leagues Baseball* and won both the Sibert Medal and a Coretta Scott King Book Award.

You worked on *We Are the Ship* for eight years. What was the process?

At first I wasn't working on a book, I was just working on paintings because I was really inspired to create artwork around the Negro Leagues. Then someone asked if I was interested in making it into a book, so then I went about trying to find an editor or a publisher who was willing to publish the book and I landed at Disney. So first I did a number of paintings and then I found the publisher. Then I started writing and put the paintings away for a while. Then when I was finished with a draft or two, I started to paint again. I couldn't do both at the same time.

How did you do your research?

I started by reading the book *Baseball* by Ken Burns, which was also a documentary. Then I started to read a lot of books on the Negro Leagues. Then I found a former Negro Leagues player here in San Diego by the name of Walt McCoy, and he was an invaluable resource because he has a very sharp mind and a very sharp memory. Later I interviewed some other players. So the book is based on my readings and my interviews.

How did you decide on your narrator's voice?

I felt it was most interesting to hear history from someone who lived it, to hear it in the first person. A lot of the interviews I read were direct interviews, and these people were speaking in that voice—"We did this," "I did that," "I remember this."

It was so much more interesting than reading rote facts in a textbook. So I thought it was a really great way to introduce this piece of history to a younger audience. It's kind of like a little kid listening to his grandfather talk about what it was like for him when he played baseball when he was in the prime of his life.

Before *We are the Ship*, did you know that you could write?

I don't know if I'm a good writer. I had a really good editor. I never really thought of myself as being any kind of a writer. I just knew how I wanted to tell this story. It was really difficult for me to tell an established writer what to write and how to write it because I knew how I wanted it to sound. So I just asked my editors if it was OK if I tried my hand at it and they were good enough to let me give it a try.

Do you plan to write more books?

I'm actually working on another book with the same editor on American history, so it's a much broader topic. But it's really interesting because I really wanted to learn more about American history—more than I learned in school.

Do you write with boys in mind? Do you write with African American children in mind?

It's more of a general audience. I don't know if I can write thinking about a specific audience. I just want to tell the story in a competent way.

Is writing and illustrating the books you do something of a mission for you?

I don't think it's really a mission. It's just part of what I do. I tell stories with words and pictures. I'm primarily an artist, but it's nice to be able to use a different part of my brain to tell stories. It's a different process, but I really enjoy it.

Paulsen, Gary. *How Angel Peterson Got His Name and Other Outrageous Tales about Extreme Sports.* Wendy Lamb Books, 2003. ISBN 0385900902. 111 p. Grades 4–8.

Gary Paulsen tells us right at the beginning of this funny book that he was a kid a long time ago. He tells us to remember two important facts:

"1. We were quite a bit dumber then.

"2. There wasn't any safety gear" (page xiiii).

And then he tells us some of the incredibly stupid and dangerous things that he and some of his friends did.

One of his friends hears that the world's fastest skier went over 74 miles an hour. He is sure he can break that record. All he has to do is buy a pair of used skis and then get someone in a very fast car to let him tie himself to that car—and then the car has to go faster than 74 miles an hour. Man, he will set the new record. He will be famous! What can possibly go wrong with a plan like that?

You will find out—with that and other plans, such as going over a waterfall in a barrel, gliding with a kite, and fighting a bear, among others. You will be laughing out loud as you read these very funny true stories.

Sandler, Michael. *Manny Ramirez and the Boston Red Sox: 2004 World Series* (World Series Superstars). Bearport Publishing, 2008. ISBN 9781597166287. 24 p. Grades 2–5.

In 2004 the Boston Red Sox had not won a World Series in 86 years. Some people thought they would never win another one. But one of their players did a lot to make their dream come true. His name was Manny Ramirez, and he was born and spent the first 13 years of his life in the Dominican Republic. Then he moved to New York City. He played baseball in high school, and his coach said he was the hardest worker he ever had. After high school, the Cleveland Indians drafted him and he spent two years playing in the minors before he moved into the major Leagues. And there he did good! He drove home more than 160 runners in one season, the first player to do that in over 60 years!

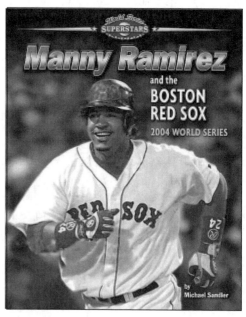

Manny Ramirez and the Boston Red Sox: 2004 World Series **by Michael Sandler.**

In 2000 he joined the Red Sox. He thought they could win the World Series, and he was right. Read all about how he became the most valuable player in the 2004 World Series.

Smith, Charles R., Jr. *Twelve Rounds to Glory: The Story of Muhammad Ali.* Illustrated by Bryan Collier. Candlewick Press, 2007. ISBN 9780763616922. 80 p. Grades 4–9.

Cassius Marcellus Clay started fighting when he was twelve years old. Somebody stole his bike. He found a cop and told him he was going to whip whoever it was stole his bike—and the cop told him he had to learn to fight and started teaching him how.

Cassius turned out to be an excellent student. He got to be such an incredible boxer that six years later he won the Gold Medal in the 1960 Olympics.

Then he became a professional boxer. He knew he was really good, and he did not mind telling everyone else that he was good too. He bragged all the time, and that drove some people crazy. In 1964 he became the world heavyweight champion when he knocked out Sonny Liston. In the ring, he said

> I am the greatest!
> I shook up the world!
> I don't have a mark on my face!
> I'm pretty.
> I'm a bad man!
> You must listen to me!
> I can't be beat!
> I'm the prettiest thing that ever lived. (page 18)

And then he changed his name to Muhammad Ali. He had become a devout Muslim and he said Cassius Clay was a slave name, so he got rid of it.

And he went on to fight and fight and get into trouble when he refused to go fight a war he wanted no part of in a faraway country called Vietnam. They told him he could no longer be champion if he would not be a soldier—and he fought that, too.

Muhammad Ali always said what he believed, and this is his story, told in a long and wonderful poem with great colorful illustrations.

Sturm, James, and Rich Tommaso. *Satchel Paige: Striking Out Jim Crow*. Jump at the Sun/Hyperion, 2007. ISBN 0786839007. 90 p. Grades 5–9.

If you have never heard of Satchel Paige, you are missing something pretty amazing. Satchel Paige may have been the greatest baseball player that ever lived. But a lot of people do not know his name because he was African American, and he was not allowed to play in Major Leagues baseball until he was 42 years old—an age when most baseball players have already retired.

He was born around 1905, and he was unbelievably good. But he did more than just prove how good Satchel Paige was. He helped his people, the poor African Americans who loved him and who loved to watch him play in the Negro Leagues. He made a lot of money compared to most, but he traveled hard and suffered a lot of discrimination and abuse.

This tells us the story of one young man, who gets struck out by Satchel in his fist big game—and also hurts his knee badly in that game, so badly that he cannot play anymore. It tells what his life was like and how Satchel Paige made his life a little happier, a little better—and a lot more hopeful.

This is a graphic novel. If you like comic books, go for it. You'll have a great time and you will learn just enough about Satchel to make you want to know a lot, lot more.

Sullivan, George. *Knockout! A Photobiography of Boxer Joe Louis*. National Geographic, 2009. ISBN 9781426303289. 64 p. Grades 4–8.

When Joe Louis started his career as a boxer in the 1930s, discrimination against African Americans was just the way it was. They got the jobs no one else wanted, they had few opportunities, and laws of segregation made inequality the way they had to live. Even in sports they had few opportunities. Professional football, baseball, and basketball teams refused to let African Americans play in the big Leagues.

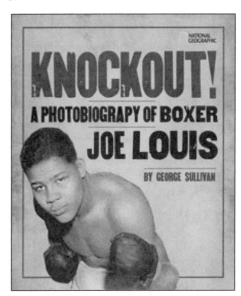

Knockout! A Photobiography of Boxer Joe Louis by George Sullivan.

Only in boxing, for some reason, were African Americans given an opportunity. And Joe Louis grabbed that opportunity and ran with it.

He had not seen much opportunity anywhere else. He grew up in the deep South, the child of a father whose own father was a slave. His parents were sharecroppers, which many people considered basically a legalized form of slavery. Joe was born in

1914 and lived in Alabama until he was 12. That's when his family moved to Detroit, where life was a lot better—until the Great Depression made life harder for nearly everybody.

But a friend of his from school invited Joe to go to a gym with him and box—and Joe was astounding. He turned out to be really good at it, and he was willing to work extremely hard to get better.

This is the story of the first African American cultural hero in America, a man who earned the respect and affection of many Americans.

Winter, Jonah. *Muhammad Ali: Champion of the World*. Illustrated by François Roca. Schwartz & Wade, 2008. ISBN 9780375836220. Unpaged. Grades 3–6.

It all started with Jack Johnson. He was black and he was proud, and white people did not like that. It didn't help that he was the best boxer in the world.

Then came Joe Louis, another great boxer. Then Sonny Liston. And then a young man named Cassius Clay, who vowed he would be the greatest ever. "Then he talked and jived and practiced and punched his way to victory, until he had won the Olympic Gold Medal."

Finally he got to fight the heavyweight champion, Sonny Liston, and he told him right then and there that he was going to beat him. And he did just that.

And now it was time to change his name. Cassius Clay, he said, was a slave name. He had become a Muslim, and now he had a Muslim name: Muhammad Ali.

And many African Americans loved him. But others were not so sure.

This is the poetic, true story of the man many believe was the greatest boxer in the history of the world. It is a fine read.

Winter, Jonah. *You Never Heard of Sandy Koufax?* Illustrated by Jonah Winter. Schwartz & Wade, 2009. ISBN 9780375837388. Unpaged. Grades 2–5.

Do you like baseball? Have you ever heard of Sandy Koufax? If you haven't, listen to what the author of this book, Jonah Winter, has to say to you: "You gotta be kidding! You never heard of Sandy Koufax?! He was only the greatest lefty who ever pitched in the game of baseball."

So maybe you ought to find out about him—and he was one interesting guy, and being the greatest lefty who ever pitched was not easy. But boy, was he good. A player on an opposing team said, "Hittin' a Koufax fastball was like trying to drink coffee with a fork."

Sandy grew up Jewish in Brooklyn, and he was a whiz at sports. Major Leagues scouts came to take a look at him. When he was only 19 years old, he was signed by the Brooklyn Dodgers. But all he did at first was sit on the bench, and he just hated it. He had to get off that bench!

Read the story of how he did it and what happened.

WORTH READING

Nonfiction books with "boy appeal" that have received positive reviews in *Booklist*, *Horn Book Guide*, and/or *School Library Journal*.

Aretha, David. *America's Team—the Dallas Cowboys* (Sensational Sports Teams). Enslow, 2007. ISBN 1598450468. 128 p. Grades 4–7.

Aretha, David. *Dodger Blue—the Los Angeles Dodgers* (Sensational Sports Teams). Enslow, 2007. ISBN 159845045X. 128 p. Grades 4–7.

Aretha, David. *Power in Pinstripes—the New York Yankees: The New York Yankees* (Sensational Sports Teams). Enslow, 2007. ISBN 1598450441. 128 p. Grades 4–7.

Aretha, David. *Tiki Barber* (Football Superstars). Chelsea House, 2008. ISBN 9780791098363. 136 p. Grades 6–up.

Aylmore, Angela. *I Like Soccer* (Things I Like). Heinemann, 2007. ISBN 140-3492662. 24 p. Grades K–2.

Barber, Tiki, and Ronde Barber. *Kickoff!* Simon & Schuster, 2007. ISBN 978-1416936183. 160 p. Grades 4–6.

Basen, Ryan. *Steve Nash: Leader On and Off the Court* (Sports Stars With Heart). Enslow, 2007. ISBN 0766028682. 128 p. Grades 5–8.

Becker, Helaine. *Skateboarding Science* (Sports Science). Crabtree Publishing, 2009. ISBN 9780778745365. 32 p. Grades 3–5.

Berman, Len. *And Nobody Got Hurt 2! The World's Weirdest, Wackiest Most Amazing True Sports Stories*. Little, Brown, 2007. ISBN 9780316067065. 136 p. Grades 3–7.

Berman, Len. *Greatest Moments in Sports*. Sourcebooks/Jabberwocky, 2009. ISBN 9781402218576. 368 p. Grades 6–9.

Bodden, Valerie. *Hiking* (Active Sports). Creative Education, 2009. ISBN 978-1583416983. 24 p. Grades K–1.

Bodden, Valerie. *Kayaking* (Active Sports). Creative Education, 2009. ISBN 978-1583416990. 24 p. Grades K–1.

Bodden, Valerie. *Running* (Active Sports). Creative Education, 2009. ISBN 978-1583417003. 24 p. Grades K–3.

Bodden, Valerie. *Scuba Diving* (Active Sports). Creative Education, 2009. ISBN 978-1583417010. 24 p. Grades K–3.

Booth, Tanis. *Football* (In the Zone). Weigl Publishers, 2009. ISBN 9781605961262. 24 p. Grades 4–7.

Boudreau, Helene. *Swimming Science* (Sports Science). Crabtree Publishing, 2009. ISBN 9780778745389. 32 p. Grades 3–5.

Bow, James. *Baseball Science* (Sports Science). Crabtree Publishing, 2009. ISBN 9780778745341. 32 p. Grades 3–5.

Bow, Patricia. *Tennis Science* (Sports Science). Crabtree Publishing, 2009. ISBN 9780778745396. 32 p. Grades 3–5.

Bowen, Fred. *No Easy Way: The Story of Ted Williams and the Last .400 Season*. Illustrated by Charles S. Pyle. Dutton Children's Books, 2010. ISBN 9780525478775. 32 p. Grades 1–3.

Brown, Monica. *Pele, King of Soccer/Pele, el Rey del Futbol*. Rayo, 2009. ISBN 9780061227790. 40 p. Grades 1–3.

Bruning, Matt. *Sports Picture Puzzles*. Capstone Press, 2009. ISBN 9781429632904. 32 p. Grades K–3.

Buckley, James, Jr. *American Leagues East* (Behind the Plate). Child's World, 2007. ISBN 1592968384. 48 p. Grades 4–6.

Buckley, James, Jr. *Pele* (DK Biography). DK, 2007. ISBN 9780756629878. 128 p. Grades 6–9.

Burgan, Michael. *Muhammad Ali: American Champion* (Graphic Biographies). Graphic Library, 2007. ISBN 1429601531. 32 p. Grades 2–6.

Casil, Amy Sterling. *Tony Hawk* (Super Skateboarding). Rosen, 2009. ISBN 9781435853911. 48 p. Grades 5–7.

Cefrey, Holly. *Competitive Skateboarding* (Super Skateboarding). Rosen, 2009. ISBN 9781435850507. 48 p. Grades 5–7.

Clendening, John. *American Leagues West* (Behind the Plate). Child's World, 2007. ISBN 1592968392. 48 p. Grades 4–6.

Cline-Ransome, Lesa, and James Ransome. *Young Pele: Soccer's First Star*. Schwartz & Wade, 2007. ISBN 9780375835995. 40 p. Grades K–4.

Cobb, Allan B. *Skating the X Games* (Super Skateboarding). Rosen, 2009. ISBN 9781435850484. 48 p. Grades 5–7.

Collins, Tracy Brown. *Babe Ruth* (Baseball Superstars). Chelsea House, 2008. ISBN 9780791095706. 122 p. Grades 5–up.

Crompton, Samuel Willard. *Barry Sanders* (Football Superstars). Chelsea House, 2008. ISBN 9780791096673. 120 p. Grades 6–up.

Crompton, Samuel Willard. *John Elway* (Football Superstars). Chelsea House, 2008. ISBN 9780791096048. 152 p. Grades 5–up.

Crompton, Samuel Willard. *Peyton Manning* (Football Superstars). Chelsea House, 2008. ISBN 9780791096055. 152 p. Grades 5–up.

Crossingham, John. *Spike It Volleyball* (Sports Starters). Crabtree Publishing, 2008. ISBN 9780778731436. 32 p. Grades 1–4.

Doeden, Matt. *The Greatest Baseball Records* (Edge Books). Capstone Press, 2008. ISBN 9781429620055. 32 p. Grades 4–9.

Doeden, Matt. *The Greatest Basketball Records* (Edge Books). Capstone Press, 2008. ISBN 9781429620062. 32 p. Grades 4–9.

Doeden, Matt. *The Greatest Hockey Records* (Edge Books). Capstone Press, 2008. ISBN 9781429620086. 32 p. Grades 4–9.

Doeden, Matt. *Jeff Gordon* (Blazers). Capstone Press, 2008. ISBN 9781429619769. 32 p. Grades 3–6.

Doeden, Matt. *Jimmie Johnson* (Blazers). Capstone Press, 2008. ISBN 9781429619776. 32 p. Grades 3–6.

Doeden, Matt. *Kasey Kahne* (Blazers). Capstone Press, 2008. ISBN 9781429619806. 32 p. Grades 3–6.

Dougherty; Terri. *The Greatest Football Records* (Edge Books). Capstone Press, 2008. ISBN 9781429620079. 32 p. Grades 4–9.

Drevitch, Gary. *Baseball! Q&A.* Collins, 2007. ISBN 0060899476. 48 p. Grades 2–4.

Eck, Ed. *Baseball in the American Leagues West Division* (Inside Major Leagues Baseball). Rosen, 2009. ISBN 9781435850415. 48 p. Grades 5–7.

Eck, Ed. *Baseball in the National Leagues Central Division* (Inside Major Leagues Baseball). Rosen, 2009. ISBN 9781435850453. 48 p. Grades 5–7.

Eck, Ed. *Baseball in the National Leagues West Division* (Inside Major Leagues Baseball). Rosen, 2009. ISBN 9781435850446. 48 p. Grades 5–7.

Ellenport, Craig. *Ladainian Tomlinson: All-Pro On and Off the Field* (Sports Stars With Heart). Enslow, 2006. ISBN 0766028208. 128 p. Grades 5–up.

Fischer, David. *American Leagues Central* (Behind the Plate). Child's World, 2007. ISBN 1592968376. 48 p. Grades 4–6.

Franks, Katie. *I Want to Be a Baseball Player* (Dream Jobs). PowerKids Press, 2007. ISBN 9781404236226. 24 p. Grades 2–4.

Gifford, Clive. *Basketball* (Personal Best). PowerKids Press, 2008. ISBN 978-1404244436. 32 p. Grades 4–8.

Gifford, Clive. *Martial Arts Legends* (Crabtree Contact). Crabtree Publishing, 2009. ISBN 9780778737988. 32 p. Grades 3–4.

Gifford, Clive. *Soccer* (Personal Best). PowerKids Press, 2008. ISBN 978-1404244412. 32 p. Grades 4–8.

Gifford, Clive. *Swimming* (Personal Best). PowerKids Press, 2008. ISBN 978-1404244436. 32 p. Grades 4–8.

Gifford, Clive. *Track and Field* (Personal Best). PowerKids Press, 2008. ISBN 9781404244429. 32 p. Grades 4–8.

Gifford, Clive. *Track Athletics* (Know Your Sport). Sea to Sea Publications, 2008. ISBN 9781597711548. 32 p. Grades 4–8.

Gifford, Clive. *Tennis* (Personal Best). PowerKids Press, 2008. ISBN 978-1597711531. 32 p. Grades 4–8.

Gigliotti, Jim. *National Leagues West* (Behind the Plate). Child's World, 2007. ISBN 1592968422. 48 p. Grades 4–6.

Gilbert, Sara. *The Story of the Detroit Tigers* (The Story of the). Creative Education, 2007. ISBN 9781583414873. 48 p. Grades K–4.

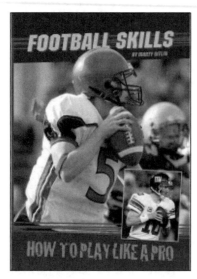

***Football Skills: How to Play
Like a Pro* by Marty Gitlin.**

Gitlin, Marty. *Football Skills: How to Play Like a Pro.* Enslow, 2008. ISBN 9780766032033. 48 p. Grades 4–6.

Gitlin, Marty. *Shaun White: Snow and Skateboard Champion* (Hot Celebrity Biographies). Enslow, 2009. ISBN 9780766032125. 48 p. Grades 5–8.

Glaser, Jason. *Ninja* (Edge Books). Capstone Press, 2006. ISBN 0736864326. 32 p. Grades 3–5.

Goldish, Meish. *Michael Phelps: Anything Is Possible!* (Defining Moments). Bearport Publishing, 2009. ISBN 9781597168557. 32 p. Grades 2–4.

Goodman, Michael E. *Montreal Canadiens* (The NHL: History and Heroes). Creative Education, 2008. ISBN 9781583416181. 42 p. Grades 4–6.

Goodman, Michael E. *The Story of the New York Rangers* (The NHL: History and Heros). Creative Education, 2008. ISBN 9781583416198. 48 p. Grades 4–6.

Hampton, Wilborn. *Babe Ruth* (UpClose). Viking, 2009. ISBN 9780670063055. 208 p. Grades 6–9.

Hanel, Rachel. *Samurai* (Fearsome Fighters). Creative Education, 2007. ISBN 9781583415382. 48 p. Grades 5–8.

Hasan, Heather. *Skateboarding Today and Tomorrow* (Super Skateboarding). Rosen, 2009. ISBN 9781435850491. 48 p. Grades 5–7.

Hasday, Judy L. *Tiger Woods: Athlete* (Black Americans of Achievement). Chelsea House, 2008. ISBN 9780791097144. 95 p. Grades 6–up.

Hatton, Caroline. *The Night Olympic Team: Fighting to Keep Drugs Out of the Games.* Boyds Mills, 2008. ISBN 9781590785669. 56 p. Grades 5–8.

Hill, Christine M. *Lance Armstrong: Cycling, Surviving, Inspiring Hope* (People to Know Today). Enslow, 2008. ISBN 0766026949. 128 p. Grades 4–7.

Hillstrom, Laurie Collier. *Pele: Soccer Superstar* (The Twentieth Century's Most Influential Hispanics). Lucent Books, 2007. ISBN 9781420500233. 104 p. Grades 7–up.

Hocking, Justin. *World's Greatest Skate Parks* (Super Skateboarding). Rosen, 2009. ISBN 9781435850460. 48 p. Grades 5–7.

Hofstetter, Adam. *Cool Careers Without College for People Who Love Sports* (Cool Careers Without College). Rosen, 2007. ISBN 140420749X. 144 p. Grades 6–up.

Horn, Geoffrey M. *Sports Therapist* (Cool Careers). Gareth Stevens, 2008. ISBN 9780836893298. 32 p. Grades 3–5.

Hubbard, Crystal. *The Last Black King of the Kentucky Derby.* Lee & Low Books, 2008. ISBN 9781584302742. 40 p. Grades 2–4.

Hudak, Heather C. *Extreme Skiing* (Extreme). Weigl Publishers, 2008. ISBN 9781590369180. 32 p. Grades 4–8.

Hyde, Natalie *Soccer Science* (Sports Science). Crabtree Publishing, 2009. ISBN 9780778745372. 32 p. Grades 3–5.

Hyland, Tony. *Divers* (Extreme Jobs). Smart Apple, 2007. ISBN 9781583407448. 32 p. Grades 4–6.

Inman, Roy. *The Judo Handbook* (Martial Arts). Rosen, 2008. ISBN 9781404213937. 256 p. Grades 5–up.

Kelley, James S. *The Atlantic Division* (Above the Rim). Child's World, 2008. ISBN 9781592969814 40 p. Grades 2–5.

Kelley, James S. *The Central Division* (Above the Rim). Child's World, 2008. ISBN 9781592969821. 40 p. Grades 3–5.

Kelley, James S. *The Northwest Division* (Above the Rim). Child's World, 2008. ISBN 9781592969838. 40 p. Grades 2–5.

Kelley, James S. *The Pacific Division* (Above the Rim). Child's World, 2008. ISBN 9781592969845. 40 p. Grades 2–5.

Kelley, James S. *The Southeast Division* (Above the Rim). Child's World, 2008. ISBN 9781592969852. 40 p. Grades 2–5.

Kelley, James S. *The Southwest Division* (Above the Rim). Child's World, 2008. ISBN 9781592969869. 40 p. Grades 2–5.

Kelley, K. C. *AFC East* (Inside the NFL). Child's World, 2008. ISBN 978-1600530010. 40 p. Grades 4–8.

Kelley, K. C. *AFC West* (Inside the NFL). Child's World, 2008. ISBN 978-1600530041. 40 p. Grades 4–8.

Kelley, K. C. *NFC East* (Inside the NFL). Child's World, 2008. ISBN 978-1592969975. 40 p. Grades 4–8.

Kelley, K. C. *NFC North* (Inside the NFL). Child's World, 2008. ISBN 978-1592969982. 40 p. Grades 4–8.

Kelley, K. C. *NFC South* (Inside the NFL). Child's World, 2008. ISBN 978-1592969999. 40 p. Grades 4–8.

Kelley, K. C. *NFC West* (Inside the NFL). Child's World, 2008. ISBN 978-1600530003. 40 p. Grades 4–8.

Klein, Adam G. *Archery* (Outdoor Adventure!). Checkerboard Library, 2008. ISBN 9781599289557. 32 p. Grades 4–6.

Klein, Adam G. *Boating (*Outdoor Adventure!). Checkerboard Library, 2008. ISBN 9781599289564. 32 p. Grades 4–6.

Klein, Adam G. *Camping* (Outdoor Adventure!). Checkerboard Library, 2008. ISBN 9781599289571. 32 p. Grades 4–6.

Klein, Adam G. *Fishing* (Outdoor Adventure!). Checkerboard Library, 2008. ISBN 9781599289588. 32 p. Grades 4–6.

Klein, Adam G. *Hiking* (Outdoor Adventure!). Checkerboard Library, 2008. ISBN 9781599289595. 32 p. Grades 4–6.

Klein, Adam G. *Hunting* (Outdoor Adventure!). Checkerboard Library, 2008. ISBN 9781599289601. 32 p. Grades 2–4.

Knutson, Jeffrey. *The Business of Skateboarding: From Board to Boardroom* (Super Skateboarding). Rosen, 2009. ISBN 9781435850514. 48 p. Grades 5–7.

Koestler-Grack, Rachel A. *Ben Roethlisberger* (Football Superstars). Chelsea House, 2008. ISBN 9780791098370. 136 p. Grades 6–up.

Koestler-Grack, Rachel A. *Brett Favre* (Football Superstars). Chelsea House, 2008. ISBN 9780791096901. 144 p. Grades 6–up.

Koestler-Grack, Rachel A. *Tom Brady*. Chelsea House, 2008. ISBN 9780791096895. 151 p. Grades 6–up.

Kummer, Patricia K. *Athletic Trainer* (Cool Careers). Cherry Lake, 2008. ISBN 9781602793033. 32 p. Grades 3–5.

Kummer, Patricia K. *Sports Medicine Doctor* (Cool Careers). Cherry Lake, 2008. ISBN 9781602793026. 32 p. Grades 3–5.

Leavitt, Caroline. *Samurai* (Edge Books). Capstone Press, 2006. ISBN 0736864334. 32 p. Grades 3–5.

Levin, Judith. *Ichiro Suzuki* (Baseball Superstars). Chelsea House, 2007. ISBN 9780791094402. 144 p. Grades 7–10.

MacDonald, James. *Hockey Skills: How to Play Like a Pro*. Enslow, 2008. ISBN 9780766032071. 48 p. Grades 4–6.

Macrae, Sloan. *Meet Eli Manning: Football's Unstoppable Quarterback* (All-Star Players). PowerKids Press, 2009. ISBN 9781435827059. 32 p. Grades 3–5.

Macrae, Sloan. *Meet Tony Parker: Basketball's Famous Point Guard* (All-Star Players). PowerKids Press, 2009. ISBN 9781435827103. 32 p. Grades 3–5.

Macrae, Sloan. *Meet Vladimir Guerrero: Baseball's Super Vlad* (All-Star Players). PowerKids Press, 2009. ISBN 9781435827073. 32 p. Grades 3–5.

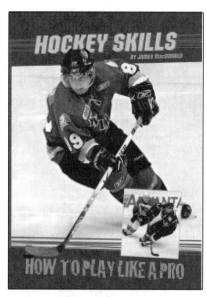

Hockey Skills: How to Play Like a Pro by **James MacDonald.**

Marcovitz, Hal. *Derek Jeter* (Modern Role Models). Mason Crest Publishers, 2008. ISBN 9781422204825. 64 p. Grades 5–8.

Marsico, Katie. *Speed Skating* (Real World Math: Sports). Cherry Lake, 2008. ISBN 9781602792500. 32 p. Grades 4–6.

Marsico, Katie, and Cecilia Minden. *Football* (Real World Math). Cherry Lake, 2008. ISBN 9781602792470. 32 p. Grades 4–6.

Marsico, Katie, and Cecilia Minden. *Running* (Real World Math). Cherry Lake, 2008. ISBN 9781602792494. 32 p. Grades 4–6.

Marsico, Katie, and Cecilia Minden. *Tennis* (Real World Math). Cherry Lake, 2008. ISBN 9781602792487. 32 p. Grades 4–6.

Mason, Paul. *Judo* (Know Your Sport). Sea to Sea Publications, 2008. ISBN 978-1597711517. 32 p. Grades 4–8.

Mattern, Joanne. *BMX* (Action Sports). Rourke Publishing, 2008. ISBN 978-1604723946. 24 p. Grades 2–5.

Mattern, Joanne. *Kickboxing* (Action Sports). Rourke Publishing, 2008. ISBN 978-1604723953. 24 p. Grades 2–5.

Mattern, Joanne. *Kiteboarding* (Action Sports). Rourke Publishing, 2008. ISBN 978-1604723960. 24 p. Grades 2–5.

Mattern, Joanne. *Paintball* (Action Sports). Rourke Publishing, 2008. ISBN 978-1604723977. 24 p. Grades 2–5.

Mattern, Joanne. *Skateboarding* (Action Sports). Rourke Publishing, 2008. ISBN 9781604723984. 24 p. Grades 2–5.

Mattern, Joanne. *Wrestling* (Action Sports). Rourke Publishing, 2008. ISBN 978-1604723991. 24 p. Grades 2–5.

McMahon, Dave. *Baseball Skills: How to Play Like a Pro*. Enslow, 2008. ISBN 9780766032040. 48 p. Grades 4–6.

Medeiros, Michael. *Steve Nash* (Remarkable People). Weigl Publishers, 2008. ISBN 9781590369913. 24 p. Grades 5–7.

Miller, Craig. *David Beckham* (Xtreme Athletes). Morgan Reynolds, 2008. ISBN 9781599350820. 100 p. Grades 6–up.

Minden, Cecilia, and Katie Marsico. *Baseball* (Real World Math). Cherry Lake, 2008. ISBN 9781602792432. 32 p. Grades 4–6.

Minden, Cecilia, and Katie Marsico. *Basketball* (Real World Math). Cherry Lake, 2008. ISBN 9781602792456. 32 p. Grades 4–6.

Minden, Cecilia, and Katie Marsico. *Soccer (*Real World Math). Cherry Lake, 2008. ISBN 9781602792449. 32 p. Grades 4–6.

Minden, Cecilia, and Katie Marsico. *Swimming* (Real World Math). Cherry Lake, 2008. ISBN 9781602792463. 32 p. Grades 4–6.

Monteverde, Matt. *Baseball in the American Leagues East Division* (Inside Major Leagues Baseball). Rosen, 2009. ISBN 9781435850408. 48 p. Grades 5–7.

Myers, Walter Dean. *Muhammad Ali: The People's Champion*. Illustrated by Alex Delinois. Collins, 2010. ISBN 9780060291310. 40 p. Grades 1–3.

Needham, Tom. *Albert Pujols: MVP On and Off the Field* (Sports Stars With Heart). Enslow, 2007. ISBN 0766028666. 128 p. Grades 5–8.

Needham, Tom. *Tiki Barber: All-Pro On and Off the Field* (Sports Stars With Heart). Enslow, 2007. ISBN 0766028658. 128 p. Grades 5–8.

Nichols, John *The Story of the Boston Bruins* (The NHL: History and Heroes). Creative Education. 2008. ISBN 9781583416143. 48 p. Grades 4–6.

Ollhoff, Jim. *Grappling* (The World of Martial Arts). ABDO & Daughters, 2008. ISBN 9781599289762. 32 p. Grades 4–6.

Ollhoff, Jim. *Martial Arts Movies* (The World of Martial Arts). ABDO & Daughters, 2008. ISBN 9781599289809. 32 p. Grades 3–5.

Ollhoff, Jim. *Masters & Heroes* (The World of Martial Arts). ABDO & Daughters, 2008. 9781599289816. 32 p. Grades 3–5.

Ollhoff, Jim. *Ninja* (The World of Martial Arts). ABDO & Daughters, 2008. ISBN 1599289822. 32 p. Grades 3–5.

Ollhoff, Jim. *Samurai* (The World of Martial Arts). ABDO & Daughters, 2008. ISBN 9781599289830. 32 p. Grades 3–5.

Ollhoff, Jim. *Weapons* (The World of Martial Arts). ABDO & Daughters, 2008. ISBN 9781599289854. 32 p. Grades 4–6.

Omoth, Tyler. *The Story of the Chicago Cubs* (The Story of the). Creative Education, 2007. ISBN 9781583414828. 48 p. Grades 3–6.

Omoth, Tyler. *The Story of the Los Angeles Dodgers* (The Story of the). Creative Education, 2007. ISBN 9781583414910. 48 p. Grades K–4.

Orr, Tamra. *Jay-Jay Okocha* (Robbie Readers). Mitchell Lane, 2006. ISBN 1584154934. 32 p. Grades 3–5.

Orr, Tamra. *Michael Owen* (Robbie Readers). Mitchell Lane, 2006. ISBN 1584154918. 32 p. Grades 3–5.

Orr, Tamra. *Ronaldo* (Robbie Readers). Mitchell Lane, 2006. ISBN 1584154926. 32 p. Grades 3–5.

O'Sullivan, Robyn. *Jackie Robinson Plays Ball* (History Chapters). National Geographic, 2007. ISBN 1426301901. 48 p. Grades 2–4.

Pawlett, Mark, and Ray Pawlett. *The Tae Kwon Do Handbook* (Martial Arts). Rosen, 2008. ISBN 9781404213968 256 p. Grades 5–up.

Pawlett, Ray. *The Karate Handbook* (Martial Arts). Rosen, 2008. ISBN 9781404213944 256 p. Grades 7–12.

Peterson, Brian. *AFC North* (Inside the NFL). Child's World, 2008. ISBN 9781602530027. 40 p. Grades 4–8.

Peterson, Brian. *AFC South* (Inside the NFL). Child's World, 2008. ISBN 9781602530034. 40 p. Grades 4–8.

Polzer, Tim. *Peyton Manning: Leader On and Off the Field* (Sports Stars With Heart). Enslow, 2006. ISBN 0766028224. 128 p. Grades 5–up.

Poolos, J. *Hank Aaron* (Baseball Superstars). Chelsea House, 2007. ISBN 9780791095362. 128 p. Grades 5–up.

Porterfield, Jason. *Baseball in the American Leagues Central Division* (Inside Major Leagues Baseball). Rosen, 2009. ISBN 9781435850422. 48 p. Grades 5–7.

Porterfield, Jason. *Baseball in the National Leagues East Division* (Inside Major Leagues Baseball). Rosen, 2009. ISBN 9781435850439. 48 p. Grades 5–7.

Powell, Ben. *Skateboarding Skills: The Rider's Guide.* Firefly Books, 2008. ISBN 9781554073603. 128 p. Grades 5–10.

Price, Sean. *Jackie Robinson: Breaking the Color Barrier* (American History Through Primary Sources). Raintree, 2008. ISBN 9781410931153. 32 p. Grades 4–6.

Reis, Ronald A. *Mickey Mantle* (Baseball Superstars). Chelsea House, 2008. ISBN 9780791095461. 130 p. Grades 5–up.

Reis, Ronald A. *Ted Williams* (Baseball Superstars). Chelsea House, 2008. ISBN 9780791095454. 130 p. Grades 5–up.

Ritschel, John. *The Kickboxing Handbook* (Martial Arts). Rosen, 2008. ISBN 9781404213951. 256 p. Grades 7–up.

Roberts, Jeremy. *Tiger Woods: Golf's Master* (Lifeline Biographies). Twenty-First Century Books, 2008. ISBN 9781580135696. 112 p. Grades 5–9.

Robinson, Tom. *Andruw Jones: All-Star On and Off the Field* (Sports Stars With Heart). Enslow, 2007. ISBN 0766028674. 128 p. Grades 5–8.

Robinson, Tom. *Basketball Skills: How to Play Like a Pro.* Enslow, 2008. ISBN 9780766032057. 48 p. Grades 4–6.

Robinson, Tom. *David Beckham: Soccer's Superstar* (People to Know Today). Enslow, 2008. ISBN 9780766031104. 128 p. Grades 4–6.

Robinson, Tom. *Derek Jeter: Captain On and Off the Field* (Sports Stars With Heart). Enslow, 2006. ISBN 0766028194. 128 p. Grades 5–up.

Robinson, Tom. *Donovan McNabb: Leader On and Off the Field* (Sports Stars With Heart). Enslow, 2007. ISBN 076602864X. 128 p. Grades 5–8.

Robinson, Tom. *Kevin Garnett: All-Star On and Off the Court* (Sports Stars With Heart). Enslow, 2007. ISBN 0766028631. 128 p. Grades 5–8.

Robinson, Tom. *Mark Marti.* Enslow, 2008. ISBN 9780766030015. 128 p. Grades 4–6.

Robinson, Tom. *Shaquille O'Neal: Giant On and Off the Court* (Sports Stars With Heart). Enslow, 2006. ISBN 0766028232 p. 128 p. Grades 5–up.

Roselius, J. Chris. *Soccer Skills: How to Play Like a Pro.* Enslow, 2008. ISBN 9780766032064. 48 p. Grades 3–6.

Roselius, J. Chris. *Tim Duncan: Champion On and Off the Court* (Sports Stars With Heart). Enslow, 2006. ISBN 0766028216. 128 p. Grades 5–8.

Rosen, Michael J. *Balls! Round 2.* Darby Creek Publishing, 2008. ISBN 9781581960662. 80 p. Grades 4–6.

Sandler, Michael. *Ben Roethlisberger* (Football Heroes Making a Difference). Bearport Publishing, 2009. ISBN 9781597167703. 24 p. Grades 2–4.

Sandler, Michael. *Brett Favre* (Football Heroes Making a Difference). Bearport Publishing, 2009. ISBN 9781597167710. 24 p. Grades 2–4.

Sandler, Michael. *Brian Urlacher* (Football Heroes Making a Difference). Bearport Publishing, 2009. ISBN 9781597167758. 24 p. Grades 2–4.

Sandler, Michael. *Cool Snowboarders* (X-Moves). Bearport Publishing, 2009. ISBN 9781597169493. 24 p. Grades 3–6.

Sandler, Michael. *David Eckstein and the St. Louis Cardinals: 2006 World Series* (World Series Superstars). Bearport Publishing, 2008. ISBN 9781597166362. 24 p. Grades K–3.

Sandler, Michael. *Derek Jeter and the New York Yankees: 2000 World Series* (World Series Superstars). Bearport Publishing, 2008. ISBN 9781597166416. 24 p. Grades K–3.

Sandler, Michael. *Donovan McNabb* (Football Heroes Making a Difference). Bearport Publishing, 2009. ISBN 9781597167727. 24 p. Grades 2–4.

Sandler, Michael. *Eli Manning and the New York Giants: Super Bowl XLII* (Super Bowl Superstars). Bearport Publishing, 2008. ISBN 9781597167369. 24 p. Grades K–3.

Sandler, Michael. *Jermaine Dye and the Chicago White Sox: 2005 World Series* (World Series Superstars). Bearport Publishing, 2008. ISBN 9781597166379. 24 p. Grades K–3.

Sandler, Michael. *Joe Montana and the San Francisco 49ers: Super Bowl XXIV* (Super Bowl Superstars). Bearport Publishing, 2008. ISBN 9781597167383. 24 p. Grades K–3.

Sandler, Michael. *Josh Beckett and the Florida Marlins: 2003 World Series* (World Series Superstars). Bearport Publishing, 2008. ISBN 9781597166393. 24 p. Grades K–3.

Sandler, Michael. *LaDainian Tomlinson* (Football Heroes Making a Difference). Bearport Publishing, 2009. ISBN 9781597167741. 24 p. Grades 2–4.

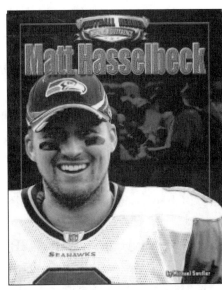

Matt Hasselbeck by **Michael Sandler.**

Sandler, Michael. *Lebron James: I Love Challenges!* (Defining Moments: Super Athletes). Bearport Publishing, 2009. ISBN 9781597168564. 32 p. Grades 3–5.

Sandler, Michael. *Matt Hasselbeck* (Football Heroes Making a Difference). Bearport Publishing, 2009. ISBN 9781597167734. 24 p. Grades 2–4.

Sandler, Michael. *Mike Lowell and the Boston Red Sox: 2007 World Series* (World Series Superstars). Bearport Publishing, 2008. ISBN 9781597167390. 24 p. Grades 4–6.

Sandler, Michael. *Randy Johnson and the Arizona Diamondbacks: 2001 World Series* (World Series Superstars). Bearport Publishing, 2008. ISBN 9781597166386. 24 p. Grades K–3.

Sandler, Michael. *Super Surfers* (X-Moves). Bearport Publishing, 2009. ISBN 9781597169530. 24 p. Grades 3–6.

Sandler, Michael. *Troy Aikman and the Dallas Cowboys: Super Bowl XXVII* (Super Bowl Superstars). Bearport Publishing, 2008. ISBN 9781597167376. 24 p. Grades K–3.

Sandler, Michael. *Troy Glaus and the Anaheim Angels: 2002 World Series* (World Series Superstars). Bearport Publishing, 2008. ISBN 9781597166409. 24 p. Grades K–3.

Savage, Jeff. *Barry Bonds* (Amazing Athletes). Lerner Publications, 2007. ISBN 9781580136112. 32 p. Grades 2–5.

Savage, Jeff. *Dallas Friday* (Amazing Athletes). Lerner Publications, 2006. ISBN 0822565951. 32 p. Grades 2–4.

Savage, Jeff. *Dave Mirra* (Amazing Athletes). Lerner Publications, 2007. ISBN 0822565935. 32 p. Grades 2–4.

Savage, Jeff. *David Beckham* (Amazing Athletes). Lerner Publications, 2007. ISBN 9780822588344. 32 p. Grades K–3.

Schilling, Vincent. *Native Athletes in Action.* 7th Generation, 2007. ISBN 978-0977918300. 128 p. Grades 4–6.

Schweitzer, Karen. *Shaun White.* Mason Crest Publishers, 2009. ISBN 978-1422204931. 64 p. Grades 6–up.

Schweitzer, Karen. *Sheryl Swoopes* (Modern Role Models). Mason Crest Publishers, 2008. ISBN 9781422204917. 64 p. Grades 6–up.

Sheen, Barbara. *Tony Hawk* (People in the News). Lucent Books, 2007. ISBN 9781420500165. 104 p. Grades 6–10.

Silbaugh, John. *National League Central* (Behind the Plate). Child's World, 2007. ISBN 1592968406. 48 p. Grades 4–6.

Skog, Jason. *Chicago Blackhawks* (The NHL: History and Heroes). Creative Education, 2008. ISBN 9781583416150. 42 p. Grades 4–6.

Slade, Suzanne. *Jackie Robinson: Hero and Athlete* (Biographies). Picture Window Books, 2008. ISBN 9781404839786. 24 p. Grades K–3.

Staff, Chronicle Books. *B Is for Baseball: Running the Bases from A to Z.* Chronicle Books, 2009. ISBN 9780811860963. 40 p. Grades K–4.

Sterngass, Jon. *Dan Marino* (Football Superstars). Chelsea House, 2008. ISBN 9780791096062. 144 p. Grades 5–up.

Sterngass, Jon. *Jerry Rice* (Football Superstars). Chelsea House, 2008. ISBN 9780791096079. 144 p. Grades 6–up.

Stewart, Mark. *The Baltimore Orioles* (Team Spirit). Norwood House Press, 2007. ISBN 1599530929. 48 p. Grades 3–5.

Stewart, Mark. *The Baltimore Ravens* (Team Spirit). Norwood House Press, 2008. ISBN 9781599532066. 48 p. Grades 4–6.

Stewart, Mark. *The Cincinnati Reds* (Team Spirit). Norwood House Press, 2008. ISBN 9781599531649. 48 p. Grades 4–6.

Stewart, Mark. *Classic Rivalries* (Ultimate 10). Gareth Stevens, 2009. ISBN 9780836891614. 48 p. Grades 3–5.

Stewart, Mark. *The Colorado Rockies* (Team Spirit). Norwood House Press, 2008. ISBN 9781599531663. 48 p. Grades 2–5.

Stewart, Mark. *The Detroit Tigers* (Team Spirit). Norwood House Press, 2007. ISBN 1599530937. 48 p. Grades 3–5.

Stewart, Mark. *The Florida Marlins* (Team Spirit). Norwood House Press, 2008. ISBN 9781599531670. 48 p. Grades 4–6.

Stewart, Mark. *The Houston Astros* (Team Spirit). Norwood House Press, 2007. ISBN 1599530945. 48 p. Grades 3–5.

Stewart, Mark. *The Jacksonville Jaguars* (Team Spirit). Norwood House Press, 2008. ISBN 9781599532097. 48 p. Grades 4–6.

Stewart, Mark. *The Kansas City Chiefs* (Team Spirit). Norwood House Press, 2008. ISBN 9781599532080. 48 p. Grades 4–6.

Stewart, Mark. *The Los Angeles Angels of Anaheim* (Team Spirit). Norwood House Press, 2006. ISBN 1599530023. 48 p. Grades 3–5.

Stewart, Mark. *The Los Angeles Dodgers* (Team Spirit). Norwood House Press, 2007. ISBN 1599530953. 48 p. Grades 3–5.

Stewart, Mark. *The Michigan Wolverines* (Team Spirit). Norwood House Press, 2009. ISBN 9781599532783. 48 p. Grades 4–6.

Stewart, Mark. *The Milwaukee Brewers* (Team Spirit). Norwood House Press, 2008. ISBN 9781599531694. 48 p. Grades 2–5.

Stewart, Mark. *The Minnesota Vikings* (Team Spirit). Norwood House Press, 2009. ISBN 9781599532103. 48 p. Grades 4–6.

Stewart, Mark. *The Oakland A's* (Team Spirit). Norwood House Press, 2008. ISBN 9781599531700. 48 p. Grades 4–6.

Stewart, Mark. *The San Diego Chargers* (Team Spirit). Norwood House Press, 2008. ISBN 9781599532059. 48 p. Grades 4–6.

Stewart, Mark. *The Seattle Seahawks* (Team Spirit). Norwood House Press, 2008. ISBN 9781599532011. 48 p. Grades 4–6.

Stewart, Mark. *The St. Louis Cardinals* (Team Spirit). Norwood House Press, 2007. ISBN 1599530961. 48 p. Grades 3–5.

Swish: The Quest for Basketball's Perfect Shot **by Mark Stewart and Mike Kennedy.**

Stewart, Mark. *The Toronto Blue Jays* (Team Spirit). Norwood House Press, 2008. ISBN 9781599531779. 48 p. Grades 4–6.

Stewart, Mark, and Mike Kennedy. *Swish: The Quest for Basketball's Perfect Shot* (Exceptional Sports Titles for Intermediate Grades). Millbrook Press, 2009. ISBN 9780822587521. 64 p. Grades 5–8.

Stewart, Mark, and Mike Kennedy. *Touchdown: The Power and Precision of Football's Perfect Play*. Millbrook Press, 2009. ISBN 9780822587514. 64 p. Grades 3–8.

Stone, Lynn. *The Rodeo*. Rourke Publishing, 2008. ISBN 9781604723878. 32 p. Grades 4–7.

Stone, Lynn. *Rodeo Barrel Racers*. Rourke Publishing, 2008. ISBN 9781604723922. 32 p. Grades 4–7.

Stone, Lynn. *Rodeo Bronc Riders*. Rourke Publishing, 2008. ISBN 9781604723885. 32 p. Grades 4–7.

Stone, Lynn. *Rodeo Bull Riders*. Rourke Publishing, 2008. ISBN 9781604723908. 32 p. Grades 4–7.

Stone, Lynn. *Rodeo Ropers*. Rourke Publishing, 2008. ISBN 9781604723892. 32 p. Grades 4–7.

Stone, Lynn. *Rodeo Steer Wrestlers*. Rourke Publishing, 2008. ISBN 978-1604723915. 32 p. Grades 4–7.

Stutt, Ryan. *The Skateboarding Field Manual*. Firefly Books, 2009. ISBN 978-1554074679. 144 p. Grades 7–up.

Tate, Nikki. *Behind the Scenes at the Racetrack: The Racehorse*. Fitzhenry and Whiteside, 2007. ISBN 9781554550180. 88 p. Grades 5–8.

Teitelbaum, Michael. *National League East* (Behind the Plate). Child's World, 2007. ISBN 1592968414. 48 p. Grades 3–5.

Thomas, Keltie. *How Soccer Works* (How Sports Work). Maple Tree, 2007. ISBN 9781897349007. 64 p. Grades 1–3.

Tieck, Sarah. *Nat & Alex Wolff* (Big Buddy Biographies). Buddy Books, 2008. ISBN 9781604531268. 32 p. Grades K–3.

Torsiello, David P. *Michael Phelps: Swimming for Olympic Gold* (Hot Celebrity Biographies). Enslow, 2009. ISBN 9780766035911. 48 p. Grades 3–5.

Turnbull, Stephen. *Real Ninja: Over 20 True Stories of Japan's Secret Assassins*. Enchanted Lion Books, 2008. ISBN 9781592700813. 48 p. Grades 4–6.

Turnbull, Stephen. *Real Samurai*. Enchanted Lion Books, 2007. ISBN 9781592700608. 48 p. Grades 4–6.

Uschan, Michael V. *David Beckham* (People in the News). Lucent Books, 2008. ISBN 9781420500547 112 p. Grades 6–up.

Warr, Peter. *The Kung Fu Handbook* (Martial Arts). Rosen, 2008. ISBN 978-1404213920. 256 p. Grades 7–12.

Watson, Galadriel Findlay. *David Beckham* (Remarkable People). Weigl Publishers, 2007. ISBN 1590366417. 24 p. Grades 3–5.

Wheeler, Jill C. *David Beckham* (Awesome Athletes). Checkerboard Library, 2006. ISBN 1599283042. 32 p. Grades 3–5.

Wiseman, Blaine. *Skateboarding* (Extreme). Weigl Publishers, 2008. ISBN 978-1590369128. 32 p. Grades 4–8.

Wiseman, Blaine. *Surfing* (Extreme). Weigl Publishers, 2008. ISBN 9781590369166. 32 p. Grades 4–8.

Wong, Stephen. *Baseball Treasures*. Collins, 2007. ISBN 0061144738. 64 p. Grades 4–7.

Woog, Adam. *Joe Montana* (Football Superstars). Chelsea House, 2008. ISBN 9780791095683. 120 p. Grades 6–up.

Woog, Adam. *Walter Payton* (Football Superstars). Chelsea House, 2008. ISBN 9780791095676. 135 p. Grades 5–up.

Wurdinger, Scott, and Leslie Rapparlie. *Kayaking*. Creative Education, 2006. ISBN 1583413975. 32 p. Grades 7–10.

Wyckoff, Edwin Brit. *The Man Who Invented Basketball: James Naismith and His Amazing Game* (Genius at Work! Great Inventor Biographies). Enslow, 2007. ISBN 0766028461. 32 p. Grades 2–4.

Young, Jeff. *Kelly Slater* (Xtreme Athletes). Morgan Reynolds, 2008. ISBN 9781599350783 112 p. Grades 6–up.

Young, Jeff. *Shaun White* (Xtreme Athletes). Morgan Reynolds, 2008. ISBN 9781599350813 112 p. Grades 6–up.

Young, Jeff C. *Dwayne Wade* (Modern Role Models). Mason Crest Publishers, 2008. ISBN 9781422204924. 64 p. Grades 6–up.

Zuehlke, Jeffrey. *Ben Roethlisberger* (Amazing Athletes). Lerner Publications, 2007. ISBN 0822576600. 32 p. Grades 2–4.

Zuehlke, Jeffrey. *Joe Mauer* (Amazing Athletes). Lerner Publications, 2007. ISBN 9780822588351. 32 p. Grades 2–5.

Chapter ————————— 2

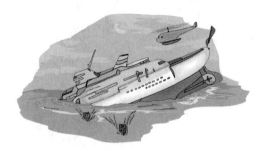

Disasters and Mysteries

Dead bodies, mysterious happenings, and disastrous events such as ship-wrecks have long been favorite reading material for boys. Books about the *Titanic*, the *Hindenburg*, Mount Saint Helens, and other famous disasters have proven themselves to be an easy sell to reluctant readers. Many of the real-life dramas in the following books overflow with action and intrigue and provide as much excite-ment as any fictional movie plot. Play up the mysterious, dangerous, and some-times even gross aspects of these books to get boys hooked on reading about these exciting true events.

BOOKTALKS

Brown, Don. *All Stations! Distress! April 15, 1912: The Day the* Titanic *Sank.* Roaring Brook Press, 2008. ISBN 978196432222. Unpaged. Grades 2–5.

Four thousand workers built the gigantic ship *Titanic* in Belfast, Ireland. It was the largest ship in the world and they said it was unsinkable. So many safety precautions had been taken.

All Stations! Distress! April 15, 1912: The Day the Titanic Sank *by Don Brown.* **Jacket shown with permission from Roaring Brook Press.**

Its first voyage was to sail from England to New York City. Some of the passengers were wealthy, but more than half of the passengers were in steerage, the cheapest lodging, most moving to America for good. On April 14, 1912, the lookouts spied an iceberg, straight ahead. The ship was going fast. It tried to turn, but there was not enough time. The ship hit the iceberg.

Below deck, water started pouring in. The ship's builder came and looked. It was awful. It was hopeless. The ship was filling fast with water and it was going to sink. It had perhaps an hour and a half left, and there were only about 20 lifeboats, not nearly enough for more than 2,000 passengers and crew members.

This is the story of the most famous shipwreck in all of history and of some of the people who lived and died that night. You will learn about the famous older couple, Isidor and Ida Straus, who owned Macy's department store. You will learn that some children were thrown into lifeboats. You will learn about the Unsinkable Molly Brown. It is one of the best true stories ever.

Cerullo, Mary M. *Shipwrecks: Exploring Sunken Cities Beneath the Sea.* Dutton Children's Books, 2009. ISBN 9780525479680. 64 p. Grades 4–8.

When a disaster of some sort causes a ship to sink, it is a horrible thing. The passengers and crew must be terrified. When a ship is caught in the grip of a hurricane or a winter storm, surely everyone must be aware that there is little hope of rescue. Almost everyone on board will probably drown.

But when a ship does sink, it is a wonderful thing for the animals that live on the bottom of the ocean. A sunken ship is an amazing hiding place—it's a place to build a home and a place to be safe from predators. New life quickly takes over in the remains of the ship.

Years later, maybe hundreds of years later, underwater archaeologists will be thrilled to learn that a sunken ship has been discovered, for by exploring it, they can find out more about the people who lived long ago.

This book tells the story of two sunken ships, the *Henrietta Maria*, which was discovered west of the Florida Keys in 1972 by searchers who were looking for something else, and the *Portland*, found off the coast of Massachusetts in 2002.

The finding of the *Henrietta Maria* was a major discovery. For a long time the searchers did not know the name of the ship, but when they discovered and cleaned the ship's bell, the name was revealed. The *Henrietta Maria* was a British ship, and research proved it sank in 1700. What was extraordinary about it is that it was a slave ship. Different sized shackles for men, women, and children were found in the wreck. (See the photos on page 11.) The good news was that there were no slaves on the ship when it sank. All 190 of them had been sold earlier in Jamaica.

Now the sunken ship was home to a huge coral community, full of colorful fish of all sorts, including a barrel sponge big enough for a human being to crawl into (see photo on page 21). The ship of horror in the past is now a home to many beautiful animals.

The *Portland* sank in colder waters, and the fish that live in it now are not so colorful. But the *Portland*, which sank in 1898, was a huge ship and could accommodate 800 passengers. It went on a journey of only a hundred miles. But the beautiful, luxurious ship sank in a winter storm.

This book is filled with tantalizing photographs and maps. It makes for a fine read.

Fradin, Judy, and Dennis Fradin. *Volcanoes* (Witness to Disaster). National Geographic, 2007. ISBN 9780792253761. 48 p. Grades 4–8.

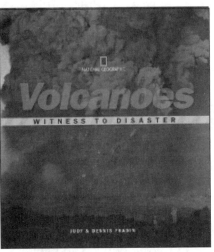

Volcanoes **by Judy Fradin and Dennis Fradin.**

One of the most famous volcanoes just came out of the ground in a cornfield in Mexico in 1943. Although the ground was trembling on the morning of February 20, the farmer and his helpers went to work anyway. Around 4:30 in the afternoon, the earth split and smoke and fiery ashes came out of it. All four people in the field ran for the nearest village. The next day lava began to pour out, and a week after the eruption started, a volcano stood about 400 feet high—about 40 stories. People could hear the noise of the eruption 120 miles away. And that is just the beginning of one of the great volcano stories in this book.

You will read about exactly what causes volcanoes to happen and how they work, and some of the other famous eruptions, including:

- The volcano in about 1640 BC in what is now Santorini, a Greek island about 70 miles from Crete. Most of Santorini collapsed into the sea, and historians believe that this could have led to the legend of Atlantis, the city buried beneath the sea.

- The eruption of Vesuvius in AD 79. It completely destroyed the cities of Pompeii and Herculaneum and covered them both completely for centuries—and left us a superb look at life long ago.

- The eruption of Mount Pelee on the island of Martinique in the Caribbean Sea. It killed all but two of the 26,000 people in the city of Saint-Pierre. One was a prisoner locked in an underground dungeon!

This book is just full of great photographs and fascinating information about volcanoes.

Freedman, Russell. *Who Was First? Discovering the Americas*. Clarion Books, 2007. ISBN 0618663916. 88 p. Grades 5–8.

We all have heard a lot about Christopher Columbus. Most people still believe that he was the guy who discovered America. We know he was not really looking to discover anything except a shorter route to a place that was already there—India. He died believing he had found that.

And how can anyone *discover* a place where millions of people already live? North and South America together almost certainly had more people than were living in all of Europe. The truth is that the ancestors of those people got there thousands of years before Columbus was even born. And many historians believe that a lot of other people who did not live in the Americas may have landed on them, "found" them, many years before Columbus made his voyage.

Russell Freedman is one of our greatest writers, and in this colorful book he tells us about some of the people (including Columbus) who may have been here long ago. One is Zheng He, a famous Chinese admiral who commanded a huge fleet of powerful ships that sailed around Asia—and who knows?—maybe a lot farther than that. Zheng He's voyages became so famous that you have probably heard of them, although under a slightly different name: Sin Bao. The sailors who sailed with him told stories that lived forever. The stories were about Sinbad the Sailor.

Other people believe that the Vikings discovered North America, or perhaps the Welsh or perhaps the Africans. It is certain that many people "discovered" it, some perhaps coming over the long-gone land bridge from Siberia, others coming on rafts or boats.

This is a wonderfully interesting true story that will make you think.

Howard, Amanda. *Robbery File: The Museum Heist* (Crime Solvers). Bearport Publishing, 2007. ISBN 1597165506. 32 p. Grades 3–5.

How on earth would you steal two Van Gogh paintings worth $3 million each? And how do you get caught?

This is a true story about a robbery that happened in the Van Gogh museum in Amsterdam in 2002. And it tells exactly how the robbers pulled it off.

For starters, they placed a ladder against the building and a sledgehammer on the roof. Nobody wondered about these things, because there was construction in the area. Then, early in the morning, the museum overnight security systems were shut down as the staff arrived. Only a few alarms were left on. The burglars climbed up the ladder and used the sledgehammer to break the skylight, dropped down into the building, and ran straight for the main gallery. They each grabbed a painting and got out before the police arrived, within two minutes.

How did they figure out how to do it? Did they make any mistakes? Did the police find them? Why would they steal something so famous that everyone they might sell it to would recognize it?

You will learn the answers to these questions in this interesting book.

Jenkins, Martin. Titanic: *Disaster at Sea.* Illustrated by Brian Sanders. Candlewick Press, 2008. ISBN 9780763637958. 32 p. Grades 4–7.

The passengers, the crew, the designers, and the builders all knew one thing: the *Titanic* was a state-of-the-art ship, brand new, luxurious, built for the ages. It could not be sunk. There were too many protections against such a thing ever happening. It was safe and it was beautiful.

But on its first trip across the ocean, it sank in one of the worst sea disasters in history.

This is the story of what happened: what was right and what went wrong and who was to blame. It is the story of why so many people died and why there were not nearly enough lifeboats for them. And of why the poorest people, the ones who had paid the least for their passage to America, died in much greater numbers than those who had paid more.

One thing that makes this book so interesting to read is the charts and time lines and interesting facts. There are photographs as well, including photos of some of the famous people on the ship and some of the kids on the ship. There is even one of the most famous photos taken, of a lifeboat full of *Titanic* passengers about to be rescued by another ship, the *Carpathia.*

This is a good look at one of the most famous true stories of all time.

MacLeod, Elizabeth. *Royal Murder: the Deadly Intrigue of Ten Sovereigns.* Annick Press, 2008. ISBN 9781554511273. 128 p. Grades 4–8.

This is a book about a great topic—royal people who were involved with murder. Either they were murdered themselves or they murdered other people. And here are ten true stories with lots of great pictures.

Some of the stories are about people you probably already know something about: Cleopatra, who managed to kill off several of her family members before she finally killed herself; Vlad the Impaler, who is more commonly called Dracula—and you won't believe the horrifying ways in which *he* killed people; and the beautiful French queen Marie Antoinette, who never killed anyone herself, but who was beheaded after spending a lot of time in a horrible prison.

Others may not be familiar. Do you know about those poor little princes in the tower? Their father had been the king of England, but he died. The older boy was still too young to be king, so his uncle Richard took over until he was old enough. The only thing keeping Richard from being king himself was those two boys—and somehow they died mysteriously in the Tower of London and Richard *did* become the king, King Richard III. They unquestionably died. But who killed them? We still are not sure who was the guilty person, but a lot of people have argued about it ever since.

Read about Luigi Lucheni, who said, "I wanted to kill a royalty. It did not matter which one" (p. 5). He got his wish. But his choice of victim made almost the entire Western world sad. Or read about Nicholas II of Russia and his beautiful wife Alexandra and their family. They lived an extravagant, lovely life without seeming to notice that their subjects were living in horrible poverty and many were starving. A lot of people hated them and let them know it when they murdered them, kids and all, in a basement.

This is an extremely interesting read.

Martin, Russell, and Lydia Nibley. *The Mysteries of Beethoven's Hair.* Charlesbridge, 2009. ISBN 9781570917141. 120 p. Grades 5–8.

The Mysteries of Beethoven's Hair by Russell Martin and Lydia Nibley.

So, what do you know about Ludwig van Beethoven? Most of us probably know he was a great composer, one of the greatest of all time. Maybe you know that he became almost completely deaf—but that did not stop him from writing music even though he could not hear it when it was played. And maybe you have heard that he had a hard life, and was extremely moody, ill much of the time, and not very happy.

Beethoven himself did not know what was the matter with him, but he knew something was horribly wrong. Why was he sick and moody and deaf? Like Beethoven, people who love his music have been wondering the same thing for almost 200 years.

If you are wondering too, you should read this fascinating book.

Shortly after Beethoven died, Ferdinand Hiller, a teenage fan of his, cut off a lock of his hair. This was something people often did; it was considered a good way to remember people. That hair became one of Hiller's most prized possessions, and he had it carefully framed. On his son Paul's thirtieth birthday, it became his birthday present.

Historians know that the family carefully guarded their prized possession for decades, but no one is quite sure what happened to it when people of Jewish descent, like the Hillers, began to flee Germany because of the Holocaust. All we know for sure is that someone, no one knows who, gave the locket to a physician in Denmark who was taking care of people fleeing the Nazis and helping them to escape. He proved a good caretaker, but years later his adopted daughter needed money and sold the hair at auction.

And that is when a lot more excitement started. Two Americans bought the hair, and now it was time for forensic scientists to take a look! Maybe they could solve the mystery of what kind of disease Beethoven had—and maybe even what caused it.

If you like real-life mysteries, this is a fine one.

Swanson, James L. *Chasing Lincoln's Killer.* Scholastic Press, 2009. ISBN 0439903548. 198 p. Grades 5–8.

Two days after the end of the Civil War, Abraham Lincoln gave a speech at the White House. He wasn't gloating, just celebrating the end of the horrible conflict.

There was a man in the audience named John Wilkes Booth, a famous, handsome actor, 26 years old, and he absolutely hated the president. He said to his friend Lewis Powell, "That is the last speech he will ever give." He meant it. John Wilkes Booth was determined to kill Lincoln.

The story of how and where he shot the president is famous. Booth was lucky; the United States of America was not. Ford's Theater, where Lincoln sat watching a play, was not well guarded, and security was not at all what it is today. Booth paid a man to watch his horse and crept into the theater, where he shot Lincoln fatally in the head. Next he leapt out of the presidential box, catching his leg on a decoration and breaking it as he fell. He ran across the stage as everyone stared in shock, and escaped. Then he had to get out of town fast.

He thought he knew what was going to happen next: everyone would clap and cheer and he would be a great hero as soon as he got to his beloved South. He had one companion, a fellow conspirator in the plot to kill Lincoln, David Herold. They met in Maryland, and almost from the get go, Booth realized he was not going to be a great hero. He was going to have to hide, and he needed medical help badly. If he was lucky, he might find good people to help—he had some names.

Booth managed to hide out for 12 days while people were searching for him everywhere. He never got far from Washington, D.C., and things did not always go well.

This story of the manhunt for Booth reads like an action story, and it's all true. It's a great read!

Walker, Sally M. *Written in Bone: Buried Lives in Jamestown and Colonial Maryland.* Carolrhoda Books, 2009. ISBN 9780822571353. 144 p. Grades 5–up.

Do you like mysteries? Do you like to look at interesting photographs? Do you wonder what people's lives were like long ago? Then this is the book for you.

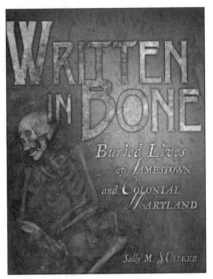

Sally Walker loves science and history and archaeology. When she researched *Written in Bone,* she got to work, and not just sitting at a computer. She started digging and sifting through soils, looking at skeletons, and watching and helping archaeologists dig up the graves of settlers who died hundreds of years ago in Maryland and Virginia. Who were these people? What did she find in their graves? Can we find out what their names were, what they worked at, or how they died?

The incredible thing is that often we can learn more about those things than anyone could imagine.

Written in Bone: Buried Lives in Jamestown and Colonial Maryland by Sally Walker.

Take the case of "The Body in the Basement" on page 54. In 2003 archaeologists began excavating the site of the former home of a tobacco planter named William Neale. Neale probably lived in the house from about 1662 to 1677. The house had a cellar, often used in old houses as a storage area. This cellar, it turned out, was also used as a trash heap. Archaeologists love trash heaps because they can learn so much from the things people throw away.

Imagine their surprise when one of the pieces of trash, with a broken piece of pottery on top of it, was a human skeleton. The body it once belonged to had been thrown carelessly in the pit like a piece of garbage.

Whose body was it? Why would anyone treat a dead person like that?

Historical records showed that the Neale family had two indentured servants. They would have paid the servants' passage from England, and then those servants basically belonged to them for a period of time, usually several years. At that time in history some indentured servants were not treated well. Some were treated horribly, as was this one. He was a teenager, and he was sick. His bones show that he had been forced to work extremely hard, and his teeth showed that he must have been in absolute agony most of the time. They were infected and would have been terribly painful. He probably was not able to work as hard as his master wanted him to. They probably got into an argument. And his master or master's wife probably killed him—and hid the body.

This is a book that is difficult to put down. All of the stories are fascinating. It is a great read with a lot of photographs.

Winchester, Simon. *The Day the World Exploded: The Earthshaking Catastrophe at Krakatoa.* Adaptation by Dwight Jon Zimmerman. Collins, 2008. ISBN 9780061239823. 96 p. Grades 5–8.

When Krakatoa, a volcano island located west of Java, erupted in 1883, it made a terrifying kind of history. "[I]t generated the loudest sound ever made, it sent pressure waves rushing around the world no fewer than seven times, it created tsunamis that killed more than thirty thousand people and it stained the skies with lurid and frighteningly apocalyptic-looking colors for some months afterward" (page 9).

So what happened? First of all we learn about volcanoes, how they are made, and the different kinds. We see lots of fine pictures—take a look at some of the famous ones on pages 18 and 19.

Then we learn about this particular volcano, Krakatoa, and the people, both native and mostly Dutch European settlers, who lived nearby. The Dutch wanted their new homes in the tropics to resemble their old ones in the Netherlands, and they even built canals. Sometimes crocodiles got into those canals!

When strange things, such as lots of steam and ash, started coming out of the volcano, a boatload of tourists came to see it up close. A few of the men took a small boat and saw it up even closer. They actually went into the crater to check out what was going on! This was Sunday, August 26, the day before the volcano blew up.

It took four explosions to destroy it the next day, and the last one could be heard thousands of miles away. By the time of the fourth explosion, thousands and thousands of people were dead from the tsunamis that hit.

There are lots of interesting photographs and a great deal of interesting information here.

Woods, Michael, and Mary B. Woods. *Mudflows and Landslides* (Disasters Up Close). Lerner Publications, 2007. ISBN 9780822565741. 64 p. Grades 4–up.

They happen a lot more than you might think, and they are always, always scary. Sometimes they come so fast that no one has time to get out of the way, and lots of people die. Sometimes they come slowly, so people can save their lives, but often not much else. You have probably seen pictures of them in the news.

They are landslides and mudflows, and they are a part of erosion, in which land changes and reforms. They have many causes, such as deforestation, overbuilding in unsafe areas, just plain old gravity, and things like hurricanes and volcanoes.

This book is full of fine color photographs of these natural disasters. Take a look at the picture on page 17 of the landslide after the 2005 Pakistan earthquake; on page 33 of the mudslide in La Conchita, California; or the landslide that closed Highway 89 in California for 18 months, on page 11.

Then read the stories that go with them. You'll hope you never live in an area that gets a disaster like these.

WORTH READING

Nonfiction books with "boy appeal" that have received positive reviews in *Booklist*, *Horn Book Guide*, and/or *School Library Journal*.

Aldridge, Rebecca. *The Sinking of the* Titanic (Great Historic Disasters). Chelsea House, 2008. ISBN 9780791096437. 112 p. Grades 7–up.

Allman, Toney. *Stonehenge* (Mysterious & Unknown). Referencepoint Press, 2008. ISBN 9781601520340. 96 p. Grades 6–9.

Baker, Julie. *The Great Whaleship Disaster of 1871*. Morgan Reynolds, 2007. ISBN 9781599350431. 144 p. Grades 6–up.

Belanger, Jeff. *Who's Haunting the White House? The President's Mansion and the Ghosts Who Live There*. Sterling, 2008. ISBN 9781402738227. 64 p. Grades 4–7.

Bennie, Paul. *The Great Chicago Fire of 1871* (Great Historic Disasters). Chelsea House, 2008. ISBN 9780791096383. 128 p. Grades 6–8.

Branley, Franklyn M. *Volcanoes* (Let's-Read-and-Find-Out Science 2). Collins, 2008. ISBN 9780060280116. 40 p. Grades 3–4.

Burns, Jan. *Crop Circles* (Mysterious Encounters). KidHaven Press, 2008. ISBN 9780737740479. 48 p. Grades 4–6.

Butler, Dori Hillestad. *F Is for Firefighting*. Pelican, 2007. ISBN 1589804201. 32 p. Grades K–2.

Caper, William. *Nightmare on the* Titanic (Code Red). Bearport Publishing, 2007. ISBN 9781597163620. 32 p. Grades 3–6.

Claybourne, Anna. *Volcanoes*. Kingfisher, 2007. ISBN 9780753461372. 64 p. Grades 3–6.

Doeden, Matt. *Hurricanes* (Pull Ahead Books). Lerner Publications, 2007. ISBN 9780822579069. 32 p. Grades K–3.

Duffield, Katy S. *The Bermuda Triangle* (Mysterious Encounters). KidHaven Press, 2008. ISBN 9780737740462. 48 p. Grades 4–6.

Farr, Richard *Emperors of the Ice: A True Story of Disaster and Survival in the Antarctic, 1910–13.* Farrar, Straus and Giroux, 2008. ISBN 9780374319755. 240 p. Grades 6–9.

Feigenbaum, Aaron. *Emergency at Three Mile Island* (Code Red). Bearport Publishing, 2007. ISBN 9781597163644. 32 p. Grades 3–6.

Feigenbaum, Aaron. *The* Hindenburg *Disaster* (Code Red). Bearport Publishing, 2007. ISBN 9781597163613. 32 p. Grades 3–6.

Fradin, Dennis, and Judy Fradin. *Hurricanes* (Witness to Disaster). National Geographic, 2007. ISBN 9781426201110. 48 p. Grades 4–7.

Fradin, Judy. *Droughts* (Witness to Disaster). National Geographic, 2008. ISBN 9781426303395. 48 p. Grades 4–6.

Fradin, Judy, and Dennis Fradin. *Earthquakes* (Witness to Disaster). National Geographic, 2008. ISBN 9781426302114. 48 p. Grades 4–7.

Ghost Society. *Ghost Files: The Haunting Truth.* HarperCollins, 2008. ISBN 9780061283956. 36 p. Grades 4–6.

Godkin, Celia. *Hurricane!* Fitzhenry and Whiteside, 2008. ISBN 9781554550807. 32 p. Grades K–3.

Goin, Miriam. *Storms!* (National Geographic Readers). National Geographic, 2009. ISBN 9781426303951. 32 p. Grades 1–3.

Green, Emily K. *Volcanoes* (Blastoff! Readers: Learning About the Earth). Children's Press, 2006. ISBN 0531178935. 24 p. Grades 2–4.

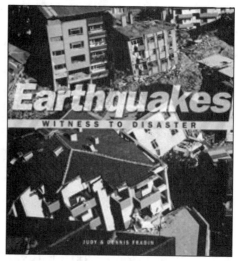

Earthquakes **by Judy Fradin and Dennis Fradin.**

Hamilton, Sue. *Air & Sea Mysteries* (Unsolved Mysteries). ABDO & Daughters, 2007. ISBN 9781599288376. 32 p. Grades 4–6.

Hamilton, Sue. *The Bermuda Triangle* (Unsolved Mysteries). ABDO & Daughters, 2007. ISBN 9781599288345. 32 p. Grades 4–6.

Hamilton, Sue. *Creatures of the Abyss* (Unsolved Mysteries). ABDO & Daughters, 2007. ISBN 9781599288369. 32 p. Grades 5–8.

Hamilton, Sue. *Lost Cities* (Unsolved Mysteries). ABDO & Daughters, 2007. ISBN 978159928832. 32 p. Grades 5–8.

Hamilton, Sue. *Monsters of Mystery* (Unsolved Mysteries). ABDO & Daughters, 2007. ISBN 9781599288352. 32 p. Grades 5–8.

Hamilton, Sue L. *Ancient Astronauts*. ABDO & Daughters, 2008. ISBN 9781599288338. 32 p. Grades 4–6.

Harbo, Christopher L. *The Explosive World of Volcanoes With Max Axiom, Super Scientist* (Graphic Science). Capstone Press, 2007. ISBN 1429601442. 32 p. Grades 5–8.

Hile, Kevin. *Ghost Ships* (Mysterious Encounters). KidHaven Press, 2009. ISBN 9780737740868. 48 p. Grades 4–6.

Ho, Oliver. *Mutants & Monsters* (Mysteries Unwrapped).Sterling, 2008. ISBN 9781402736421. 96 p. Grades 5–9.

Jurmain, Suzanne. *The Secret of the Yellow Death: A True Story of Medical Sleuthing*. Houghton Mifflin, 2009. ISBN 9780618965816. 112 p. Grades 6–10.

Kallen, Stuart A. *Communication with the Dead* (The Library of Ghosts & Hauntings). Referencepoint Press, 2009. ISBN 9781601520890. 80 p. Grades 4–8.

Kallen, Stuart A. *Haunted Houses* (The Mysterious & Unknown). Referencepoint Press, 2007. ISBN 1601520263. 96 p. Grades 5–8.

Kallen, Stuart A. *The Loch Ness Monster* (The Mysterious & Unknown). Referencepoint Press, 2008. ISBN 9781601520593. 104 p. Grades 4–6.

Kallen, Stuart A. *Vampires* (The Mysterious & Unknown). Referencepoint Press, 2008. ISBN 9781601520296. 104 p. Grades 4–6.

Koestler-Grack, Rachel A. *The Johnstown Flood of 1889* (Great Historic Disasters). Chelsea House, 2008. ISBN 9780791097632. 101 p. Grades 6–up.

Kupperberg, Paul. *The Influenza Pandemic of 1918–1919* (Great Historic Disasters). Chelsea House, 2008. ISBN 9780791096406. 120 p. Grades 6–8.

La Pierre, Yvette. *Neandertals: A Prehistoric Puzzle* (Discovery!). Twenty-First Century Books, 2007. ISBN 9780822575245. 112 p. Grades 6–up.

Lace, William W. *The Curse of King Tut* (The Mysterious & Unknown). Referencepoint Press, 2007. ISBN 1601520247. 104 p. Grades 5–8.

Lace, William. *Ghost Hunters* (The Mysterious & Unknown).Referencepoint Press, 2009. ISBN 9781601520913. 80 p. Grades 4–8.

Lace, William W. *The* Hindenburg *Disaster of 1937* (Great Historic Disasters). Chelsea House , 2008. ISBN 9780791097397. 120 p. Grades 7–10.

Lace, William W. *King Arthur* (The Mysterious & Unknown). Referencepoint Press, 2008. ISBN 9781601520333. 104 p. Grades 4–6.

Lindeen, Mary. *Anatomy of a Volcano* (Shockwave: Science). Children's Press, 2007. ISBN 9780531177914. 36 p. Grades 3–6.

Linneá, Sharon. *Lost Civilizations* (Mysteries Unwrapped*)*. Sterling, 2009. ISBN 9781402739842. 96 p. Grades 4–7.

Lynette, Rachel. *The Abominable Snowman* (Monsters). KidHaven Press, 2007. ISBN 9780737734485. 48 p. Grades 4–6.

Marcovitz, Hal. *Poltergeists* (The Library of Ghosts & Hauntings). Referencepoint Press, 2009. ISBN 9781601520937. 80 p. Grades 4–8.

Mason, Paul. *Into the Fire: Volcanologists* (Scientists at Work). Heinemann, 2007. ISBN 9781403499509. 32 p. Grades 4–6.

Mason, Paul. *The Mystery of Stone Circles* (Can Science Solve?). Heinemann, 2008. ISBN 9781432910235. 32 p. Grades 4–6.

Matthews, John. *King Arthur: Dark Age Warrior and Mythic Hero* (Prime Time History). Rosen, 2008. ISBN 9781404213647. 127 p. Grades 9–up.

McCormick, Lisa Wade. *Ghosts: The Unsolved Mystery* (Blazers: Mysteries of Science). Capstone Press, 2009. ISBN 9781429623278. 32 p. Grades 4–6.

McHugh, Janet. *The Great Chicago Fire* (Code Red). Bearport Publishing, 2007. ISBN 9781597163606. 32 p. Grades 3–6.

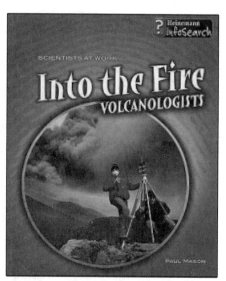

Into the Fire: Volcanologists
by Paul Mason.

Micklos, John. *Unsolved: What Really Happened to Amelia Earhart?* (Prime). Enslow, 2007. ISBN 0766023656. 128 p. Grades 4–8.

Miller, Karen. *Monsters and Water Beasts: Creatures of Fact or Fiction?* Henry Holt, 2007. ISBN 9780805079029. 96 p. Grades 4–8.

Newton, Michael. *Unsolved Crimes* (Criminal Investigations). Chelsea House, 2008. ISBN 9780791094143. 120 p. Grades 7–up.

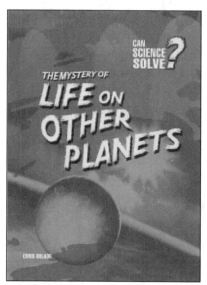

The Mystery of Life on Other Planets by Chris Oxlade.

Noyes, Deborah. *Encyclopedia of the End: Mysterious Death in Fact, Fancy, Folklore, and More.* Houghton Mifflin, 2008. ISBN 9780618823628. 160 p. Grades 6–10.

Oxlade, Chris. *The Mystery of ESP* (Can Science Solve?). Heinemann, 2008. ISBN 9781432910211. 32 p. Grades 4–6.

Oxlade, Chris. *The Mystery of Life on Other Planets* (Can Science Solve?). Heinemann, 2008. ISBN 978-1432910204. 32 p. Grades 4–6.

Oxlade, Chris. *The Mystery of the Death of the Dinosaurs* (Can Science Solve?). Heinemann, 2008. ISBN 9781432910242. 32 p. Grades 4–6.

Oxlade, Chris. *The Mystery of Vampires and Werewolves* (Can Science Solve?). Heinemann, 2008. ISBN 9781432910228. 32 p. Grades 4–6.

Parks, Peggy J. *ESP* (The Mysterious & Unknown). Referencepoint Press, 2007. ISBN 1601520255. 96 p. Grades 5–8.

Parks, Peggy J. *Witches* (The Mysterious & Unknown). Referencepoint Press, 2007. ISBN 9781601520319. 96 p. Grades 6–9.

Peterson, Judy Monroe. *Braving Volcanoes: Volcanologists* (Extreme Scientists). PowerKids Press, 2008. ISBN 9781404245259. 24 p. Grades 3–5.

Rau, Dana Meachen. *Firefighter* (Benchmark Rebus). Benchmark, 2007. ISBN 9780761426172. 24 p. Grades K–1.

Riley, Joelle. *Earthquakes* (Pull Ahead Books). Lerner Publications, 2007. ISBN 9780822579052. 32 p. Grades K–3.

Robson, David. *The Devil* (Mysterious Encounters). KidHaven Press, 2007. ISBN 9780737737806. 48 p. Grades 4–6.

Rubin, Ken. *Volcanoes & Earthquakes* (Insiders). Simon & Schuster, 2007. ISBN 9781416938620. 64 p. Grades 4–7.

Rusch, Elizabeth. *Will It Blow? Become a Volcano Detective at Mount St. Helens.* Sasquatch, 2007. ISBN 1570615101. 46 p. Grades 4–6.

Scher, Linda. *The Texas City Disaster* (Code Red). Bearport Publishing, 2007. ISBN 9781597163637. 32 p. Grades 3–6.

Schreiber, Anne. *Volcanoes!* (National Geographic Readers). National Geographic, 2009. ISBN 9781426302879. 32 p. Grades 1–3.

Simon, Seymour. *Hurricanes.* Collins, 2007. ISBN 9780061170720. 32 p. Grades 2–5.

Slavicek, Louise Chipley. *The San Francisco Earthquake and Fire of 1906* (Great Historic Disasters). Chelsea House, 2008. ISBN 9780791096505. 128 p. Grades 6–up.

Sloate, Susan. *The Secrets of Alcatraz* (Mysteries Unwrapped). Sterling, 2008. ISBN 9781402735912. 96 p. Grades 5–9.

Stewart, Gail. *UFOs* (The Mysterious & Unknown). Referencepoint Press, 2007. ISBN 9781601520302. 95 p. Grades 6–9.

Stewart, Gail B. *Ghosts* (The Mysterious & Unknown). Referencepoint Press, 2008. ISBN 9781601520326. 104 p. Grades 4–6.

Temple, Bob. *The* Titanic*: An Interactive History Adventure* (You Choose Books). Capstone Press, 2007. ISBN 9781429611824. 112 p. Grades 3–6.

Thomas, William David. *Mountain Rescuer* (Cool Careers). Gareth Stevens Publishing, 2008. ISBN 9780836891959. 32 p. Grades 4–7.

Treaster, Joseph B. *Hurricane Force: In the Path of America's Deadliest Storms* (New York Times). Kingfisher, 2007. ISBN 0753460866. 128 p. Grades 6–up.

Walker, Kathryn. *Mysteries of the Bermuda Triangle* (Unsolved!). Crabtree Publishing, 2008. ISBN 9780778741572. 32 p. Grades 3–5.

Wetzel, Charles. *Mysteries Unwrapped: Haunted U.S.A.* Sterling, 2008. ISBN 9781402737350. 96 p. Grades 5–8.

Woog, Adam. *Mummies* (The Mysterious & Unknown). Referencepoint Press, 2008. ISBN 9781601520548. 104 p. Grades 6–9.

Worth, Richard. *Massacre at Virginia Tech: Disaster & Survival* (Deadly Disasters). Enslow, 2008. ISBN 9780766032743. 48 p. Grades 4–6.

Zoehfeld, Kathleen Weidner. *Curse of King Tut's Mummy* (A Stepping Stone Book). Random House, 2007. ISBN 0375938621. 112 p. Grades 1–3.

Chapter

Gross and Disgusting

$$3$$

Many librarians, teachers, and caregivers are female and may shy away from these titles, but this is a cardinal rule of books for boys—you cannot go wrong with gross. Boys love things that are disgusting, messy, horrifying, and gross. Hiding behind most of these books about bugs, bodily functions, dead bodies, and underwear is a big dose of science and even social history. So find these books at your library or bookstore and get them into the hands of boys.

BOOKTALKS

Davies, Nicola. *What's Eating You? Parasites—The Inside Story.* Illustrated by Neal Layton. Candlewick Press, 2007. ISBN 9780763634605. 64 p. Grades 4–8.

This book has bad news for us. Every animal has a habitat, a place where it lives, but parasites have a unique habitat. They live on other animals. For some parasites, the animals they live on are human beings! More than 430 different kinds of parasites can live on or in a human body. And every one of us has at least some! Think of head lice, think of body lice, think of fleas, think of tapeworms . . . do you want to stop thinking?

In this book you will learn about the ectoparasites, which live outside the body, and the endoparasites, which live inside it.

And what do you need to be, to be a parasite? You need to be small, often very small, and you need to be adaptable. So most parasites are invertebrates, such as insects, worms, and single-celled animals. And you need to be adaptable because your environment is not stable. Think of a person—going inside, going outside, taking a bath, getting in a car or a plane—the human environment changes frequently.

There are lots of illustrations here, and some really gross-you-out information.

Deem, James M. *Bodies from the Ice: Melting Glaciers and the Recovery of the Past.* Houghton Mifflin, 2008. ISBN 9780618800452. 58 p. Grades 5–8.

Glaciers are melting all over the world. It is a problem. In many parts of the world, glaciers are the main drinking water supply. What will happen to those areas if all the glaciers disappear? But the melting is also an opportunity, because when glaciers melt, all sorts of things that were buried in the glaciers in the past—sometimes hundreds or even thousands of years ago—start turning up. Some of those things are the bodies of human beings.

This book is loaded with great photographs and illustrations and riveting information about the bodies that scientists, hikers, and mountain climbers are finding, many purely by chance.

The most famous frozen body ever found is the iceman, who was named Otzi (rhymes with tootsie). Erika and Helmut Simon were climbing the Similaun Mountain in Italy near the Austrian border. The weather had been warm, and the snow was melting everywhere. On their way back, they found a body. Helmut took a photo. They reported their discovery to the police.

When the police came, it did not take them long to realize that this was not a recently dead body. In fact, this might be a very old body. An unusual ax was nearby. The body's clothing was strange.

No one had a clue that they were involved in a major archaeological find. They were not as careful as they might have been with either the body or the area surrounding it.

They should have been. The body was about 5,300 years old! There are great photos of the body and lots of interesting information. It turns out that Otzi had been killed in a fight! You'll enjoy reading about him.

Other fascinating bodies included are those of a soldier who died about 1595 and of a woman from about 1700—both from the Alps; the mummified bodies of children found in the Andes Mountains in South America; and a body of a man named George Mallory, who tried to climb Mount Everest in the Himalayas in 1924. It was not his first attempt. People have been wondering for years whether he made it to the top before he fell to his death, and everyone thought that if his body could ever be found, the mystery would be solved. They were wrong. The body was found, but it did not solve the mystery at all! We still don't know.

If you have never seen a glacier, you should go looking for one soon. Who knows what you might discover in it?

If you enjoy this book, be sure to read James Deem's *Bodies from the Bog* and *Bodies from the Ash.*

Author Profile: James Deem

James Deem, who taught English to under-prepared college students for almost 27 years, is best known for his "Bodies" books for children—*Bodies from the Bog*, *Bodies from the Ash*, and *Bodies from the Ice*. His thorough method of research has taken him around the globe in search of primary source material.

What made you start to write nonfiction for kids?

First, let me say that I don't like the word nonfiction. I hate it. The fact that it's defined negatively is really detrimental. Fiction and nonfiction are like twins. Fiction is the good twin—the one that everyone adores—just cute as a button. The problem with nonfiction is that's the twin nobody wants to hang out with. It's like the stereotypical evil twin, the one that's hard to like because it's too serious. I think of fiction as "stories." I think of nonfiction as "true stories." So I prefer the "true stories" name rather than nonfiction.

My wife and I have two sets of twin children, and it was our first set of twin daughters that got me involved writing "true stories." When they were born somebody asked me to consider writing a ghost book. That was before I was published. I thought I would write a book that was not scary—one that would make my children not be afraid of ghosts because that was one of the things that petrified me as a child. So I started researching the subject of ghosts one day and ended up writing my very first nonfiction book, although people have a hard time thinking of it as nonfiction. And that was *How to Find a Ghost*. And of course my daughters as they grew up read it and got scared of ghosts anyway, so it didn't really matter.

How did your "Bodies" series come about?

The last "How To" book I did was called *How to Make a Mummy Talk*. A large part was about bog bodies, and it was just illustrated with cartoons. My editor and I had a conversation after that book came out and she said you really ought to do a book about bog bodies and it could be a picture book. And as soon as she said that I thought it was the kind of picture book I would want to do. I love picture books for my children, but they're not the kind of thing I thought I could ever write—the cutesy picture books. That's not my kind of thing. But as soon as she said I could do bog bodies in a picture book I thought, "Oh, yes I can." So that was the beginning and how *Bodies from the Bog* came about. After that came *Bodies from the Ash* and *Bodies from the Ice*.

Do you write with boys in mind?

I tend to write non-gender-specific books. I'm not thinking I'm going to write this for boys or I'm going to write this for girls. I'm basically just writing a book that I would have liked to read, and I find it easier for me in doing the research and writing if I just think of my childhood and keep it open in that way.

How do you research your books?

When I start to research a book I'm not an expert on the subject. In fact, I really like being ignorant. The less I know the better, because usually if I do know something it's wrong and I find that out pretty quickly as I do the research. The very first thing I do is try to read as much as I can on the subject. I try not to read things written for children, because I find that many nonfiction books for children are not particularly good. I don't mean the award-winning ones or the ones by great nonfiction authors, but the run-of-the-mill. Usually the authors have not done good research. They haven't traveled to see things. They're using the same old stories and the same old things that have been passed down over the years. What I do is I read what scientists and historians have written. I do fairly extensive reading on whatever the topic is. As I do that, I then make decisions about places I would want to go and the people I would want to meet. I make up a list and start going places and I start contacting people to arrange interviews. Some people don't want to be bothered, especially if they hear it's a children's book. You can't always get the access you would like, so I work with what I have. Once I've done the research, which can take a couple of years, I'll sit down and start writing. So all together the process of doing the research and writing can take between two and three years.

What was the most exciting research moment you have had while researching a book?

I get to see some incredible things I never thought I would get to see. One of the times that I went to Pompeii I had permission to go into some of the buildings that are permanently closed. I had three different tour guides from the different guide stations at Pompeii, and they had keys and they took me in. These are the kinds of buildings they would never open to tourists, so they would only be open to researchers. Just to breathe the air in these buildings and see what was there was phenomenal. I went to Pompeii five times. To even go once is unbelievable, so to have been there five times and to walk the streets and picture myself living back then was a dream come true.

Just recently I'm working on a new book and had to make a quick trip to the Netherlands. The book is going to be on facial reconstruction, which is what scientists do when they find a skull and want to know what the person actually looked like when he was alive. In the Netherlands I watched a forensic artist recreate a face on a skull for two days—14 hours the first day and 10 hours the next day, watching him put a face made out of clay on this skull. It was one of the most fascinating things I've ever seen.

Krull, Kathleen, and Paul Brewer. *Fartiste.* Illustrated by Boris Kulikov. Simon & Schuster, 2008. ISBN 9781416928287. Unpaged. Grades 2–5.

It seems unbelievable, but this is a true story.

When Joseph Pujol was a kid in Marseille, France, about 150 years ago, he loved to go swimming in the ocean. One day, in the water, he realized he had an extremely unusual talent—he was able to do some pretty amazing things with his farts! He breathed in air and expelled it—and he could imitate gunshots and make music. In the army, he completely cracked up his comrades.

When he grew up, he became a baker, married, and had ten kids—and not enough money. He started performing as a clown, but then decided to use his own natural abilities. He started playing music with his farts onstage, and he became a big, big star. Presidents, royalty, and famous people of all sorts came to see him and laugh and laugh. You'll love reading about him!

Murphy, Glenn. *Why Is Snot Green? And Other Extremely Important Questions (and Answers).* Illustrated by Mike Phillips. Roaring Brook Press, 2009. ISBN 9781596435001. 236 p. Grades 4–8.

Glenn Murphy, the author of this book, knows what questions kids want to know the answers to. He is an educational presenter in a science museum, and he gets asked these questions all the time. So he decided to write this book. If you want to have a great time, sit down, open it up, and take a look. You won't be able to stop reading.

Here are a few examples:

- If we started digging a hole and kept on going, could we really dig all the way to China? Well, no. One reason is that China is not directly opposite North America. If you could dig that hole, you would come out somewhere in the Indian Ocean! But Mr. Murphy tells us several other excellent reasons why you could not dig down that deep. Part of the problem is that you won't believe how hot it is down there.

- Do animals fart like people do? Well, anything that digests farts, because it is an important part of the digestive process. But Mr. Murphy even gives us a list of the top ten animals that fart—in order by stinkiness! The termite, of all things, is at the top of the list.

- Why do we walk on two legs instead of four? Guess what? Nobody is really sure what the answer is, though there are a lot of theories. You'll enjoy reading them and figuring out which one *you* think is the best answer.

- Where do tsunamis come from? How do they get so big? How come they are so dangerous? See if you can find the answers yourself.

Platt, Richard. *Doctors Did What?! The Weird History of Medicine.* Two-Can Publishing, 2006. ISBN 1587285800. 64 p. Grades 4–8.

You may not like going to the doctor, but wait till you hear what it was like in the past. Learning about the history of medicine is a scary thing. "Less than 150 years ago, doctors knew how to cure only a few of the diseases that can kill us or make our lives miserable and painful. About 250 years before that, they barely understood anything about how the human body works. And before that, medicine was little more than prayer, luck, magic, and superstition" (page 3).

Here are some great facts you will discover:

- In ancient Mesopotamia, doctors made a lot of money doing surgery. But if it didn't work, the surgeon might have his hand cut off!

- A doctor in ancient Greece named Hippocrates believed it was a good thing to eat well and to rest—and that would make the body heal naturally. He was the first one to point this out. Other ancient Greeks were not so smart. They had some really weird ideas that got in the way of scientific fact for 2,000 years. Read about it on page 11.

- Ancient India and ancient China were way ahead of Europeans in their treatment of diseases. Indian surgeons had a great idea. When they had an open wound, they would put soldier ants around it. The ants grabbed the edges of the wound and pulled them together. Then the surgeons grabbed each ant at the waist and snapped it in two. The ant's pincers then worked like stitches do today. They held the wound together. Look at the picture on page 12.

- People did not understood what caused the Black Plague that killed millions of people. Today we know that fleas on rats spread it—and we can cure it with modern drugs.

- Quack medicines promised everything. Some even promised to grow a new leg if yours was amputated. Most of them did not work at all—but their sellers could make a lot of money.

- A big development was anesthesia. People could have surgery and not feel the pain. Imagine having major surgery while wide awake and fully conscious!

Prepare to be grossed out and fascinated!

Author Profile: Richard Platt

Richard Platt, author of more than 80 nonfiction books for children, uses his photography and design training to write heavily illustrated books full of the kind of fun facts that boys love. He initially planned to be a photographer but slipped into writing for children through a fortunate turn of events.

How did you get your start in writing nonfiction for kids?

Many years ago I went to work for Dorling Kindersley as an editor, and I was working on the *Dorling Kindersley Children's Encyclopedia*. We were working through each of the topics in the encyclopedia and we got to sex and reproduction, and the chief editor and the designer were closeted in a smoke-filled room trying to work out how they could present this topic in a way that was direct and honest for children and at the same time was not likely to offend the Idaho potato farmer. This became such a joke that I produced a page about it in the style of the encyclopedia that was circulated around the company. So through this I established a reputation for having a sense of humor. Later, Stephen Biesty, the illustrator, brought some samples of his work to Peter Kindersley and Peter was very impressed by them. Steve's illustrations were very witty, but his jokes were rather dry. So Peter Kindersley tried to think of who they could link up with Steve to leaven his dry drawings with some slapstick humor. Because of my earlier prank I got the job. It was one of those things where your career turns in the most odd and peculiar way for the most ridiculous of reasons. So that was how I got a start in writing nonfiction.

You have done quite a few Eyewitness books for Dorling Kindersley. What is the process for writing those books?

They're a publishing phenomenon, and they were very influential in changing the way children's books, in fact in the way all books, are produced, really. The formula is very rigid, as you can see by comparing any two of the Eyewitness books. Each book has to consist of 29 double-page spreads. I would work up how to divide the topic into 29 and how to arrange those subtopics in a logical way so you could work your way through the book. And once they'd given me the OK on it I would do a picture list of the pictures I ideally wanted them to find. They would go away and find the pictures or they would commission the photographer and they would lay the pages out. They would supply me with a layout with a word count on it, and I would write captions and main text to the length they had supplied. It's a mechanical way of working, but once you've done it four or five times you get used to it. It has produced some wonderful books—not just the ones I've written, but I mean generally some of the Eyewitness series are truly wonderful and give me an insight in the subject that you can't, or couldn't, find at the time in any other book.

Do you choose the books you will write?

More often it's a question of the publisher saying we would like a book about so-and-so, and increasingly publishing is driven by the series. Publishers are reluctant to produce a book on a single subject as a stand-alone volume. They find it easier to sell the rights to a series to foreign publishers, and because of the cost of publishing heavily illustrated books, obtaining foreign co-editions is vitally important. So frequently the publisher will approach me with book ideas.

How many books are you working on at one time?

Probably no fewer than three and sometimes as many as six or seven. That's if you include the whole process, from planning the book at one end to checking proofs at the other end. At the moment I'm working on a Web site for the USS *Constitution*, Old Ironsides. I'm working on a book about codes and ciphers for Collins. And what else am I doing? I'm finishing off a Through Time book on New York. That's almost done. I'm working on a book about pirates. I'm working on a book about Ellis Island and an Irish child who goes to New York for

Walker Books (Candlewick Press in the United States). And that's it at the moment. So quite a lot, simultaneously.

Do you write with boys in mind when you're writing books for young people?

Not really. I think that my writing is sometimes identified as the kind of writing that gets boys reading, but I don't consciously do that, and I try to introduce female characters whenever I can and I try to avoid gender stereotyping. There is a perception in publishing that girls will read books with a male lead character but boys will not read books that have a female lead character. That's a stereotype; I'm not sure how true it is. But certainly there is a sort of subtle pressure from publishers sometimes.

Visit Richard Platt online at http://www.richardplatt.co.uk.

Platt, Richard. *They Ate What?! The Weird History of Food* (Weird History). Two-Can Publishing, 2006. ISBN 1587285770. 48 p. Grades 4–8.

There are a lot of things that many modern people will not eat. Period. In North America, hardly anyone wants to eat horsemeat, or bugs, or dogs, or lots of other food that people in other places in the world might consider delicious.

This book is loaded with drawings and photographs, and gives us a lot of information about what people ate in the past and continue to eat today—and some of it may surprise you. Here are some things you'll read about.

- Coprolites are fossilized feces—or poop. Scientists love to find them, because by examining them they can tell what people and animals ate in the past. There is even a name for the study of this kind of fossil: paleoscatology.

- A popular dish in ancient Rome was roasted dormouse. A dormouse is a little smaller than a squirrel. Romans trapped them and stuck them in a jar and fattened them up with hazelnuts and acorns. They got so fat that they had to break the jar to get them out!

- Read the list of table manners from the Middle Ages on page 9. Here's one: "When you use your fingers to blow your nose, wipe them on your clothes, not the tablecloth." How would your teacher like that if you tried it in school?

- Many people around the world eat rats! Look at the picture on page 25.

- How about worms? Would you like to try one? Look at the pictures on pages 34 and 35.

And that is just the beginning. You will have fun with this one!

Prishmann, Deirdre A. *Poop-Eaters: Dung Beetles in the Food Chain* (Fact Finders). Capstone Press, 2008. ISBN 9781429612654. 32 p. Grades 3–5.

Dung beetles are a wonderful gift to the earth. They get rid of animal waste in a really effective way. If you have ever stepped on dog poop, you know it is really yucky. Isn't it great that someone or something else has to clean it up? And that is what dung beetles do.

They are an important part of the food chain—they break down waste and return the nutrients to the soil. And this book tells us all about them.

Here are three amazing dung beetle facts:

- They do not eat or drink anything but poop. They get everything they need from it.

- They can bury more than 250 times their weight in one day.

- They eat their own poop.

You will learn about the different types of dung beetles—the tunnelers, the dwellers, the thieves, and the rollers. Guess what each kind does!

If you aren't grossed out too easily, you will have a lot of fun with this book.

Raum, Elizabeth. *The Story Behind Toilets* (True Stories). Heinemann, 2009. ISBN 9781432923501. 32 p. Grades 3–7.

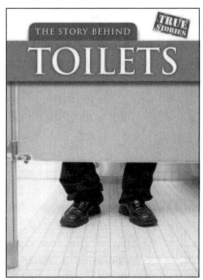

The Story Behind Toilets **by Elizabeth Raum.**

In the United States most people say they have to go to the restroom or to the bathroom. They mean it! Our bodies need to get rid of waste. It is an important part of our life. And for most of us, that means using a toilet. This book tells us the fascinating story of toilets.

Long ago, people just used the outdoors to go to the bathroom. They did not live in towns or cities, so there was plenty of space to do that. But once they did begin to live in villages and cities, proper disposal of waste became a problem. By the time of ancient Rome, sewer systems were developed. Look at the picture of the 12-man toilet on page 7—it was used in what is now Tunisia.

Some people used chamber pots, which they either sat directly on or which were put in the bottom of chairs designed for that purpose. On page 8, look at that fancy chamber pot. It has a picture of a man's face on it. It was made in the 1770s in colonial America. It has a picture of King George III of England on it. People could go to the bathroom right on the king's head!

The first flush toilet was designed more than 400 years ago, but it did not catch on. By the late 1770s, however, flush toilets did start to catch on. But you needed running water for them to work, and a lot of people did not have that.

This book is loaded with great information. Do you know you can still take tours of the sewers of Paris? Or that toilet paper was first sold in the United States in 1857? Or that a man in Korea has built his home to look like a giant toilet? Do you know about dual-flush toilets or the kind of toilets they use in space? You'll have a lot of fun finding out.

Rosenberg, Pam. *Blecch! Icky, Sticky, Gross Stuff in Your School.* (Icky, Sticky, Gross-Out Books). Illustrated by Beatriz Helena Ramos. Child's World. 2008. ISBN 9781592968992. 24 p. Grades 2–4.

> Would you believe that the tray you pick up in the cafeteria is a *lot* germier than the toilet seat in the restroom? Like *ten* times as germy? Well, it is.
>
> This book is just full of gross things we encounter almost every day at school, such as:
>
> - Your mouth is the germiest part of your body—about 100 million microscopic critters live there.
>
> - Borrowing another kid's comb may get you something you do not want: lice.
>
> - Cockroaches love to eat food you forget to take out of your locker. They like sweat, too. Some female cockroaches can produce half a million babies every year!
>
> You will be grossed out by the information in this book for sure.

Swain, Ruth Freeman. *Underwear: What We Wear Under There.* Illustrated by John O'Brien. Holiday House, 2008. ISBN 0823419207. 32 p. Grades 1–4.

> The first underwear was probably what we call the breechcloth—a strip of leather worn between the legs and looped over a cord tied around the waist. Many Native Americans wore these. But when people learned to weave cloth, they wore loincloths, like Tarzan—strips of fabric wrapped around the waist and through the legs, then tucked in. They protected people's private parts—and are still worn in parts of the world today.
>
> There was some underwear by the Middle Ages in Europe, but it was just filthy. It was only washed a few times a year!
>
> You will learn a lot about the history of underwear—and believe me, you would not want to wear a corset. Some men wore them, too, not just women! And women wore skirts that were as much as six feet wide. They also wore hoop skirts, usually made from whalebone or steel. They could fly right up and show everything, which meant you had to be careful to wear lots of underwear.
>
> You will learn about bloomers, long johns, union suits, and much, much more. You will have a lot of fun learning about underwear.

Walker, Richard. *Ouch! How Your Body Makes It Through a Very Bad Day.* DK, 2007. ISBN 9780756625368. 72 p. Grades 5–8.

> Interesting! Yucky! Disgusting! Amazing!
>
> Those are a few of the feelings you experience when you start looking through this book.
>
> We get a look at what goes on inside and outside our bodies when all sorts of things happen, from the scary and threatening to the normal, both pleasant and unpleasant. There are lots of color pictures and illustrations that show us exactly what happens. Here are a few samples:
>
> - Your eyelids snap shut the minute you sneeze. It is virtually impossible to keep your eyes open and sneeze at the same time.

- "Bone is as strong as steel but six times lighter, making the skeleton robust and easy to move" (page 15).

- Don't ever squeeze pimples, however bad they look. Your face might look a lot worse—permanently—if you do. Check out the facts on pages 16 through 19.

- Look at the magnified photograph of a scab on page 25. It looks yucky, but it really is a wonderful thing that protects us in all sorts of ways.

- Learn about some of the pathogens and parasites we can have in and on our bodies on pages 40 and 41. The tapeworm can be more than 16 feet long—and live right inside us!

- What exactly goes on when you choke? Check it out on pages 56 and 57.

- How do our tongues detect good and bad tastes? What makes us suspicious that a food may not be good? Read about that on pages 58–59.

And that's just the beginning. You'll have lots of fun learning how our bodies really work.

WORTH READING

Nonfiction books with "boy appeal" that have received positive reviews in *Booklist*, *Horn Book Guide*, and/or *School Library Journal*.

Barnhill, Kelly Regan. *Do You Know Where Your Water Has Been? The Disgusting Story Behind What You're Drinking* (Sanitation Investigation). Capstone Press, 2008. ISBN 9781429619950. 32 p. Grades 3–7.

Barnhill, Kelly Regan. *Sewers and the Rats That Love Them: The Disgusting Story Behind Where It All Goes* (Sanitation Investigation). Capstone Press, 2008. ISBN 9781429619981. 32 p. Grades 3–7.

Carney, Elizabeth. *Mummies* (National Geographic Readers). National Geographic, 2009. ISBN 9781426305290. 32 p. Grades K–2.

Day, Jeff. *Don't Touch That! The Book of Gross, Poisonous, and Downright Icky Plants and Critters*. Chicago Review Press, 2008. ISBN 9781556527111. 112 p. Grades 3–6.

Dipucchio, Kelly. *Sipping Spiders Through a Straw: Campfire Songs for Monsters*. Scholastic Press, 2008. ISBN 9780439584012. Unpaged. Grades 2–5.

Sewers and the Rats That Love Them: The Disgusting Story Behind Where It All Goes by Kelly Regan Barnhill.

Donovan, Sandy. *Hawk & Drool: Gross Stuff in Your Mouth* (Gross Body Science). Millbrook Press, 2009. ISBN 978- 0822589662. 48 p. Grades 3–5.

Goldish, Meish. *Baby Bug Dishes* (Extreme Cuisine). Bearport Publishing, 2009. ISBN 9781597167581. 24 p. Grades 3–6.

Goldish, Meish. *Bug-a-licious* (Extreme Cuisine). Bearport Publishing, 2009. ISBN 9781597167574. 24 p. Grades 2–5.

Goldish, Meish. *Deadly Praying Mantises* (No Backbone! the World of Invertebrates). Bearport Publishing, 2008. ISBN 9781597165822. 24 p. Grades K–3.

Goldish, Meish. *Disgusting Hagfish* (Gross-Out Defenses). Bearport Publishing, 2008. ISBN 9781597167192. 24 p. Grades 2–3.

Hawk & Drool: Gross Stuff in Your Mouth **by Sandy Donovan.**

Baby Bug Dishes **by Meish Goldish.**

Bug-a-licious **by Meish Goldish.**

Disgusting Hagfish **by Meish Goldish.**

Goldish, Meish. *Spider-tizers and Other Creepy Treats* (Extreme Cuisine). Bearport Publishing, 2009. ISBN 9781597167598. 24 p. Grades 2–3.

Harris, Elizabeth Snoke. *Yikes! Wow! Yuck!* Sterling, 2008. ISBN 1579909302. 112 p. Grades 4–7.

Hynson, Colin. *You Wouldn't Want to Be an Inca Mummy! A One-Way Journey You'd Rather Not Make* (You Wouldn't Want to). Franklin Watts, 2007. ISBN 0531187446. 32 p. Grades 4–8.

Katz, Alan. *Smelly Locker: Silly Dilly School Songs.* Margaret K. McElderry Books, 2008. ISBN 9781416906957. 32 p. Grades 1–5.

***Spider-tizers and Other Creepy Treats* by Meish Goldish.**

Katz, Alan, and David Catrow. *On Top of the Potty: And Other Get-Up-and-Go Songs.* Margaret K. McElderry Books, 2008. ISBN 9780689862151. 32 p. All ages.

Larsen, C. S. *Crust and Spray: Gross Stuff in Your Eyes, Ears, Nose, and Throat* (Gross Body Science). Millbrook Press, 2009. ISBN 9780822589648. 48 p. Grades 3–5.

Lew, Kristi. *Clot & Scab: Gross Stuff About Your Scrapes, Bumps, and Bruises* (Gross Body Science). Millbrook Press, 2009. ISBN 9780822589655. 48 p. Grades 3–5.

Lunis, Natalie. *Deadly Black Widows* (No Backbone! the World of Invertebrates). Bearport Publishing, 2008. ISBN 9781597166676. 24 p. Grades 1–3.

Lunis, Natalie. *Gooey Jellyfish* (No Backbone! the World of Invertebrates). Bearport Publishing, 2007. ISBN 9781597165105. 24 p. Grades 1–3.

Lunis, Natalie. *Leggy Centipedes* (No Backbone! The World of Invertebrates!). Bearport Publishing, 2009. ISBN 9781597167529. 24 p. Grades K–3.

Lunis, Natalie. *Portuguese Man-of-War: Floating Misery* (Afraid of the Water). Bearport Publishing, 2009. ISBN 9781597169462. 24 p. Grades 2–4.

Lunis, Natalie. *Stinging Scorpions* (No Backbone! The World of Invertebrates!). Bearport Publishing, 2009. ISBN 9781597167567. 24 p. Grades K–3.

Matthews, Rupert. *You Wouldn't Want to Be a Mayan Soothsayer! Fortunes You'd Rather Not Tell* (You Wouldn't Want to). Franklin Watts, 2007. ISBN 978-0531187463. 32 p. Grades 4–8.

Miller, Connie Colwell. *Garbage, Waste, Dumps, and You: The Disgusting Story Behind What We Leave Behind* (Sanitation Investigation). Capstone Press, 2008. ISBN 9781429619967. 32 p. Grades 3–7.

Miller, Connie Colwell. *Getting to Know Your Toilet: The Disgusting Story Behind Your Home's Strangest Feature* (Sanitation Investigation). Capstone Press, 2008. ISBN 9781429619974. 32 p. Grades 3–7.

Murphy, Glen. *How Loud Can You Burp? More Extremely Important Questions (and Answers).* Illustrated by Mike Phillips. Roaring Brook Press, 2009. ISBN 9781596435063. 284 p. Grades 5–9.

Murray, Julie. *Backyard* (That's Gross! a Look at Science). Buddy Books, 2009. ISBN 9781604535532. 32 p.

Murray, Julie. *The Body* (That's Gross! a Look at Science). Buddy Books, ISBN 9781604535549. 32 p. Grades 2–5.

Murray, Julie. *Home* (That's Gross! a Look at Science). Buddy Books, 2009. ISBN 9781604535556. 32 p. Grades 2–5.

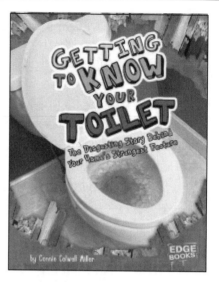

Getting to Know Your Toilet: The Disgusting Story Behind Your Home's Strangest Feature **by Connie Colwell Miller.**

Murray, Julie. *Hospital* (That's Gross! a Look at Science). Buddy Books, 2009. ISBN 9781604535563. 32 p. Grades 2–5.

Murray, Julie. *School* (That's Gross! a Look at Science). Buddy Books, 2009. ISBN 9781604535570. 32 p. Grades 2–5.

Murray, Julie. *Underwater* (That's Gross! a Look at Science). Buddy Books, 2009. ISBN 9781604535587. 32 p. Grades 2–5.

Neuman, Pearl. *Bloodsucking Leeches* (No Backbone! the World of Invertebrates!). Bearport Publishing, 2009. ISBN 9781597167550. 24 p. Grades K–3.

Nichols, Catherine. *Tricky Opossums* (Gross-Out Defenses). Bearport Publishing, 2008. ISBN 9781597167185. 24 p. Grades K–3.

Pipe, Jim. *You Wouldn't Want to Be an Aristocrat in the French Revolution! A Horrible Time in Paris You'd Rather Avoid* (You Wouldn't Want to). Franklin Watts, 2007. ISBN 0531187454. 32 p. Grades 4–8.

Pipe, Jim. *You Wouldn't Want to Be Cleopatra! An Egyptian Ruler You'd Rather Not Be.* Franklin Watts, 2007. ISBN 9780531187268. 32 p. Grades 3–6.

Rosenberg, Pam. *Ack! Icky, Sticky, Gross Stuff Underground* (Icky, Sticky, Gross-Out Books). Child's World, 2007. ISBN 9781592969005. 24 p. Grades 2–3.

Rosenberg, Pam. *Eek! Icky, Sticky, Gross Stuff in Your Food* (Icky, Sticky, Gross-Out Books). Child's World, 2007. ISBN 9781592968954. 24 p. Grades 2–3.

Rosenberg, Pam. *Eew! Icky, Sticky, Gross Stuff in Your Body* (Icky, Sticky, Gross-Out Books). Child's World, 2007. ISBN 9781592968947. 24 p. Grades 2–3.

Somervill, Barbara A. *Fleas: Feasting on Blood* (Bloodsuckers). PowerKids Press, 2007. ISBN 9781404238053. 24 p. Grades 3–5.

Somervill, Barbara A. *Leeches: Waiting in the Water* (Bloodsuckers). PowerKids Press, 2007. ISBN 9781404238015. 24 p. Grades 3–5.

Somervill, Barbara A. *Mosquitoes: Hungry for Blood* (Bloodsuckers). PowerKids Press, 2007. ISBN 9781404238022. 24 p. Grades 3–5.

Williams, Dinah. *Shocking Seafood* (Extreme Cuisine). Bearport Publishing, 2009. ISBN 9781597167611. 24 p. Grades 3–6.

Williams, Dinah. *Slithery, Slimy, Scaly Treats* (Extreme Cuisine). Bearport Publishing, 2009. ISBN 9781597167628. 24 p. Grades 4–6.

Chapter ——————— 4

Creepy-Crawly Creatures: Bugs, Reptiles, and Amphibians

Animals are the subject of hundreds of new children's books each year. How do you decide which ones to spend your money on? Start with well-reviewed books about high-interest subjects. Look for great photography to capture their attention (see the Nic Bishop books below—no one can match his stunning photographs). Kids have a fascination with the natural world, so capitalize on it. You cannot go wrong with bugs, snakes, lizards, frogs, and other creepy-crawly creatures.

BOOKTALKS

Bishop, Nic. *Nic Bishop Butterflies and Moths.* Scholastic Press, 2009. ISBN 9780439877572. 48 p. Grades 1–5.

If you have never read a Nic Bishop book before, you cannot even imagine what you are missing. And if you ever thought butterflies and moths were pretty but not very interesting, you are in for a big surprise.

Bishop is not only an amazing photographer, but he has a lot of great stories to tell. Start looking at the book and you won't be able to stop.

Here are a few of the wonderful things you will learn:

- Moth eggs are tiny, maybe as big as a grain of sand. Then they turn into caterpillars.

- Most caterpillar mothers lay their eggs on the favorite food plant of the young—so the minute the caterpillar gets out, it has a handy food supply close by.

- The glasswing butterfly from the Amazon rainforest is shown on page 30. It has transparent wings—look right through them.

- The luna moth, shown on page 37, is considered one of the most beautiful moths in North America. It only lives for about a week—and it does not even have a mouth. It lives on the food stored in its body when it was a caterpillar.

- Look at the photo of the snake on page 17. The surprise is that this is not a snake—it is a caterpillar. You won't believe it till you see it—and then read Bishop's astounding story of how he got that photo on pages 46–47.

You will be astounded by this book—guaranteed.

Author Profile: Nic Bishop

Writer and photographer Nic Bishop had many adventures growing up in places such as New Guinea, Sudan, and Bangladesh. His PhD in biology and incredible skills as a photographer have led him to pursue the adventurous life while writing some astounding books for young readers.

I know from your Web site that you weren't a reader when you were a child. Did you read anything at all as a boy?

I didn't read at all really. When I was about 12 or 14 I started reading books a little bit—maybe one a year at the most. The first books I started taking an interest in were nonfiction books—adventure books—books about people sailing around the world or people exploring the Amazon rainforest or something. I was very much into exploring when I was in my teenage years. So that was really when I first started taking any interest in books and even then it was a fairly casual interest. I've never been a serious and heavy-duty reader.

What do you read now as an adult?

I read more now. I read a lot of nonfiction. I tend to read science books and I read about the history of exploration—books about Captain Cook sailing around the world and things like this. My tastes haven't changed all that much.

Do you write with boys in mind? Do you write things you would have wanted to read as a boy?

I'm never writing with boys in mind at all. I'm just writing for my own pleasure about things I'm interested in. I'm a biologist and I think living things are amazing. Since I am a photographer I get a lot of firsthand experience with animals. I've seen them or maybe held them in my hand or followed them in the wild. They are amazing and very real to me because I've had this personal contact with them. The main driving force is what I find interesting.

You have done so much exploring and adventuring in your life. Did you have regular jobs to make some money before you became a successful writer?

I went to university in England and after that I didn't have any particular career in mind. I just knew I didn't like living in England because I'd been raised so much overseas when I was younger. I decided to go off and have an adventure because I'd always liked outdoor exploration and adventure. I traveled out to New Zealand with no particular plan. I just traveled overland on local transport, buying bus tickets and things. I got to New Zealand and I did do jobs there, but they were just casual jobs working as a waiter or I worked as a technician at the university for a while. I planted trees for a while. I did all sorts of things, mainly so I could have lots of time to go off hiking into the mountains and things like that. Then I did a PhD in New Zealand and when I was about 30 I realized I had to actually follow some sort of career path. I knew at that stage that I really enjoyed taking photographs, so that's when I decided that I might as well go into doing books. I also knew I'd rather be self-employed than work for a company. I much preferred being outdoors and observing firsthand. I thought doing books would be a good way of having that firsthand experience. I thought I'd be able to use my interest in photography in producing books.

You began writing and photographing books for adults. Was it hard to break into children's publishing?

When I first started I never had any particular reason to do children's books because I didn't read children's books when I was young. I did about four or five fairly large adult books, which take about one or two years apiece, which is pretty slow going. A children's publisher contacted me because it was apparent that young readers liked my close-up photographs of frogs and other small animals. I took these photographs for adults, but children seemed to like them and it kind of surprised me at first. Up till then I'd just never even thought about it, but it made a lot of sense for me to do children's books. I could still do the same style of photography that I'd always done. I didn't need to change much. So I moved into children's books.

Are you planning to stick with children's books?

Yes. I'll never do any more adult books. It didn't take me long to switch from one to the other because adult books take so long. It's two years or so and so much goes wrong in two years—your publisher gets sold or your editor gets sacked or something. You have so much invested in this book and the money's not coming in and after a year you're sick of doing it. You know you've had enough of this book, but you've got to keep going for another year to finish it. It's just so stressful. But children's books take between three months and six months each, so you're still having fun and then you're on to the next one. And I find other children's authors and children's publishers more friendly. Other adult authors are much more guarded about their work because they have so much invested in each book and a lot of ego wrapped up in them. So I much prefer working in children's books.

How do you choose the books you will work on?

I've never worked on any publisher's suggestion. It's entirely what I want to do. But they hint occasionally of course. They might say why don't we do a book on so-and-so and usually it's an idea I've thought of already because it's so obvious. I just work on ideas that I want to do and usually we agree on the same thing.

Which comes first, the writing or the photography?

When I plan a book I first think about the photographs I want to include. Some people think that photographs are just a random process, that you go walking around in Africa or wherever you're going to take pictures and you just see things. But that's not the way most photographers work. I'm a pretty controlled person, so when I start doing one of these books I think about what sort of photographs I need to give a broad picture of the animal that I'm going to feature. I'll write a list of different sorts of animals I want in the book and what I want these animals to be doing—whether I want the animal laying eggs or eating or hunting or running. Of course you can't get everything you want because nature is somewhat random. Some things I would just never manage to find, and other things I might find that I never expected. So there is a bit of a mixture. But I am pretty pre-planned in these books. And I certainly can't write until I've taken the photographs because it's entirely hopeless to expect to get a particular picture.

I know you've had many amazing experiences doing your research and photography. Can you tell about any research moments that really stand out in your mind?

Yes and no. People think I must have lots of dangerous moments because it seems risky, but I'm a very controlled and planned sort of person. I'm usually fairly cautious in the way I do things. I try and avoid anything going wrong on these trips. They can be amazing all the same. For example, Sy Montgomery and I did the book on tree kangaroos and that was really neat because I grew up in Papua New Guinea between the ages of 14 and 18. And so to go back when I was approaching 50 was amazing. After all those years I could still speak pidgin English, and in the evenings when we finished looking for tree kangaroos I could swap stories with local guides and that was great. That's one amazing thing that I remember.

Bishop, Nic. *Nic Bishop Frogs*. Scholastic Press, 2008. ISBN 0439877555. 48 p. Grades 3–6.

Even if frogs creep you out, you are going to love looking through this book. It has the most amazing photographs and information. Nic Bishop spent a lot of time getting the perfect pictures of the many frogs in the book. Take a look at these pages:

- On pages 8 and 9, look at the picture of the African bullfrog. He is a baby, but he can weigh up to three pounds when he grows up. Wow! Check out the picture of a grown-up one on page 40. Bishop tells us that frogs have lungs, but they also breathe through their skin—but only if the skin is damp. If a frog ever dries out completely, it will die.

- You can see the insides of glass frogs! Look at the picture on page 11. No one knows why they are transparent, but you can see the heart, stomach, and other organs. Bishop tells us that frogs do not have rib bones, which means they can squeeze through some tight places.

- Maybe the most amazing photograph in the book is on page 14. The frog is leaping straight out of the water to catch a caterpillar. At the end of the book, Bishop tells us exactly how he took this incredible picture.

- Poison dart frogs are brightly colored. That is a warning to other animals. Don't eat me! It works, too. Just licking one of these frogs can make you sick. South and Central American natives use these to make their arrow points poisonous. They rub the point on the frog and they have created a lethal weapon. Take a look at a couple of these frogs on pages 24 and 25, and also on page 42.

You will not believe what you will find out about frogs!

Goldish, Meish. *Smelly Stink Bugs* (No Backbone! the World of Invertebrates). Bearport Publishing, 2008. ISBN 9781597165808. 24 p. Grades 1–4.

Stink bugs got their name because of one interesting thing: they have stinky smelling liquid inside their bodies that they spray when they get scared. It's yucky!

There are more than 4,000 kinds of them, and many are brightly colored. They have beaks, not teeth, and they use their beaks like straws. They drink the liquid from plants or the blood from bodies of other insects. They are pretty good at camouflaging themselves to look like their surroundings. Take a look at the picture on pages 16–17.

This book tells about their lives. It has great pictures and is fun to read.

Smelly Stink Bugs **by Meish Goldish.**

Markle, Sandra. *Sneaky, Spinning Baby Spiders*. Walker & Company, 2008. ISBN 9780802796974. 32 p. Grades 3–5.

Baby spiders are called spiderlings, and this book shows us some incredible photographs of a lot of them. The facts are pretty interesting, too! Here are a few:

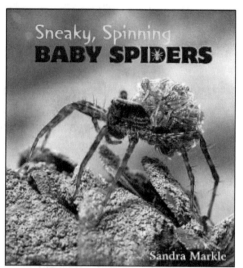

Sneaky, Spinning Baby Spiders
by Sandra Markle.

- Look at the photo on page 7 of the silk strands, called spinnerets, shooting out of a spider's rear end. "When the spider fastens the silk to something—even its own leg—and pulls, the liquid is transformed into a solid strand five times stronger than a steel wire of the same thickness!"

- Female spiders are bigger than males—and dangerous to males. So male spiders wait until the female starts feeding and then they rush in to mate.

- Look at the photo of the crab spider rushing out to defend her egg sac from an ant. She is killing it!

- Spiders aren't looking to bite or hurt people. The only time they do that is when they are afraid of being attacked themselves. Spiders are wonderfully helpful to us because they eat a lot of insects that harm people—like mosquitoes and flies, for instance.

Nirgiotis, Nicholas. *Killer Ants*. Illustrated by Emma Stevenson. Holiday House, 2009. ISBN 9780823420346. Unpaged. Grades 2–5.

Many of the more than 13,000 species of ants are peaceful, but not all. This book tells us the true story of the several different kids of flesh-eating killer ants. They work in huge groups, biting their victims with powerful jaws and tearing them to pieces. Many of them sting while doing this. These are mostly army ants that live in South and Central America, but there also are red fire ants in the southern United States and bull-dog ants in Australia.

Let's take a look at some of the information.

- Army ants live in large colonies of hundreds of thousands to millions. They do not build nests. Instead they build a temporary home using their own bodies as walls and roofs. Look at the picture on page 9. The bivouac keeps the queen of the ant colony and her babies safe.

- All the worker ants are female. The male ants are the only ants in the colony with wings. They mate with young queens in other colonies and live only two days.

- There are too many army ants in a column for anything to fight. Instead, even the largest animals just run away. If the animals are caught, "the workers sting them to subdue them. Then they rip them into small pieces with their powerful jaws and carry the booty of animal pieces to the bivouac to be eaten" (page 16). Yuck!

- Fire ants, described on pages 22 and 23, are often called "the ants from hell." To be stung by one feels like being burned with a match. It is not just one match, for usually many fire ants bite at the same time. Fire ants came to the United States in 1918 in a ship from South America being loaded in Mobile, Alabama.

- Ants have been around since before dinosaurs. If you want to see one of nature's oldest life forms, go outside and look.

Turner, Pamela S. *The Frog Scientist* (Scientists in the Field). Photographs by Andy Comins. Houghton Mifflin, 2009. ISBN 9780618717163. 58 p. Grades 4–8.

You may have read about it or heard about it. Strange things are happening to frogs. The frog population is going way down, and deformed frogs are being born—lots and lots of them. And the world would have a lot more bugs in it if it weren't for frogs. We need them. Now scientists are trying to figure out what is going on.

This is the story of one scientist, Dr. Tyrone Hayes, and his assistants and the research they are doing to solve the mystery. Their work includes catching frogs, taking them to laboratories, dissecting them, comparing frogs that grow up without pesticides in their water with frogs who grow up with pesticides, especially one called atrazine, and in general finding out everything they possibly can about frogs. After all, if tiny amounts of pesticides in water have a devastating impact on frogs and their bodies, might those pesticides also damage human beings? We need to know.

Dr. Hayes is a pretty cool guy. By the time he was five years old, he knew he liked frogs. He says, "I tell kids, if there is something you like doing, stick with it!" (p. 9).

Frogs proved to be a great thing in which to specialize. At an international conference in 1989, several scientists had discovered that there seemed to be fewer amphibians in their part of the world. Put all of that information together and you realize this is not something that is happening at a local level. It is happening all over the world. Some frogs have already disappeared forever, becoming extinct.

This book is loaded with wonderful photographs of frogs and the people who are studying them. It is a wonderful look at a terrible mystery.

WORTH READING

Nonfiction books with "boy appeal" that have received positive reviews in *Booklist*, *Horn Book Guide*, and/or *School Library Journal*.

Armentrout, David, and Patricia Armentrout. *Blood Suckers* (Weird and Wonderful Animals). Rourke Publishing, 2008. ISBN 9781604723014. 32 p. Grades 2–4.

Bredeson, Carmen. *Fun Facts About Alligators!* (I Like Reptiles and Amphibians!). Enslow, 2007. ISBN 9780766027862. 24 p. Grades K–2.

Bredeson, Carmen. *Fun Facts About Frogs!* (I Like Reptiles and Amphibians!). Enslow, 2007. ISBN 9780766027886. 24 p. Grades K–2.

Bredeson, Carmen. *Fun Facts About Lizards!* (I Like Reptiles and Amphibians!). Enslow, 2007. ISBN 0766027899. 24 p. Grades K–2.

Bredeson, Carmen. *Fun Facts About Salamanders!* (I Like Reptiles and Amphibians!). Enslow, 2007. ISBN 9780766027909. 24 p. Grades 1–3.

Bredeson, Carmen. *Fun Facts About Snakes!* (I Like Reptiles and Amphibians!). Enslow, 2007. ISBN 9780766027879. 24 p. Grades K–2.

Bredeson, Carmen. *Fun Facts About Turtles!* (I Like Reptiles and Amphibians!). Enslow, 2007. ISBN 9780766027855. 24 p. Grades 1–3.

Bredeson, Carmen. *Poison Dart Frogs Up Close* (Zoom in on Animals!). Enslow, 2008. ISBN 9780766030770. 24 p. Grades 1–3.

Bredeson, Carmen. *Tarantulas Up Close* (Zoom in on Animals!). Enslow, 2008. ISBN 9780766030763. 24 p. Grades 1–3.

Camisa, Kathryn. *Hairy Tarantulas* (No Backbone! the World of Invertebrates). Bearport Publishing, 2008. ISBN 9781597167048. 24 p. Grades 1–3.

Campbell, Sarah C., and Richard P. Campbell. *Wolfsnail: A Backyard Predator.* Boyds Mills, 2008. ISBN 9781590785546. 32 p. Grades K–2.

Poison Dart Frogs Up Close by **Carmen Bredeson.**

Hairy Tarantulas by Kathryn Camisa.

Coates, Jennifer. *Lizards* (Our Best Friends). Eldorado Ink. 2008. ISBN 9781932904314. 112 p. Grades 7–12.

Coxon, Michele. *Termites on a Stick.* Star Bright Books, 2008. ISBN 9781595721211. 32 p. Grades K–1.

Davies, Andrew. *Super-Size Bugs.* Sterling, 2008. ISBN 9781402753404. 28 p. Grades 2–6.

Dixon, Norma. *Focus on Flies*. Fitzhenry and Whiteside, 2008. ISBN 9781550051285. 32 p. Grades 3–6.

Dussling, Jennifer. *Deadly Poison Dart Frogs* (Gross-Out Defenses). Bearport Publishing, 2008. ISBN 9781597167208. 24 p. Grades 2–3.

Gaines, Ann. *Top 10 Reptiles and Amphibians for Kids* (Top Pets for Kids With American Humane). Enslow, 2008. ISBN 9780766030749. 48 p. Grades 2–5.

Gibbons, Gail. *Snakes*. Holiday House, 2007. ISBN 0823421228. 32 p. Grades 1–3.

Glaser, Linda. *Dazzling Dragonflies: A Life Cycle Story* (Linda Glaser's Classic Creatures). Millbrook Press, 2007. ISBN 9780822567530. 32 p. Grades K–3.

Deadly Praying Mantises **by Meish Goldish.**

Goldish, Meish. *Deadly Praying Mantises* (No Backbone! the World of Invertebrates). Bearport Publishing, 2008. ISBN 978-1597165822. 24 p. Grades K–3.

Goldish, Meish. *Goliath Bird-Eating Tarantula: The World's Biggest Spider* (Supersized!). Bearport Publishing, 2007. ISBN 1597163899. 24 p. Grades 1–3.

Goldish, Meish. *Hidden Walkingsticks* (No Backbone! the World of Invertebrates). Bearport Publishing, 2008. ISBN 9781597166461. 24 p. Grades K–3.

Goldish, Meish. *Jumping Spiders* (No Backbone! the World of Invertebrates). Bearport Publishing, 2008. ISBN 9781597167055. 24 p. Grades 1–3.

Goldish, Meish. *Leaping Grasshoppers* (No Backbone! the World of Invertebrates). Bearport Publishing, 2008. ISBN 9781597165860. 24 p. Grades K–3.

Goldish, Meish. *Spooky Wolf Spiders* (No Backbone! the World of Invertebrates). Bearport Publishing, 2008. ISBN 9781597167062. 24 p. Grades 1–3.

Goldish, Meish. *Tricky Trapdoor Spiders* (No Backbone! the World of Invertebrates). Bearport Publishing, 2008. ISBN 9781597167079. 24 p. Grades 1–3.

Hall, Kirsten. *Leatherback Turtle: The World's Heaviest Reptile* (Supersized!). Bearport Publishing, 2007. ISBN 1597163937. 24 p. Grades K–2.

Haney, Johannah. *Turtles* (Great Pets). Benchmark, 2007. ISBN 9780761427094. 48 p. Grades 2–4.

Harrison, David L. *Bugs*. Front Street, 2007. ISBN 9781590784518. 56 p. Grades K–3.

Hartley, Karen. *Stick Insect*. Heinemann, 2008. ISBN 9781432912352. 32 p. Grades K–3.

Hartley, Karen, Chris MacRo, and Philip Taylor. *Flea* (Heinemann First Library). Heinemann, 2008. ISBN 9781432912406. 32 p. Grades K–3.

Houran, Lori Haskins. *Bloody Horned Lizards* (Gross-Out Defenses). Bearport Publishing, 2008. ISBN 9781597167178. 24 p. Grades 2–3.

Huggins-Cooper, Lynn. *Creepy Crawlers* (QEB Awesome Animals).QEB Publishing, 2008. ISBN 9781595665614. 32 p. Grades 4–7.

Huggins-Cooper, Lynn. *Revolting Reptiles* (QEB Awesome Animals). QEB Publishing, 2008. ISBN 9781595665645. 32 p. Grades 4–7.

Huggins-Cooper, Lynn. *Slimy Sliders* (QEB Awesome Animals). QEB Publishing, 2008. ISBN 9781595665652. 32 p. Grades 4–7.

Kaufman, Gabriel. *Saltwater Crocodile: The World's Biggest Reptile* (Supersized!). Bearport Publishing, 2007. ISBN 1597163961. 24 p. Grades K–3.

Lang, Aubrey. *Baby Sea Turtle* (Nature Babies). Fitzhenry and Whiteside, 2007. ISBN 9781550417289. 32 p. Grades 2–4.

Leavitt, Amie Jane. *Care for a Pet Tarantula* (How to Convince Your Parents You Can.) (Robbie Readers). Mitchell Lane, 2007. ISBN 9781584156031. 32 p. Grades 2–4.

Lockwood, Sophie. *Ants* (World of Insects). Child's World, 2007. ISBN 781-592968176 40 p. Grades 4–6.

Lockwood, Sophie. *Beetles* (World of Insects). Child's World, 2007. ISBN 159-2968198. 40 p. Grades 4–6.

Lockwood, Sophie. *Dragonflies* (World of Insects). Child's World, 2007. ISBN 978-1592968213. 40 p. Grades 4–6.

Lockwood, Sophie. *Flies* (World of Insects). Child's World, 2007. ISBN 978-1592968220. 40 p. Grades 4–6.

Lunis, Natalie. *Deadly Black Widows* (No Backbone! the World of Invertebrates). Bearport Publishing, 2008. ISBN 9781597166676. 24 p. Grades 1–3.

Lunis, Natalie. *Leggy Centipedes* (No Backbone! the World of Invertebrates!) Bearport Publishing, 2009. ISBN 9781597167529. 24 p. Grades K–3.

Lunis, Natalie. *Komodo Dragon: The World's Biggest Lizard* (Supersized!). Bearport Publishing, 2007. ISBN 9781597163927. 24 p. Grades K–2.

Lunis, Natalie. *Stinging Scorpions* (No Backbone! the World of Invertebrates!). Bearport Publishing, 2009. ISBN 9781597167567. 24 p. Grades K–3.

Lunis, Natalie. *Wiggly Earthworms* (No Backbone! the World of Invertebrates!). Bearport, 2009. ISBN 9781597167512. 24 p. Grades K–3.

Markle, Sandra. *Hornets: Incredible Insect Architects* (Insect World). Lerner Publications, 2007. ISBN 9780822572978. 48 p. Grades 2–5.

Markle, Sandra. *Insects: Biggest! Littlest!* Boyds Mills, 2009. ISBN 9781590785126. 32 p. Grades 1–3.

Markle, Sandra. *Luna Moths: Masters of Change* (Insect World). Lerner Publications, 2007. ISBN 9780822573029. 48 p. Grades 2–5.

Markle, Sandra. *Praying Mantises: Hungry Insect Heroes* (Insect World). Lerner Publications, 2007. ISBN 9780822573005. 48 p. Grades 2–5.

Markle, Sandra. *Termites: Hardworking Insect Families* (Insect World). Lerner Publications, 2007. ISBN 9780822573012. 48 p. Grades 2–5.

Marsico, Katie. *A Komodo Dragon Hatchling Grows Up* (Scholastic News Nonfiction Readers). Children's Press, 2007. ISBN 9780531174777. 24 p. Grades 1–2.

Mattern, Joanne. *Anacondas* (First Facts). Capstone Press, 2008. ISBN 9781429619202. 24 p. Grades 2–4.

Mattern, Joanne. *Boa Constrictors* (First Facts). Capstone Press, 2008. ISBN 9781429619226. 24 p. Grades 2–4.

Mattern, Joanne. *Copperheads* (First Facts). Capstone Press, 2008. ISBN 9781429619257. 24 p. Grades 2–4.

Mattern, Joanne. *Rattlesnakes* (First Facts). Capstone Press, 2008. ISBN 9781429619264. 24 p. Grades 2–4.

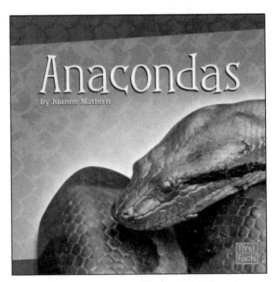

Anacondas **by Joanne Mattern.**

McGavin, George C. *Amazing Insects and Spiders* (Amazing Life Cycles). Gareth Stevens, 2007. ISBN 9780836888997. 32 p. Grades 3–5.

Moffett, Mark. *Face to Face with Frogs* (Face to Face with Animals). National Geographic, 2008. ISBN 9781426302053. 32 p. Grades 4–6.

Mortensen, Lori. *In the Trees, Honey Bees!* Illustrated by Chris Arbo. Dawn, 2009. ISBN 9781584691143. Unpaged. Grades K–3.

Murawski, Darlyne A. *Face to Face with Caterpillars* (Face to Face with Animals). National Geographic, 2007. ISBN 1426300522. 32 p. Grades 3–6.

Packard, Mary. *Goliath Beetle: One of the World's Heaviest Insects* (Supersized!). Bearport Publishing, 2007. ISBN 1597163880. 24 p. Grades K–2.

Peterson, Megan Cooley. *The Pebble First Guide to Spiders* (Pebble Books). Capstone Press, 2008. ISBN 9781429617123. 32 p. Grades K–1.

Petrie, Kristin. *Ants* (Bugs!). ABDO & Daughters, 2008. ISBN 9781604530629. 32 p. Grades 3–5.

Petrie, Kristin. *Beetles* (Bugs!). ABDO & Daughters, 2008. ISBN 9781604530636. 32 p. Grades 3–5.

Petrie, Kristin. *Box Elder Bugs* (Bugs!). ABDO & Daughters, 2008. ISBN 978-1604530643. 32 p. Grades 3–5.

Petrie, Kristin. *Centipedes* (Bugs!). ABDO & Daughters, 2008. ISBN 978-1604530650. 32 p. Grades 3–5.

Petrie, Kristin. *Cockroaches* (Bugs!). ABDO & Daughters, 2008. ISBN 978-1604530667. 32 p. Grades 3–5.

Petrie, Kristin. *Fleas* (Bugs!). ABDO & Daughters, 2008. ISBN 9781604530674. 32 p. Grades 3–5.

Petrie, Kristin. *Flies* (Bugs!). ABDO & Daughters, 2008. ISBN 9781604530681. 32 p. Grades 3–5.

Petrie, Kristin. *Grasshoppers* (Bugs!). ABDO & Daughters, 2008. ISBN 978-1604530698. 32 p. Grades 3–5.

Petrie, Kristin. *Lice* (Bugs!). ABDO & Daughters, 2008. ISBN 9781604530704. 32 p. Grades 3–5.

Petrie, Kristin. *Ticks* (Bugs!). ABDO & Daughters, 2008. ISBN 9781604530728. 32 p. Grades 3–5.

Petrie, Kristin. *Walking Sticks* (Bugs!). ABDO & Daughters, 2008. ISBN 978-1604530735. 32 p. Grades 3–5.

Pitts, Zachary. *The Pebble First Guide to Lizards* (Pebble Books). Capstone Press, 2008. ISBN 9781429617109. 24 p. Grades K–3.

Polydoros, Lori. *Crocodiles: On the Hunt* (Blazers). Capstone Press, 2009. ISBN 9781429623148. 32 p. Grades 1–4.

Pringle, Lawrence. *Alligators and Crocodiles! Strange and Wonderful.* Boyds Mills, 2009. ISBN 9781590782569. 32 p. Grades 2–5.

Rene, Ellen. *Investigating Spiders and Their Webs* (Science Detectives). PowerKids Press, 2008. ISBN 9781404244825. 24 p. Grades 3–6.

Riehecky, Janet. *Cobras: On the Hunt* (Blazers). Capstone Press, 2009. ISBN 9781429623179. 32 p. Grades 1–4.

Rompella, Natalie. *Don't Squash That Bug! The Curious Kid's Guide to Insects* (Lobster Learners). Lobster Press, 2007. ISBN 9781897073506. 32 p. Grades 2–4.

Ryder, Joanne. *Toad by the Road*: *A Year in the Life of These Amazing Amphibians.* Henry Holt, 2007. ISBN 080507354X 40 p. Grades 1–4.

Sexton, Colleen. *Praying Mantises* (Blastoff Readers: World of Insects). Children's Press, 2007. ISBN 9780531175699. 24 p. Grades 1–3.

Simon, Seymour. *Snakes.* Collins, 2007. ISBN 0061140961. 32 p. Grades 2–5.

Simon, Seymour. *Spiders.* Collins, 2007. ISBN 9780060891046. 32 p. Grades 2–5.

Singer, Marilyn. *Venom.* Darby Creek Publishing, 2007. ISBN 9781581960433. 96 p. Grades 4–8.

Smith, Molly. *Green Anaconda: The World's Heaviest Snake* (Supersized!). Bearport Publishing, 2007. ISBN 1597163910. 24 p. Grades K–3.

Smith, Molly. *Helpful Ladybugs* (No Backbone! the World of Invertebrates). Bearport Publishing, 2008. ISBN 9781597165846. 24 p. Grades K–3.

Smith, Molly. *Speedy Dragonflies* (No Backbone! the World of Invertebrates). Bearport Publishing, 2008. ISBN 9781597165839. 24 p. Grades K–3.

Somervill, Barbara A. *Fleas: Feasting on Blood* (Bloodsuckers). PowerKids Press, 2007. ISBN 9781404238053. 24 p. Grades 3–5.

Somervill, Barbara A. *Leeches: Waiting in the Water* (Bloodsuckers). PowerKids Press, 2007. ISBN 9781404238015. 24 p. Grades 3–5.

Somervill, Barbara A. *Mosquitoes: Hungry for Blood* (Bloodsuckers). PowerKids Press, 2007. ISBN 9781404238022. 24 p. Grades 3–5.

Squire, Ann O. *Chinese Giant Salamander: The World's Biggest Amphibian* (Supersized!). Bearport Publishing, 2007. ISBN 9781597163866. 24 p. Grades K–2.

St. Pierre, Stephanie. *Dragonfly* (Heinemann First Library). Heinemann, 2008. ISBN 9781432912383. 32 p. Grades K–3.

St. Pierre, Stephanie. *Earwig* (Heinemann First Library). Heinemann Educational Books, 2008. ISBN 9781432912390. 32 p. Grades K–3.

St. Pierre, Stephanie. *Pillbug* (Heinemann First Library). Heinemann, 2008. ISBN 9781432912369. 32 p. Grades K–3.

Stevens, Kathryn. *Lizards* (Pet Care for Kids). Child's World, 2009. ISBN 978-1602531857. 24 p. Grades K–2.

Stevens, Kathryn. *Turtles* (Pet Care for Kids). Child's World, 2009. ISBN 978-1602531871. 24 p. Grades K–2.

Stewart, Melissa. *Snakes!* (National Geographic Readers). National Geographic, 2009. ISBN 9781426304293. 32 p. Grades K–3.

Stidworthy, John. *Queen Alexandra's Birdwing: The World's Largest Butterfly* (Supersized!). Bearport Publishing, 2007. ISBN 1597163953. 24 p. Grades K–3.

Swanson, Diane. *Bugs Up Close*. Kids Can, 2007. ISBN 9781554531387 40 p. Grades 3–5.

Swinburne, Stephen R. *Armadillo Trail: The Northward Journey of the Armadillo*. Boyds Mills, 2009. ISBN 9781590784631. 32 p. Grades K–4.

Theodorou, Rod. *Amphibians* (Animal Babies/2nd Edition). Heinemann, 2007. ISBN 1403492417. 32 p. Grades K–2.

Theodorou, Rod. *Reptiles* (Animal Babies). Heinemann, 2007. ISBN 1403492468. 32 p. Grades K–2.

Wallach, Van. *Cobras* (First Facts). Capstone Press, 2008. ISBN 978-1429619233. 24 p. Grades 2–4.

Wallach, Van. *Garter Snakes* (First Facts). Capstone Press, 2008. ISBN 9781429619240. 24 p. Grades 2–4.

White, Nancy. *Crafty Garden Spiders* (No Backbone! the World of Invertebrates). Bearport Publishing, 2008. ISBN 9781597167031. 24 p. Grades 1–3.

Williams, Brian. *Amazing Reptiles and Amphibians* (Amazing Life Cycles). Gareth Stevens, 2007. ISBN 9780836888980. 32 p. Grades 3–5.

Wilson, Hannah. *Life-Size Reptiles* (Life-Size Series). Sterling, 2007. ISBN 9781402745423. 28 p. Grades 3–5.

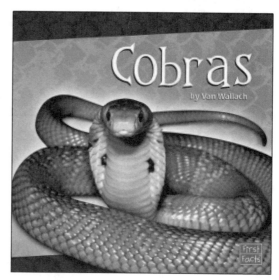

Cobras **by Van Wallach.**

Chapter —5

Prehistoric Creatures

Even the youngest boys seem to have a fascination with dinosaurs and other prehistoric creatures. Feed their interest with up-to-date books containing the newest facts and discoveries about these mysterious creatures. But be careful—scientific theories about dinosaurs change rapidly, and a five-year-old book is probably too old. Keep your dinosaur books up-to-date. And don't limit yourself just to dinosaur books. Other prehistoric creatures such as paleo bugs and saber-toothed cats can be equally fascinating.

BOOKTALKS

Bradley, Timothy J. *Paleo Bugs: Survival of the Creepiest.* Chronicle Books, 2008. ISBN 9780811860222. 48 p. Grades 5–8.

Prehistoric bugs—what were they like? We know that many of the dinosaurs were huge. What about the bugs? Were they big too?

Some of them were colossal. Take a look at page 22. That is an arthropleura, and fossils indicate that some were seven feet long. It had many feet and an armored, segmented body. Today the giant African millipede can be as big as eight inches long, and even that is pretty huge.

Insects are arthropods. Take a look at the chart on page 9 to find out what that means—they have hard shells, no backbones, and joined legs, and their bodies are often divided into segments. They have many pairs of limbs.

Look at the prehistoric cockroaches that lived about 290 million years ago. They have not changed much. "The lowly cockroach is one of the most successful creatures on Earth, due to its amazing ability to adapt to changes in its environment" (page 26). Even if human beings die out or disappear, the cockroaches will still be around. Isn't that a lovely thought?

On page 32, check out the aphodites, the ancient dung beetles. They collected animal dung and thus cleaned up after bigger animals. Their descendants are still around!

This book is full of great information and excellent color illustrations.

Brewster, Hugh. *Dinosaurs in Your Backyard*. Illustrated by Alan Barnard. Abrams Books for Young Readers, 2009. ISBN 9780810970991. 32 p. Grades 3–5.

Dinosaurs in Your Backyard
by Hugh Brewster.

Have you ever wondered who or what was living on the land where you live long ago? How about millions of years ago? What was the land like? Was it land or was it an ocean? And did dinosaurs live there?

Maybe you think that dinosaurs only lived in what is the western part of North America. That's wrong! More than 85 kinds of dinosaurs lived all over North America, and scientists are constantly discovering their fossils.

This book tells us the stories of some of these dinosaurs. "As long as a school bus and as heavy as two elephants, *T. rex* had the most powerful bite of any animal that has ever lived. Its huge teeth were serrated like steak knives and could chomp right through flesh and bones" (page 6).

Good old Tyrannosaurus rex was scary, all right, but he had some competition. Look at the Elasmosaur and the Mosoaur, which lived in the oceans that once covered the middle of the continent. Check out the Corythosaurus on pages 14–15. They weighed up to five tons and were 30–33 feet long!

Learn about the dinosaurs they call walking tanks, because they were armored with spikes. Maybe the most famous one is the Ankylosaur, but the Euoplocephalus had a bony tail that looked like a club. That tail could weigh as much as 66 pounds and could break the leg of any dinosaur that tried to attack it.

If you like dinosaurs, you'll learn a lot about them by reading this fun book.

Long, John. *Dinosaurs* (Insiders). Simon & Schuster, 2007. ISBN 9781416938576. 64 p. Grades 4–8.

For about 95 million years, dinosaurs were pretty much the most powerful creatures on earth. And then they died out. And we are still not 100 percent sure how that happened.

But we *are* 100 percent sure that we are learning more and more about dinosaurs almost every single day, and this neat book has a lot of great information about a lot of different kinds of dinosaurs. Here are some samples:

- The microraptor, pictured on page 17, was about the size of a chicken. It had wings on both its arms and its legs! So it looked and acted like it had four wings.

- Most scientists think the killer event that started the mass extinction of the dinosaurs happened in Mexico, in the Yucatan Peninsula. There is a crater almost 125 million miles wide.

- A meteorite struck there and undoubtedly caused all sorts of changes in the climate. Read about it on pages 18 and 19.

- We are not sure how horned dinosaurs, such as Protoceratops, used their bony frills and horns. They may have been like antlers, for self-defense and charging, or they may have been to attract a mate, like a peacock does today.

- Look at the pictures of the dinosaur eggs and the dinosaur babies on pages 26 and 27. A lot of dinosaurs were good parents.

- By looking at fossils, we can learn a lot about how the dinosaur body works. See a cross-section of the best dinosaur mummy we have so far, Leonardo, on pages 32 and 33.

You will love the great information you will find in this interesting book.

Manning, Mick, and Brita Granstrom. *Dino-dinners*. Holiday House, 2007. ISBN 0823420892. Unpaged. Grades 1–4.

What did dinosaurs eat? Yes, we know there were plant eaters and meat eaters —but what kinds of plants or meat did they eat?

It depended, of course, on where they were and what was available.

Every two pages have a wonderful color picture of the dinosaur, and then some excellent and interesting information on the sides—giving you specifics. Some of it is sort of gross!

Read about Oviraptor: "I eat pinecones, shellfish, and nuts—crunchy eggs can be tasty too. Best of all, a fat, crispy beetle snatched from the top of dinosaur poop." Oviraptor, we learn had a strong beak, sort of like a bird's beak, and it could easily crush egg shells, bones, nuts and shellfish.

It is fun and it is fascinating. You will enjoy looking through this book.

Author Profile: Patrick O'Brien

Patrick O'Brien, author and illustrator of *You Are the First Kid on Mars*, began his publishing career by illustrating books about pirates and knights. He then decided to do his own writing so he could paint what he wanted to paint. He specializes in historic and prehistoric subjects, including saber-toothed tigers, maritime history, and the disaster of the *Hindenburg*.

Were you a reader when you were a child?

Yes I was. I had four brothers and my mother says she used to go to the library every week and throw books on each of our beds. So we always had lots of books in the house and I was a big reader. Of course, in those days we didn't have so much competition from video games and cable TV. My favorite books were *Treasure Island* and *Tom Sawyer*. And I used to read the Hardy Boys. For nonfiction, I used to read a lot about Indians and colonial times.

What made you start to write nonfiction for kids?

I'm really an illustrator, and the reason I started writing the books is that it gave me a chance to paint what I wanted to paint. When I was illustrating other people's texts I had to follow what they had written. For me it's more interesting if I get to do exactly what I want to do. Another reason I write nonfiction is that it's what I'm interested in. It's what I read for fun. When I read recreationally it's almost entirely nonfiction. I almost never read a novel. I write about what I find interesting and what I hope kids will find interesting and that my editor will agree that kids might find interesting.

Which comes first for you—the art or the writing?

Both come together at the same time. When you're just doing the writing you need to know what the pictures are going to be so you know what you don't need to write and vice versa. I'm sketching out the pictures at the same time as I'm sketching out the words so I know how they're going to complement each other.

Do you write with boys in mind?

No, I don't. There's no reason why girls can't like knights or trains or pirates or prehistoric creatures. I just write what interests me and what interested me as a kid. I'm a boy, so that's the way it comes out. All that stuff like knights and pirates and ships and dinosaurs is all the stuff that kids like and I still like, so that's what I'm writing about.

Are you shifting into outer space with your new book about Mars?

All my books up until now have been on prehistoric or historic subjects. *You Are the First Kid on Mars* is the first time I've done something about the future. It kind of springs from books I read as a child. In particular there was one called *You Will Go to the Moon* and it was written in 1959 so it was before we had ever been to the moon. It was speculative. That's how this book is. It's a realistic depiction of how NASA currently feels we actually would colonize Mars.

How did you create the art for this book?

It's the first book that I did on the computer. I did it with a program called Painter. It was fun because it's a change. I spend every working day in my studio painting, so it's nice to have a change and do it on my computer. A lot of people think the computer makes it easy. You just push the spaceship button and you get a spaceship. You push the astronaut button and you get a picture of an astronaut. But it's not like that at all. You still have to draw everything. You still have to invent the spaceships and you still have to draw everything just the way you have to draw it in the real world. The boy in that book is my eight-year-old son. I tried to make it look as much like him as I could just for fun. I pose for all the characters in my books, and I don't make it look like myself because I don't want it to look like the same person in all my books. In this case I purposely tried to make it look like him.

O'Brien, Patrick. *Sabertooth*. Henry Holt, 2008. ISBN 9780805071054. Unpaged. Grades 2–5.

The saber tooth is extinct, and there were several kinds of saber-toothed cats. They had two enormous teeth that hung from their mouths like knives and let them bite through just about anything.

The most famous saber-toothed cat was Smilodon. It lived until about 10,000 years ago. Take a look at the picture of its skeleton and see some of its features. Its long teeth are "canine" teeth. Humans have canine teeth too—do you know which ones they are?

Smilodons could not run long distances, but they could sneak up on big animals and bite them. Look at the great illustrations of them doing just that.

Other animals had saber teeth as well, including some bears, bear-dogs, and even birds.

We have learned a lot about smilodons because of the La Brea tar pits in what is now downtown Los Angeles, California. Prehistoric animals fell into the stick black tar and couldn't get out. They died—and their remains are telling us a great deal about what life was like in ancient times.

Walker, Sally M. *The Search for Antarctic Dinosaurs* (On My Own Science). Illustrated by John Bindon. Millbrook Press, 2007. ISBN 9780822567493. 48p. Grades 1–3.

Do you know how cold it is in Antarctica? Even in the summer, it is usually about 25 to 30 degrees below zero. It is hard to work there; hard to move there; hard to do just about everything when it is so cold.

And do you know what digging for dinosaurs is like? You have to be very careful. When you see something that looks like it could be a fossil, you must do everything you can not to harm it in any way.

So—can you imagine what it would be like to dig for dinosaurs in Antarctica?

That is just what Dr. William Hammer and his crew do. They get reports from people who have seen rocks that look like fossils, and they go there and carefully, very carefully, start digging up the bones.

And Antarctica turns out to be a great place to find dinosaurs! Scientists have discovered that it was not always as cold as it is now, and dinosaurs, kinds that have never been discovered anywhere else, are right there.

The Search for Antarctic Dinosaurs by Sally Walker.

This tells the story of a true dinosaur hunt. You'll enjoy reading about it.

Williams, Judith. *The Discovery and Mystery of a Dinosaur Named Jane.* Enslow, 2007. ISBN 9780766027305. 48 p. Grades 3–4.

Scientists and volunteers looking for dinosaurs in the badlands of Montana were having a bad day. In fact, they were having a bad trip. It was hot and they had been looking for fossils for days and no one had found anything.

Then it happened. First, a few volunteers found some dinosaur parts—and then two volunteers spotted a toe bone at the base of a tall slope. And it looked a lot like that toe bone might be just a small part of a much bigger fossil. The bone was hollow. That meant the fossil was a meat eater. But the people from the Burpee Museum in Rockford, Illinois, had used up all their time. They had to go back home and wait a whole year to come back and start digging.

This is the true story of how they dug and what they found there—and what kind of a dinosaur it turned out to be! There are lots of great photos as well.

If you like dinosaurs, give this book a try.

WORTH READING

Nonfiction books with "boy appeal" that have received positive reviews in *Booklist*, *Horn Book Guide*, and/or *School Library Journal*.

Allen, Judy. *Dinosaurs* (I Wonder Why [Flip the Flaps]). Kingfisher, 2008. ISBN 9780753462218. 32 p. Grades 1–3.

Barner, Bob. *Dinosaurs Roar, Butterflies Soar!* Chronicle Books, 2009. ISBN 9780811856638. 32 p. Grades 1–3.

Brown, Charlotte Lewis. *Beyond the Dinosaurs: Monsters of the Air and Sea* (I Can Read Book 2). HarperCollins, 2007. ISBN 9780060530563. 32 p. Grades K–3.

Cohen, Roger. *Danger in the Desert: True Adventures of a Dinosaur Hunter* (Sterling, Point Books). Sterling, 2008. ISBN 9781402757068. 208 p. Grades 6–9.

Collard, Sneed B., III. *Reign of the Sea Dragons.* Charlesbridge, 2008. ISBN 9781580891240. 61 p. Grades 5–8.

Dingus, Lowell. *Dinosaur Eggs Discovered: Unscrambling the Clues* (Discovered). Twenty-First Century, 2007. ISBN 978-0822567912. 112 p. Grades 6–up.

Dixon, Dougal. *Amazing Dinosaurs.* Boyds Mills, 2007. ISBN 9781590785379. 128 p. Grades 5–7.

Dixon, Dougal. *The World of Dinosaurs: And Other Prehistoric Life.* Barron's Educational Series, 2008. ISBN 9780764140822. 112 p. Grades 4–6.

Eamer, Claire. *Super Crocs and Monster Wings: Modern Animals' Ancient Past.* Annick Press, 2008. ISBN 9781554511303. 96 p. Grades 4–7.

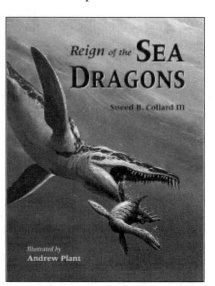

***Reign of the Sea Dragons* by Sneed B. Collard III.**

Florian, Douglas. *Dinothesaurus: Prehistoric Poems and Paintings.* Beach Lane Books, 2009. ISBN 9781416979784. 56 p. Grades K–3.

Gibbons, Gail. *Dinosaurs!* Holiday House, 2008. ISBN 9780823421435. 32 p. Grades K–1.

Goecke, Michael P. *Baryonyx* (Dinosaurs). ABDO & Daughters, 2007. ISBN 159-9286947. 32 p. Grades 1–3.

Goecke, Michael P. *Camarasaurus* (Dinosaurs). ABDO & Daughters, 2007. ISBN 159-9286955. 32 p. Grades 1–3.

Goecke, Michael P. *Compsognathus* (Dinosaurs). ABDO & Daughters, 2007. ISBN 159-9286963. 32 p. Grades 1–3.

Goecke, Michael P. *Giganotosaurus* (Dinosaurs). ABDO & Daughters, 2007. ISBN 159-9286971. 32 p. Grades 1–3.

Goecke, Michael P. *Oviraptor* (Dinosaurs). ABDO & Daughters, 2007. ISBN 159-928698X. 32 p. Grades 1–3.

Goecke, Michael P. *Pachycephalosaurus* (Dinosaurs). ABDO & Daughters, 2007. ISBN 1599286998. 32 p. Grades 1–3.

Goldish, Meish. *The Oviraptor Adventure: Mark Norell and the Egg Thief* (Fossil Hunters). Bearport Publishing, 2006. ISBN 1597162582. 32 p. Grades 3–5.

Halls, Kelly Milner. *Dinosaur Parade: A Spectacle of Prehistoric Proportions.* Lark, 2008. ISBN 9781600592676. 32 p. Grades K–3.

Henry, Michel. *Raptor: The Life of a Young Deinonychus.* Abrams Books for Young Readers, 2007. ISBN 0810957752. 32 p. Grades K–3.

Holtz, Thomas R. *Dinosaurs: The Most Complete, Up-to-Date Encyclopedia for Dinosaur Lovers of All Ages.* Random House, 2007. ISBN 9780375924194 4. 32 p. Grades 5–up.

Hughes, Monica. *Flying Giants* (I Love Reading: Dino World). Bearport Publishing, 2007. ISBN 1597165417. 24 p. Grades K–2.

Jeffrey, Gary. *Elasmosaurus: The Long-Necked Swimmer* (Graphic Dinosaurs Set 2). PowerKids Press, 2008. ISBN 9781435825055. 32 p. Grades 2–5.

Jeffrey, Gary. *Stegosaurus: The Plated Dinosaur* (Graphic Dinosaurs). Rosen, 2009. ISBN 9781435825031. 32 p. Grades 2–5.

Korb, Rena B. *Discovering Ichthyosaurus* (Dinosaur Digs). Magic Wagon, 2008. ISBN 9781602701076. 32 p. Grades 3–4.

Korb, Rena B. *Discovering Pteranodon* (Dinosaur Digs). Magic Wagon, 2008. ISBN 9781602701083. 32 p. Grades 3–4.

Korb, Rena B. *Discovering Tyrannosaurus Rex.* Magic Wagon, 2008. ISBN 9781602701090. 32 p. Grades 3–4.

Korb, Rena B. *Discovering Velociraptor* (Dinosaur Digs). Magic Wagon, 2008. ISBN 9781602701106. 32 p. Grades 3–4.

Landau, Elaine. *Pterorsaurs.* Children's Press, 2006. ISBN 0531168299. 48 p. Grades 2–4.

Lommel, Cookie. *Dinosaurs* (Insiders). Simon & Schuster, 2007. ISBN 978-1416938576. 64 p. Grades 5–8.

Lunis, Natalie. *Ocean Monsters* (Dino Times Trivia). Bearport Publishing, 2009. ISBN 9781597167130. 24 p. Grades K–3.

Lunis, Natalie. *Pet-Sized Dinos* (Dino Times Trivia). Bearport Publishing,2008. ISBN 9781597167109. 24 p. Grades 1–3.

Lunis, Natalie. *Sky Terrors* (Dino Times Trivia). Bearport Publishing, 2008. ISBN 9781597167147. 24 p. Grades 1–3.

Lunis, Natalie. *The Tiny Titanosaurs: Luis Chiappe's Dinosaur Nests* (Fossil Hunters). Bearport Publishing, 2007. ISBN 1597163732. 32 p. Grades K–2.

Savage Slashers **by Natalie Lunis and Nancy White.**

Lunis, Natalie, and Nancy White. *Savage Slashers* (Dino Times Trivia). Bearport Publishing, 2008. ISBN 9781597167093. 24 p. Grades 1–3.

Manning, Mick, and Brita Granstrom. *Woolly Mammoth.* Frances Lincoln, 2009. ISBN 9781845078607. 32 p. Grades K–3.

Manning, Phillip. *Dinomummy.* Kingfisher, 2007. ISBN 9780753460474. 64 p. Grades 4–6.

Markle, Sandra. *Outside and Inside Woolly Mammoths* (Outside and Inside). Walker Books, 2007. ISBN 9780802795892. 40 p. Grades 4–8.

Matthews, Rupert. *Dinosaur Combat* (Dinosaur Dig). QEB Publishing, 2009. ISBN 9781595665508. 32 p. Grades 3–6.

Matthews, Rupert. *Dinosaur Families* (Dinosaur Dig). QEB Publishing, 2009. ISBN 9781595665485. 32 p. Grades 3–6.

Matthews, Rupert. *Dinosaur Foods* (Dinosaur Dig). QEB Publishing, 2008. ISBN 9781595665515. 32 p. Grades 3–6.

Matthews, Rupert. *Dinosaurs in Action* (Dinosaur Dig). QEB Publishing, 2009. ISBN 9781595665492. 32 p. Grades 3–6.

Munro, Roxie. *Inside-Outside Dinosaurs.* Marshall Cavendish, 2009. ISBN 978-0761456247. 40 p. Grades K–1.

Peterson, Judy Monroe. *Fossil Finders: Paleontologists* (Extreme Scientists). PowerKids Press, 2008. ISBN 9781404245242. 24 p. Grades 3–5.

Sereno, Paul C. *Supercroc: Paul Sereno's Dinosaur Eater* (Fossil Hunters). Bearport Publishing, 2006. ISBN 1597162558. 32 p. Grades 3–5.

Shone, Rob. *Diplodocus: The Whip-Tailed Dinosaur* (Graphic Dinosaurs). PowerKids Press, 2008. ISBN 9781435825048. 32 p. Grades 2–5.

Shone, Rob. *Giganotosaurus: The Giant Southern Lizard* (Graphic Dinosaurs Set 2). PowerKids Press, 2008. ISBN 9781435825024. 32 p. Grades 2–5.

Spilsbury, Louise, and Richard Spilsbury. *Dinosaur Hunters: Paleontologists* (Scientists at Work). Heinemann, 2007. ISBN 978-1403499479. 32 p. Grades 4–6.

Dinosaur Hunters: Paleontologists **by Louise Spilsbury and Richard Spilsbury.**

Stewart, David. *Dinosaurs!* (World of Wonder). Franklin Watts, 2008. ISBN 9780531205419. 32 p. Grades K–3.

Thomson, Sarah L. *Extreme Dinosaurs! Q&A*. Collins, 2007. ISBN 9780060899714. 48 p. Grades 3–5.

White, Nancy. *Giant-O-Saurs* (Dino Times Trivia). Bearport Publishing, 2008. ISBN 9781597167116. 24 p. Grades 1–3.

Zimmerman, Howard. *Armored and Dangerous* (Dino Times Trivia). Bearport Publishing, 2008. ISBN 9781597167123. 24 p. Grades 1–3.

Zoehfeld, Kathleen Weidner. *Dinosaur Tracks* (Let's-Read-and-Find-Out Science 2). Collins, 2007. ISBN 0060290242 40 p. Grades 1–3.

Chapter 6

American Journeys

The history of the United States is full of things that boys love—heroes and villains, tragedy and war, and people overcoming great difficulties. However, it is not always easy to get kids interested in reading about history. How you talk about these titles is important. Focus on the action, the unexplained mysteries, the humor, and the occasionally gory details to capture boys' interest and draw them into some outstanding stories.

BOOKTALKS

Allen, Thomas B. *Remember Valley Forge: Patriots, Tories, and Redcoats Tell Their Stories*. National Geographic, 2007. ISBN 9781426301490. 64 p. Grades 5–9.

Have you ever heard of Valley Forge? What do you know about it, if you have? Do you think of the Revolutionary War and soldiers who are almost starving and have no warm clothes? Do you think of snow and bitter cold and George Washington practically begging the Continental Congress to send food and supplies for his men, who were deserting like crazy—and no wonder!

When the 13 colonies decided they wanted to be free to govern themselves, they were not very well organized. They were not in a good position to fight a war and take care of the men who volunteered to fight for the cause of freedom. They did not have enough money, they had no supplies, and they had inefficient methods of dealing with problems.

Remember Valley Forge: Patriots, Tories, and Redcoats Tell Their Stories **by Thomas B. Allen.**

Such was the situation George Washington, the commander of the colonial army, had to deal with. He found what he hoped was a safe space for his men. They would build flimsy little huts in the snow and their enemies, the British, would live it up by staying in the city of Philadelphia and having a lot of parties (most armies did not fight during the winter).

George Washington was not the father of our country for nothing. He was a brilliant and wise man, and he was determined to do the best for the soldiers under his command. This is the story of the second winter of the Revolutionary War and the amazing things that happened—and the help that often came from unexpected places. There are many pictures, and this is a fine read.

Brown, Don. *Let It Begin Here! April 19, 1775: The Day the American Revolution Began.* Roaring Brook Press, 2008. ISBN 9781596432215. Unpaged. Grades 2–5.

By 1775 the king of England and his colonists in America were ready to fight. The king had declared that the Americans were going to have to pay for the recent North American war, the French and Indian War. The colonials were disgusted. No one stood up for their rights. They had no representatives in the British parliament. They called it, "taxation without representation."

General Gage, the British military commander, declared that the biggest bullies were the people of Boston. And he was probably right. They were complaining and acting out against the British. They had held the famous "Boston Tea Party." They were angry when Gage stole a lot of their gunpowder, and they vowed it would not happen again.

So, on April 18, when they heard that Gage was organizing another gunpowder raid, a man named Paul Revere, who had organized a committee to look out for the colonials, set out to warn the people in Lexington, Massachusetts. It was there that two leaders named John Hancock and Samuel

Let It Begin Here! April 19, 1775: The Day the American Revolution Began **by Don Brown. Jacket shown with permission from Roaring Brook Press.**

Adams were staying. Paul Revere made it, and all the men believed that Gage was coming to steal their gunpowder supply there.

The Lexington militia got together. Their captain was John Parker, who was dying of tuberculosis. That didn't stop him. He led them straight to the town's center. And there he waited for the British.

And what happened next changed the history of the world. This is a fine look at the very beginning of the Revolutionary War.

A Boy Named Beckoning: The True Story of Dr. Carlos Montezuma, Native American Hero **by Gina Capaldi.**

Capaldi, Gina. *A Boy Named Beckoning: The True Story of Dr. Carlos Montezuma, Native American Hero.* Adapted and illustrated by Gina Capaldi. Carolrhoda Books, 2008. ISBN 9780822576440. 32 p. Grades 4–7.

What happened to a five-year-old Native American boy named Wassaja (which means "beckoning") should never happen to anyone. He lived with his people, about 150 of them, including his parents, two sisters, and an infant brother, in the Arizona territory in 1871. One night enemies, Pima Indians, attacked his village. He hid but was found and captured, then taken, terrified and lonely, to their larger village. In about a week the Pima sold him as a slave.

Slavery of black people had been outlawed in the United States after the Civil War. Slavery of Native Americans continued.

But Wassaja finally had some luck, for the man who purchased him did not want a slave. He wanted an adopted son. He was a photographer named Carol Gentile, an immigrant from Italy, and he was kind and good to the boy, whom he renamed Carlos Montezuma.

What Carlos accomplished was incredible. He graduated from college at the age of 17, and became a physician, a teacher, and a man who wanted to help his people— and he did.

One of the wonderful things about this book is the many photographs.

Fleischman, Sid. *The Trouble Begins at 8: A Life of Mark Twain in the Wild, Wild West.* Greenwillow Books, 2008. ISBN 9780061344312. 224 p. Grades 5–up.

Mark Twain is one of the most famous writers who ever lived, and he was also one of the funniest. But he was not always Mark Twain—that was a name he chose for himself. And his life was not always funny.

And in this book, Sid Fleischman, who is pretty funny himself, tells us how Mark grew up and how he became famous—in the days of the California Gold Rush.

Samuel Clemens was the real name of the kid who grew up to become Mark Twain. There is a picture of him on page 15. He is holding up the printer's woodblock letters that spell the name Sam. And he grew up poor, in Hannibal, Missouri. But he had lots of ideas about how he might become rich, even though he did not much like school. One of those ideas was that he might become a pilot, a steamboat pilot, on the river that he loved—the Mississippi. Not only was that a good job, but it gave him the new name he would use for most of his life (read the book to find out where that name Mark Twain came from).

Sam frequently got into trouble of one sort and another, and when the Civil War started, his job as a pilot pretty much ended. He joined the Confederate Army for a couple of weeks, but he didn't like that. He and his brother decided to head for the gold in the West.

This is a very funny book, and you will laugh out loud at many of the things Mark said.

Fradin, Dennis Brindell. *Duel! Burr and Hamilton's Deadly War of Words.* Illustrated by Larry Day. Walker Books, 2008. ISBN 0802795838. Unpaged. Grades 2–4.

Why would two brilliant, powerful, important men want to kill each other so badly that they decided to have a duel? Whoever killed the other would win.

It happened in New Jersey in 1804. Aaron Burr was the vice president of the United States. Alexander Hamilton had signed the Constitution and was an important government figure and had been chief aide to George Washington during the Revolutionary War. You would think these two men could work things out and learn to live with each other.

But they could not.

Duel! Burr and Hamilton's Deadly War of Words **by Dennis Brindell Fradin.**

They just hated each other. They met as members of Washington's staff, and Burr didn't like the fact that Washington favored Hamilton—and even got rid of Burr because he thought he was a troublemaker. Then they were often on opposite sides of legal cases in New York City. Each was constantly putting down the other and saying bad things about him to anyone who would listen.

Finally Burr could not take it anymore and wrote a note demanding that Hamilton either apologize or fight a duel. Hamilton accepted the latter.

Read this book to find out what happened in the most famous duel in our country's history.

Halfmann, Janet. *Seven Miles to Freedom: The Robert Smalls Story.* Illustrated by Duane Smith. Lee & Low Books, 2008. ISBN 9781600602320. Unpaged. Grades 3–6.

Robert Smalls, born a slave, started working in the house of his owner, Mr. McKee, when he was about six years old—and McKee liked him. By the time he was 12, McKee sent him to work waiting tables in Charleston (he had to give his master the money he made), but Robert was fascinated by all the ships and activity he saw on the waterfront.

He got permission to work there, and worked himself up to becoming a wheelman, a man of color who piloted boats. He was good at it—and popular. He married, had a child, and decided to buy his family's freedom. That took a lot of saving, and there was not enough time because the Civil War started and business fell way off in the South. He could not get a job as a pilot, so he took one as a deckhand—and helped the Confederate Army set up its defenses.

He got promoted to wheelman. He learned all sorts of good things. He knew he wanted the Yankees to win, but what could he do? He was a slave.

And then he got an idea. What if he could steal a ship? And carry his friends and their families and his own family away with him! Would it work? It would be terribly dangerous.

This is the story of one of the most famous escapes in all of history. You will find Robert Smalls to be an amazing fellow.

Hendrix, John. *John Brown: His Fight for Freedom.* Abrams Books for Young Readers, 2009. ISBN 9780810937897. 40 p. Grades 3–6.

In 1840 John Brown treated African Americans very differently from the way most white people did back then. A lot of people thought slavery was a terrible thing and were willing to help slaves escape, but John took it a step further. He thought black people were equal to white people. He invited them to dinner at his home and he called them "Mister" and "Mrs." and "Miss" as a sign of respect.

John was an abolitionist, like his father. They were devout Christians and ran stops on the Underground Railroad, safe places where escaping slaves could hide.

A lot of people thought John went too far. One day at church, he looked around and saw all the black people were in the back pew. He traded his nice front pew for their back one. He absolutely believed that the way black people were treated was horrible. He had important, powerful, influential black friends, people like Harriet Tubman and Frederick Douglass. Douglass said John was the first white man who ever said he would be willing to die to eliminate slavery.

In 1854 John went to Kansas to fight slavery—and put a terrible stain on his reputation and memory. The state was called Bloody Kansas, as it was going to join the union and there was a fight about whether it would be a free state of a slave state. John, traveling with his sons, attacked five pro-slavery supporters and killed them all with broadswords. After that people thought he was insane.

But John kept on fighting. He grew a long beard so people would not recognize him. And then, in 1859, he conceived a magnificent idea. He did not want a Civil War in the United States. There was a big federal armory in Harpers Ferry, Virginia. John decided to attack it, leading 21 of his men, and show the South he meant business. And the attack was a disaster.

John Brown continues to capture our attention, over 150 years after he was hanged. This is some story.

Kennedy, Robert F., Jr. *Robert Smalls: The Boat Thief* (American Heroes). Illustrations by Patrick Faricy. Hyperion, 2008. ISBN 9781423108023. 40 p. Grades 4–6.

In May 1862 America was in the middle of the Civil War. The Confederates had held Charleston harbor for a year. Not much good had happened to the Union.

But something amazing happened one night. Nine slaves commandeered the Confederate commander's gunship and delivered it straight to the Union army.

And the leader of those slaves was a 23-year-old man named Robert Smalls. This is his story.

Robert was talented and intelligent. Though he was not taught to read as a child (most masters did not want their slaves to know how to do such an important thing), he had demonstrated his abilities and willingness to work hard, and he was taught how to navigate the harbors and sail any kind of boat. He could read maps and charts. Even his master was impressed, and let Robert keep a small part of the wages that others paid him. Robert had married at age 19, and he wanted to buy his wife and family and himself—but it was going to take a long time. Unless he could think of something!

He did think of something, and he grabbed that opportunity—and he brought his own family and the families of the other escaping slaves with him the night that he decided the time had come to steal the ship. Everyone knew what a dangerous thing it was to do, and they all agreed that if they were caught, they would blow up the ship and die rather than return to slavery.

This is one of the most incredible true stories you will ever read. Look at the wonderful illustrations—and find out what happened to Robert.

Krensky, Stephen. *A Man for All Seasons: The Life of George Washington Carver.* Illustrated by Wil Clay. Amistad, 2008. ISBN 9780060278854. Unpaged. Grades 3–5.

Moses and Susan Carver owned their slave baby George, and even after the Civil War ended and slavery was abolished, they raised George and his brother, whose parents had died. The Carvers helped both boys learn to read and write and count, and George learned fast and well.

By the time he was 12, he left home looking for ways to get an education—and he succeeded. He was not afraid of hard and menial work. He wrote, "I never saw anybody doing anything with his hands that I couldn't do with mine." He graduated from high school, and when he couldn't find a college that would accept non-white students, he began farming.

At first George seemed like a young man who was not sure what he wanted, but he sorted it all out. He found a college in Iowa that would accept him, started painting, and got really interested in botany, the study of plants. His college asked him to stay on and teach when he graduated.

And then George received a letter from Booker T. Washington, president of the Tuskegee Institute in Alabama, the most famous black man in America. He wanted George to come teach with him.

And George started his life work.

"George Washington Carver spent his whole life fostering his love of growing things. Unlike others who tried to conquer nature with chemicals and pesticides, Carter viewed nature as his partner. He took equal pleasure in a beautiful rose and the hundreds of uses he devised for the peanut."

George was a wonderful human being. You will enjoy reading about him.

Murphy, Jim. *The Real Benedict Arnold*. Clarion Books, 2007. ISBN 0395776090. 264 p. Grades 5–up.

Was he really the most evil thing since Satan himself? In the Revolutionary War, many people thought so.

What do you know about Benedict Arnold? Most people know one basic thing: he was a bad guy. He was a traitor to the American side of the American Revolution. He was a general, a high-ranking officer with a lot of power. But he sold out his country. He needed money, so he agreed to betray his country. He sold plans to the British that would enable them to defeat American forces and capture a lot of soldiers. He was a man with no honor at all.

Jim Murphy is one of our very best writers. In this riveting book, he takes a good hard look at that man—and comes up with someone you can understand and even sympathize with. For Benedict Arnold was a wonderful soldier, a man who made considerable sacrifices to support the revolution, a man who spent his own money to keep his soldiers fed and clothed and was an excellent officer who got right into the thick of battle and did many brave and heroic deeds there—especially compared to many other officers who never went anywhere near danger.

Plus he did not really need money. He had a lot of property in the colonies, and part of the reason he wanted the money from the British was to replace the possessions he knew he would lose if he went over to the other side.

But Benedict Arnold, who gave so much to the revolution, got very little back. He got a lot of grief, as a matter of fact. He made enemies who put him down with the revolutionary leaders and deprived him of the promotions he felt he deserved. Often those leaders said that his legitimate expenses should not be compensated. And that was just the beginning.

If you read this book, you will begin to understand why Benedict Arnold was angry—and maybe you will begin to understand why he decided to do what he did. And maybe you will, in the end, feel sorry for him.

It is a fine read.

Author Profile: Jim Murphy

Jim Murphy, known for his award-winning historical books for children, remembers reading Ernest Hemingway, James Michener, and Charles Dickens when he was young. He turned to reading and later writing nonfiction when a seventh-grade teacher got him hooked on history.

What got you started reading when you were young?

My father refinished furniture and he taught me to refinish furniture. I found an old bookcase in my house and redid it and it looked beautiful. Then it was sitting in my room and people would come in and say, "Why aren't there any books?" so I went around the house and gathered books up and put them in the bookcase. Then people would say, "Have you read the books?" and I felt kind of foolish saying that I just put them in there to make it look nice. So I read all of those books, and once I finished that I went on reading nonstop to this day.

What did you do after graduating from college?

I was an English major and I wanted to get into publishing on the editorial side. But I couldn't type, and so right out of college I actually worked in construction in New York City working on skyscrapers. I was a tin knocker, so we were the second group that went up after the iron workers put up the iron. After a while I did get a job in publishing with Clarion Books and I worked as an editor for seven or eight years. Then I decided to become a freelance writer. That editorial job did two things that were very important. First, it let me see how other people's manuscripts were developed from an idea through a proposal and into the writing and revision stage. That gave me a lot of confidence in terms of thinking about my own projects. Second, it allowed me to meet people. I was at an ALA conference and an editor said, "What's new with you?" and I said I was going to leave Clarion to write. She asked what I was thinking of writing and I didn't know. Later we had a meeting and came up with the idea of doing unusual inventions, which became my first book, *Weird and Wacky Inventions*. So the first book went very smoothly and that was nice, but then I didn't sell another book for another two and a half years. So I did put in some time struggling.

Do you write with boys in mind when you're writing books for young people?

Not really. I have to be honest. What I do is, I do lots of research trying to come up with topics that interest me. And then when I write the books I think in terms of a wide variety of readers, boys and girls, but mostly I'm thinking about talking to readers who might not know anything about the subject. I try to be direct and clear about the information I'm giving. I do think in terms of trying to engage readers in terms of creating some sort of action line. So I look for topics that have a beginning, middle, and end, like the Chicago Fire for instance. It started small and spread and became a large consuming force in Chicago, then eventually it ended, so it has a natural story line.

How do you research your typical nonfiction book?

It varies from book to book, but essentially I see it as detective work. And I begin by choosing a broad topic. I need to educate myself and give myself a crash course in whatever this topic is. So for instance, with *The Truce*, I had to read a lot of general histories about World War I and that started me off thinking about what the topic would be. When I began I did not think about doing a book on the Christmas truce of 1914. I was thinking about some other kind of book on World War I, one possibly focusing on the African American troops. But then I shifted from that idea when I learned about the Christmas truce and then it became very specific because then I had to go searching for company histories and then I had to find out what the truth was because some people dispute whether the truce was really as large as other people claimed it to be. It becomes this process where I get a piece of information and then I search very carefully to make sure it's truthful and to find out if there are any firsthand accounts that I can include. So the research moves along at a very deliberate pace as I'm hunting out facts and trying to build the story up.

Which of the books you've written is your favorite?

I really enjoyed doing *The American Plague*. It's about the yellow fever epidemic in Philadelphia in 1793. At first I had not known very much about it and it was a surprise to find out that there had been such a massive epidemic in an American city. As I started to write I decided very consciously not to tell readers any of our modern knowledge about yellow fever until the very last chapter. And therefore they would experience the book with the same sort of knowledge that people in 1793 had. And then suddenly it became a medical mystery and I had a lot of fun putting together a nonfiction book that sort of left clues along the way and sort of let kids decipher some pieces of it.

Murphy, Jim. *A Savage Thunder: Antietam and the Bloody Road to Freedom.* Margaret K. McElderry Books, 2009. ISBN 9780689876332. 103 p. Grades 5–9.

On September 5, 1862, Robert E. Lee led his troops into enemy territory—Maryland. The brilliant general had a strategy. He was invading the North to destroy its will to fight and to move the war away from his beloved South. He was not in the best shape physically. A few days earlier, he had fallen while trying to restrain his horse. His hands had been injured and he wore clumsy splints. The horses and the men made it across the Potomac on foot or horseback; Lee had to ride in an ambulance.

But Lee never let physical pain or inconvenience stop him.

The leader of the Union Army was George McClellan, beloved by his men but a man who always hesitated in every situation. When haste and quick decision making were essential, McClellan could be counted on to procrastinate. He was always afraid that his soldiers were outnumbered, and they never were. He was absolutely the wrong man in the wrong place at the wrong time. And his Commander-in-Chief, President Abraham Lincoln, agonized about it.

McClellan didn't like Lincoln either. He called him "an idiot . . . nothing more than a well-meaning baboon" (page 10). No wonder the Union was not doing well.

The South was doing very well. At that point, England and France were seriously considering recognizing the Confederacy as a separate, independent nation. The big problem was slavery, which neither country wished to appear to condone. But the war and the South's ceasing shipping cotton to England had caused a major economic crisis in England's mills, which fired thousands of workers and cut the pay of hundreds of thousands.

Added to all of this was the president's desire to free the slaves. But he did not feel he could do it when the war was going so poorly for the Union. He wanted a victory, one that would make the Emancipation Proclamation come from a leader whose side was winning. The Union needed to win the battle that was going to happen in Maryland—the battle of Antietam.

This is the story of that battle, and it is confusing and wild and crazy and terrifying and sometimes even funny (read the excerpt from the letter Union Private William Brearley, age 16, wrote to his father, on page 67). It is an amazing story of the bloodiest day in the history of the United States of America.

Nelson, Scott Reynolds, with Marc Aronson. *Ain't Nothing but a Man: My Quest to Find the Real John Henry.* National Geographic, 2008. ISBN 9781426300004. 64 p. Grades 5–9.

Most people know the story of John Henry, the railroad man who raced with a steam engine—and won. But he also died from wearing himself out.

It's a great story. It would be an even greater story if it were true. But was it? Most people weren't sure and couldn't find out. Scott Nelson wanted it to be true and set out to find out who John Henry really was and where and when his story happened.

There are lots of songs about John Henry. Some have names in them. Could some of those names be real names of real people? Could some of those names be clues?

Scott Nelson decided he was going to find out.

What he found out is pretty horrible, but pretty wonderful too. He suspects that one of the reasons there was so much mystery around John Henry was that he was a convict in prison. But why would convicts in prison be working on railroads?

There are lots of great photographs in this excellent book. If you like mysteries and John Henry, you'll want to check this one out.

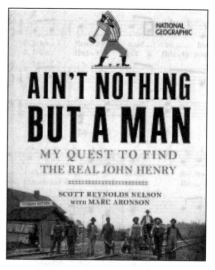

Ain't Nothing but a Man: My Quest to Find the Real John Henry **by Scott Reynolds Nelson.**

Nelson, Vaunda Micheaux. *Bad News for Outlaws: The Remarkable Life of Bass Reeves, Deputy U.S. Marshal.* Illustrations by R. Gregory Christie. Carolrhoda Books, 2009. ISBN 9780822567646. Unpaged. Grades 1–5.

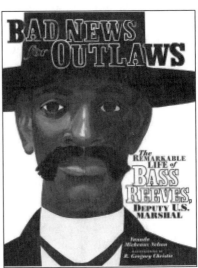

Bass Reeves may have been the most extraordinary deputy U.S. marshal of all time. He must have been somebody really special. He was born a slave in Texas sometime in the 1840s. His owner taught Bass to hunt and shoot and even took Bass with him when he fought in the Civil War. But something happened: Bass ran away and headed straight for Indian Territory out west and hid until the Civil War ended and the slaves were freed. He went on to marry and raise a family of 11 kids in Arkansas.

But there were a lot of bad guys in the Indian Territory. A judge named Isaac C. Parker was brought in to clean up the area. He hired 200 deputy marshals—and Bass was one of them. Judge Parker trusted him more than any of the others. Bass was a crack shot and would take as long as it took to find and bring in a fugitive.

Bad News for Outlaws: The Remarkable Life of Bass Reeves, Deputy U.S. Marshal **by Vaunda Micheaux Nelson.**

And, boy, there are some good stories about some of the fugitives he found and how he brought them in. Once he even had to arrest his own son!

You will enjoy reading the story of this unusual man's amazing life.

Sandler, Martin W. *Lincoln Through the Lens: How Photography Revealed and Shaped an Extraordinary Life.* Walker Books, 2008. ISBN 9780802796660. 96 p. Grades 5–up.

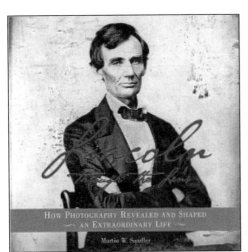

Lincoln Through the Lens: How Photography Revealed and Shaped an Extraordinary Life **by Martin W. Sandler.**

This is a different look at the man most people believe was the greatest president the United States ever had. It tells and shows us how the new invention of the camera influenced both his life and his career. There are some amazing photographs in the book.

The earliest surviving American photograph was taken in 1839, when Lincoln was 30 years old. Within a few years, he was having his picture taken, and he had no idea that one day more people would be more eager to photograph him than any other person in the country.

Look at the photo on page 10 of Lincoln with a bunch of Union officers. He was tall, almost 6 feet 4 inches, and he wore a tall hat on top of that, and he liked to stand in the middle of the picture so everyone naturally looked at him first. He knew what he was doing!

On page 21, there is a photo of Lincoln wearing a white suit. He was a prominent lawyer in Springfield, Illinois, and he often wore white in court. But it looks different to us. We are used to seeing him always dressed in black.

On page 41 is the photo that Lincoln said won him the election for president. It was taken by Matthew Brady, and he posed Lincoln with books, in front of a pillar, and he raised Lincoln's shirt collar higher so it would cover his scrawny neck!

On page 69 is a mind-boggling photo. It shows Lincoln (who was accidentally rubbed out of the original negative) at his second inauguration. Not far behind him is John Wilkes Booth, who would kill him a few weeks later, and in front of him are several of the rest of the men who planned his assassination.

This book will give you a lot to look at and think about. It is a fine read.

Sheinkin, Steve. *King George: What Was His Problem? Everything Your Schoolbooks Didn't Tell You About the American Revolution.* Illustrated by Tim Robinson. Roaring Brook Press, 2008. ISBN 9781596433199. 195 p. Grades 5–up.

This book gives you all sorts of interesting and often funny facts about the American Revolution—things you probably never read before.

Things really got going in the American colonies after the French and Indian War, which ended in 1763. The British had to keep 10,000 soldiers in North America to keep the peace, and that cost money. The British decided to tax the colonists—and they called it the Stamp Act. The colonists hated it. How come *they* did not have a say in how they were governed? Relations between the colonies and the British government went downhill fast.

Here are some of the great bits of information:

King George: What Was His Problem? Everything Your Schoolbooks Didn't Tell You About the American Revolution by Steve Sheinkin. Jacket shown with permission from Roaring Brook Press.

- The taxman in Boston, Andrew Oliver, woke up one morning to learn that a life-sized doll of him had been hanged on an elm tree. Pinned to it was a poem: "What greater joy did New England see, than a stamp man hanging on a tree?" (p. 5). How would *you* feel?

- When the Continental Congress met in Philadelphia to discuss independence, they argued about everything. John Adams said, "That if someone had declared that three plus two equaled five, members would have wasted a couple of days debating the issue" (p. 17).

- Thomas Jefferson apparently did not think July 4, 1776, was such a big deal. On that day he wrote only two things in his diary—the temperature and the fact that he had purchased seven pairs of women's gloves.

- A great English writer named Samuel Johnson wondered why the colonists were yelping for liberty when they had slaves. People have been wondering about that ever since.

- More than 2,500 soldiers died from disease, cold, and hunger at Valley Forge. It was not a good winter for the rebels.

- A slave named James Armistead asked his owner if he could help with the revolution. His owner said yes and he went to the Continental Army and was assigned to work as a spy in the British camp. He got some great information! But after the British surrendered, he had to go back to being a slave again, until Lafayette arranged for him to get his freedom in 1787.

- When the British finally surrendered at Yorktown in 1781, they did not behave like gentlemen. They threw down their guns to break them so the Americans could not use them, and some of them cried.

If you enjoy history and interesting trivia, you will have a great time with this book.

Spradlin, Michael. *Daniel Boone's Great Escape*. Illustrated by Ard Hoyt. Walker Books, 2008. ISBN 0802795811. Unpaged. Grades 2–4.

Daniel Boone had an awful lot of adventures, but maybe one of his most exciting was the time he was captured by a party of Shawnee warriors. It was 1778, and he was on the wild frontier, catching food for his men. Boone had just killed a buffalo and had no useful weapons. He tried to run away, but soon gave up. The Shawnee took him to their war chief, Blackfish, who told Boone they were going to attack the Kentucky forts and drive out the settlers. Daniel negotiated. He said his men would surrender and he would lead the Shawnees to their camp. That happened—he must have been a pretty convincing person.

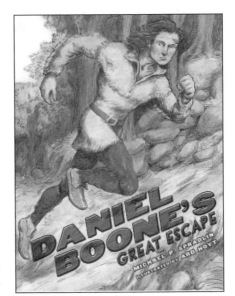

Daniel Boone's Great Escape **by Michael Spradlin.**

Over the course of a few months, Boone was adopted into the tribe and found a good life in the Shawnee village, but he knew he had to warn and save his family and friends.

He decided he had to escape, and he had to plan for it.

And this is the exciting story of how he did it!

Stark, Ken. *Marching to Appomattox: The Footrace That Ended the Civil War*. G. P. Putnam's Sons, 2009. ISBN 9780399242120. Unpaged. Grades 4–7.

How did the most horrible war of all in American history end? Do you know where it happened and who was there? This book, loaded with neat illustrations, tells us all about it. And it makes for a great story.

In the first week of April 1865, 80,000 Union Army soldiers were chasing the strongest army of the South, the Confederate Army of Northern Virginia. The Union Army leader, Ulysses S. Grant, wanted to do one thing above all: to stop the war and capture his foe, Robert E. Lee's, army without fighting another battle. Could he do it?

Only 30,000 Confederates were marching, and they were hungry. Starving, really. They had almost no rations and were eating horse food. Some of them were deserting to go back home. And all of them were bone tired.

This is the true story of what happened to both armies along the way—the people who greeted them, the two great generals, both of them afraid. Just before the end, Robert E. Lee said, "There is nothing left me to do now but to go and see General Grant, and I would rather die a thousand deaths."

Was he right to worry? Read the book and find out.

St. George, Judith. *Stand Tall, Abe Lincoln.* Illustrated by Matt Faulkner. Philomel Books, 2008. ISBN 9780399241741. Unpaged. Grades 3–5.

Most people would say that Abraham Lincoln had a really tough childhood—and they would be right. Abe was born in Kentucky in 1809, and his mother Nancy loved him dearly.

From the time he was very young, he was expected to do lots of chores. Once a neighbor gave him a baby pig, and that pig became Abe's pet. But in the fall his father killed the pig for pork for the winter. Abe was so unhappy that he ran away from home for two days.

Abe got to go to school for a while, once in a while. The schools he went to were called "blab" schools because everyone talked and did their lessons aloud—at the same time! Abe made friends and loved reading.

And then, after the family moved to Indiana, his mother died. Abe and his sister had only their father, and he could not do everything. He decided he needed to get another wife—and he did just that. Abe was worried sick. What if he did not like his new stepmother?

He did not have to worry. She loved Abe, and she brought books. She even bawled out Abe's dad when he tried to make him do chores all of the time instead of reading!

This is a wonderful true story with colorful, fun illustrations. You'll enjoy learning about the childhood of the man many think was the greatest American president ever.

Turner, Ann. *Sitting Bull Remembers.* Paintings by Wendell Minor. HarperCollins, 2007. ISBN 9780060514006. Unpaged. Grades 1–4.

In this somewhat fictionalized version of a sad true story, Sitting Bull, now caged on a reservation, remembers his happy childhood and his great victories as a warrior. Minor's compelling illustrations are based on Sitting Bull's own pictographs.

Yaccarino, Dan. *Go, Go America.* Scholastic Press, 2008. ISBN 0439703387. 80 p. Grades 1–5.

The Farley family takes a road trip across America, and state by state we see the places they go and the things they learn. This is just filled with fun facts, such as:

- Levi Hutchins of Concord, New Hampshire, invented the first alarm clock in 1787.

- The first person to go over Niagara Falls in a barrel was a 63-year-old retired schoolteacher named Annie Taylor.

- In Hartford, Connecticut, it is illegal to cross the street while you are walking on your hands.

- You better not slurp your soup in New Jersey. It is illegal there.

- The oldest zoo in the country is the Philadelphia Zoo.

And that is just the beginning. Reading this is a lot of fun!

WORTH READING

Nonfiction books with "boy appeal" that have received positive reviews in *Booklist*, *Horn Book Guide*, and/or *School Library Journal*.

Alter, Judy. *John Barclay Armstrong: Texas Ranger*. Bright Sky Press, 2007. ISBN 9781931721868. 59 p. Grades 4–7.

Blakely, Gloria. *Johnnie Cochran: Attorney and Civil Rights Advocate* (Black Americans of Achievement). Chelsea House, 2006. ISBN 0791091120. 160 p. Grades 6–1.2.

Crowe, Chris. *Thurgood Marshall* (Up Close). Viking, 2008. ISBN 9780670062287. 208 p. Grades 6–12.

Croy, Anita. *Ancient Pueblo: Archaeology Unlocks the Secrets of America's Past* (National Geographic Investigates). National Geographic, 2007. ISBN 9781426301315. 64 p. Grades 4–6.

Denenberg, Barry. *Lincoln Shot: A President's Life Remembered*. Feiwel & Friends, 2008. ISBN 9780312370138. 40 p. Grades 4–6.

Dougherty, Terri. *America's Deadliest Day: The Battle of Antietam* (Bloodiest Battles). Edge Books, 2008. ISBN 9781429619356. 32 p. Grades 4–6.

Drucker, Malka. *Portraits of Jewish American Heroes*. Dutton, 2008. ISBN 9780525477716. 96 p. Grades 3–6.

Garland, Michael. *Americana Adventure*. Dutton, 2008. ISBN 9780525479451. 32 p. Grades 1–3.

Gormley, Beatrice. *Malcolm X: A Revolutionary Voice* (Sterling Biographies). Sterling, 2008. ISBN 9781402758010. 128 p. Grades 4–6.

Green, Carl R. *Billy the Kid* (Outlaws and Lawmen of the Wild West). Enslow, 2008. ISBN 9780766031739. 48 p. Grades 3–5.

Green, Carl R. *Butch Cassidy* (Outlaws and Lawmen of the Wild West). Enslow, 2008. ISBN 9780766031753. 48 p. Grades 4–6.

Green, Carl R. *Jesse James* (Outlaws and Lawmen of the Wild West). Enslow, 2008. ISBN 9780766031722. 48 p. Grades 4–6.

Green, Carl R. *Wild Bill Hickok* (Outlaws and Lawmen of the Wild West). Enslow, 2008. ISBN 9780766031777. 48 p. Grades 4–6.

Green, Carl R. *Wyatt Earp* (Outlaws and Lawmen of the Wild West). Enslow, 2008. ISBN 9780766031746. 48 p. Grades 4–6.

Greene, Jacqueline Dembar. *The Triangle Shirtwaist Factory Fire* (Code Red). Bearport Publishing, 2007. ISBN 9781597163590. 32 p. Grades 3–6.

Hampton, Wilborn. *Elvis Presley* (Up Close). Viking, 2007. ISBN 9780670061662. 192 p. Grades 7–up.

Jesse James **by Carl R. Green.**

Harness, Cheryl. *The Remarkable Rough-Riding Life of Theodore Roosevelt and the Rise of Empire America* (Cheryl Harness Histories). National Geographic, 2007. ISBN 1426300085. 144 p. Grades 4–7.

Kennedy, Robert F., Jr. *Robert F. Kennedy, Jr.'s American Heroes: Joshua Chamberlain and the American Civil War.* Hyperion, 2007. ISBN 1423107713. 48 p. Grades 3–5.

Kent, Deborah. *The Tragic History of the Japanese-American Internment Camps* (From Many Cultures, One History). Enslow, 2008. ISBN 9780766027978. 128 p. Grades 4–6.

Landau, Elaine. *The Battle of Gettysburg: Would You Lead the Fight?* (What Would You Do?). Enslow, 2008. ISBN 9780766029033. 48 p. Grades 3–6.

Landau, Elaine. *The California Gold Rush: Would You Go for the Gold?* (What Would You Do?). Enslow, 2008. ISBN 9780766029019. 48 p. Grades 3–6.

Landau, Elaine. *George Washington Crosses the Delaware: Would You Risk the Revolution?* (What Would You Do?). Enslow, 2008. ISBN 9780766029040. 48 p. Grades 3–6.

Landau, Elaine. *The Louisiana Purchase: Would You Have Made the Deal?* (What Would You Do?). Enslow, 2008. ISBN 9780766029026. 48 p. Grades 3–6.

Landau, Elaine. *The Revolutionary War Begins: Would You Join the Fight?* (What Would You Do?). Enslow, 2008. ISBN 9780766029002. 48 p. Grades 3–6.

Leavitt, Amie Jane. *The Battle of the Alamo: An Interactive a History Adventure* (You Choose Books). Capstone Press, 2008. ISBN 9781429613545. 112 p. Grades 3–9.

Lynch, Wayne. *Everglades* (Our Wild World). NorthWord, 2007. ISBN 1559719702. 64 p. Grades 4–7.

Malam, John. *You Wouldn't Want to Be a Worker on the Statue of Liberty! A Monument You'd Rather Not Build* (You Wouldn't Want To: American History). Franklin Watts, 2008. ISBN 9780531207000. 32 p. Grades 3–5.

The Revolutionary War Begins: Would You Join the Fight? by Elaine Landau.

Margulies, Philip, and Maxine Rosaler. *The Devil on Trial: Witches, Anarchists, Atheists, Communists, and Terrorists in America's Courtrooms.* Houghton Mifflin, 2008. ISBN 9780618717170. 224 p. Grades 7–10.

National Museum of the American Indian. *Do All Indians Live in Tipis? Questions and Answers from the National Museum of the American Indian.* Collins, 2007. ISBN 9780061153013. 129 p. Grades 8–up.

How to Get Rich on the Oregon Trail: My Adventures among Cows, Crooks & Heroes on the Road to Fame & Fortune by William Reed, Age 15 by Tod Olson.

Olmstead, Kathleen. *Matthew Henson: The Quest for the North Pole* (Sterling, Biographies). Sterling, 2008. ISBN 978140276-60600. 128 p. Grades 5–8.

Olson, Tod. *How to Get Rich on the Oregon Trail: My Adventures among Cows, Crooks & Heroes on the Road to Fame & Fortune by William Reed, Age 15.* Illustrations by Scott Allred and Gregory Proch. National Geographic, 2009. ISBN 9781426304125. 48 p. Grades 4–8.

Rabin, Staton. *Mr. Lincoln's Boys: Being the Mostly True Adventures of Abraham Lincoln's Troublemaking Sons Tad and Willie.* Viking, 2008. ISBN 9780670061693. 40 p. Grades 2–4.

Reis, Ronald A. *The Dust Bowl* (Great Historic Disasters). Chelsea House, 2008. ISBN 9780791097373. 128 p. Grades 6–up.

Rinaldo, Denise. *White House Q&A* (Smithsonian. Q&A). Collins, 2008. ISBN 9780060899660. 48 p. Grades K–3.

Robson, David. *The Kennedy Assassination* (The Mysterious & Unknown). Referencepoint Press, 2008. ISBN 9781601520364. 96 p. Grades 4–6.

Rompella, Natalie. *Famous Firsts: The Trendsetters, Groundbreakers, and Risk-Takers Who Got America Moving!* (My America). Lobster Press, 2007. ISBN 9781897073551. 48 p. Grades 3–7.

Ruffin, Frances E. *Frederick Douglass: Rising Up from Slavery* (Sterling Biographies). Sterling, 2008. ISBN 9781402757990. 128 p. Grades 4–6.

Selzer, Adam. *The Smart Aleck's Guide to American History.* Delacorte, 2009. ISBN 9780385906135. 326 p. Grades 8–up.

Seuling, Barbara. *One President was Born on Independence Day: And Other Freaky Facts About the 26th Through 43rd Presidents* (Freaky Facts). Picture Window Books, 2008. ISBN 9781404841185. Unpaged. Grades K–4.

Sheinkin, Steve. *Two Miserable Presidents: Everything Your School Books Didn't Tell You About the Civil War.* Roaring Brook Press, 2008. ISBN 9781596433205 256 p. Grades 4–6.

Stanley, George Edward. *Davy Crockett: Frontier Legend* (Sterling Biographies). Sterling, 2008. ISBN 9781402754999. 128 p. Grades 4–6.

Stein, R. Conrad. *Escaping Slavery on the Underground Railroad* (From Many Cultures, One History). Enslow, 2008. ISBN 9780766027992. 128 p. Grades 4–6.

Tanaka, Shelley. *Amelia Earhart: The Legend of the Lost Aviator.* Abrams Books for Young Readers, 2008. ISBN 9780810970953. 48 p. Grades 2–4.

Thompson, Gare. *Riding with the Mail: The Story of the Pony Express* (History Chapters). National Geographic, 2007. ISBN 9781426301926. 48 p. Grades 2–4.

Tieck, Sarah. *Brooklyn Bridge* (All Aboard America Set 3). ABDO & Daughters, 2008. ISBN 9781599289342. 24 p. Grades K–3.

Tieck, Sarah. *Empire State Building* (All Aboard America). Buddy Books, 2008. ISBN 9781599289359. 24 p. Grades K–3.

Tieck, Sarah. *Jamestown* (All Aboard America). Buddy Books, 2008. ISBN 978-1599289366. 24 p. Grades K–3.

Tieck, Sarah. *Monticello* (All Aboard America). Buddy Books, 2008. ISBN 978-1599289373. 24 p. Grades K–3.

Tieck, Sarah. *Niagara Falls* (All Aboard America). Buddy Books, 2008. ISBN 978-1599289380. 24 p. Grades K–3.

Tieck, Sarah. *Oregon Trail* (All Aboard America). Buddy Books, 2008. ISBN 978-1599289397. 24 p. Grades K–3.

Vila, Laura. *Building Manhattan*. Viking, 2008. ISBN 9780670062843. 40 p. Grades 3–5.

Walker, Paul Robert. *Remember the Alamo: Texians, Tejanos, and Mexicans Tell Their Stories* (Remember). National Geographic,2007. ISBN 9781426300103. 64 p. Grades 4–8.

Warrick, Karen Clemens. *Alamo: Victory or Death on the Texas Frontier* (America's Living History). Enslow, 2008. ISBN 9780766029378 128 p. Grades 4–6.

Weatherford, Carole Boston. *I, Matthew Henson: Polar Explorer*. Walker Books, 2007. ISBN 0802796885. 32 p. Grades 3–5.

Woods, Michael. *Seven Wonders of Ancient North America* (Seven Wonders). Twenty-First Century Books, 2008. ISBN 9780822575726. 80 p. Grades 5–7.

Yolen, Jane. *Johnny Appleseed: The Legend and the Truth*. HarperCollins, 2008. ISBN 9780060591359. 32 p. Grades K–3.

Chapter  7

Animals

You can't argue with success. Kids love animals, and it seems like more books about animals are published each year than on any other topic. How do you choose among all these titles? First and foremost, look for excellent photography and an engaging narrative. And when selecting books for boys, look for the scary, the funny, and the gross details to hook them. Use these lists to fill your library with irresistible books about a topic that is a perennial favorite.

BOOKTALKS

Ablow, Gail. *A Horse in the House and Other Strange but True Animal Stories*. Illustrated by Kathy Osborn. Candlewick Press, 2007. ISBN 9780763628383. Unpaged. Grades 3–5.

Kathy Osborn really liked reading unusual stories about animals in the news, and she decided she would love to draw pictures of those stories. Her publisher paired her up with a writer, and they produced this book of fun, strange, and downright weird true stories.

You'll have a lot of fun reading about things like:

- The rabbit who was genetically engineered to glow a bright green color.

- The real wedding of two all-dressed-up donkeys.

- The parrot who terrified three burglars and made them drop their weapons and lie flat on the floor until help came.

- The elephant who has false teeth.

- The greyhound who got contact lenses so he could race better.

These stories seem unbelievable, but they really happened!

Arnold, Caroline. *Super Swimmers: Whales, Dolphins, and Other Mammals of the Sea*. Illustrated by Patricia J. Wynne. Charlesbridge, 2007. ISBN 9781570915888. 32 p. Grades 3–5.

All sorts of mammals swim in the sea, and their lives are adapted for living in the water. As the book says, "Most marine animals are shaped like torpedoes, with small heads and long, round torsos that narrow at the tail. Their limbs are usually short, or, in some cases, not there at all. The animals' ears are small; sometimes they are simply holes in their heads. Their skin is mostly bare or covered in sleek fur" (p. 6). A lot of them have a thick layer of fat called blubber underneath their skin—to keep them warm. This book has lots of great facts:

- Look at the picture of the breathing holes that seals make, on page 9.

- Once whale hunters caught a really unusual whale. It had a giant squid in its stomach. That squid weighed 440 pounds and was 40 feet long. Yikes!

- Baby walruses often ride on their mothers' backs. See the picture on page 13.

- No one knows why whales and dolphins suddenly jump out of the water. It is called breaching. Look at the picture on page 18.

- Walruses sometimes use their tusks as ice picks.

- Sea otters can stay underwater for up to five minutes.

- Polar bears can swim 60 miles or even more in open water.

This is a fun topic to explore.

Arnosky, Jim. *Jim Arnosky's All About Manatees*. Scholastic Press, 2008. ISBN 9780439903615. Unpaged. Grades 2–4.

Adult manatees are about ten to eleven feet long and weigh more than 1,000 pounds. They are relatives of elephants, and they are gentle, plant-eating animals. No one tries to eat them (they are way too big to attack!), and they leave everybody else alone.

In the United States, the only place where manatees exist in the wild is off the coast of Florida. Lots of times they like to live near power plants, because power plants discharge warm water, and manatees have to have warm water or they will die. Water needs to be above 68 degrees, which is pretty warm.

One thing that manatees have to do that causes terrible problems is stay close to the top of the water in order to breathe. They breathe every two to three minutes. This means that power boats with propellers sometimes hit them—and cut them—and even cut off parts of their bodies.

Manatees are gentle, lovable animals, and they have been endangered because living in the ocean in the twenty-first century is dangerous indeed.

You will enjoy reading about these interesting animals.

Arnosky, Jim *Parrotfish and Sunken Ships: Exploring a Tropical Reef.* Collins, 2007.
   ISBN 9780688171247. Unpaged. Grades 1–4.

   The only tropical reef in the United States is in the Florida Keys, and Jim Arnosky
   and his wife took their little boat out about 15 miles and saw all sorts of wonderful
   things. Arnosky describes them and creates beautiful color illustrations of animals
   like puffer fish, nurse sharks, stingrays, sea turtles, and hermit crabs—and also pictures of the vegetation in the area, not to mention sunken ships.

Bishop, Nic. *Nic Bishop Marsupials.* Scholastic Press, 2009. ISBN 9780439877589. 48 p.
   Grades 3–6.

   It's difficult to find photographs better than the ones Nic Bishop takes. In this
   book he searches the world to find marsupials, which, as he tells us, are mammals, just
   like cats, dogs, horses, and us. But marsupials do something that is different from
   other mammals. They give birth to babies that are tiny, sometimes tinier than a grain
   of rice. Those babies are way too undeveloped to be separated from their mothers.

   Fortunately, those mothers usually have pouches that the babies crawl straight
   into after they are born. They grab on to their mother's nipple and don't let go until
   they are old enough to leave the pouch.

   The only marsupial found in the United States is the Virginia opossum, the one
   famous for playing dead so well. That opossum is now living as far north as Canada. It
   eats almost anything, including our garbage!

   There are opossums in Central and South America. Take a look at the puzzled one
   on page 11. The reason it looks so curious is that it found something strange. It is sniff-
   ing Nic's camera!

   On page 14, look at the mother kangaroo—kangaroos are the most famous marsupial—fighting with her baby, which is called a joey. They are not going to hurt each
   other—this fight is just for practice.

   On page 24, look at the photo of the koala mother and her joey. Koalas have their
   pouches on their backs, so they look different from kangaroo pouches. On page 25 you
   will learn a gross (to us) benefit of having the pouch on the back.

   On pages 28 and 29 are the most amazing photos in the book—showing a sugar
   glider possum flying through the air!

   Marsupials are animals that are always interesting. You will be delighted by this
   book with its wonderful photos.

Carson, Mary Kay. *Emi and the Rhino Scientist* (Scientists in the Field). With photographs
   by Tom Uhlman. Houghton Mifflin, 2007. ISBN 9780618646395. 57 p. Grades 5–8.

   Emi is a rare and endangered Sumatran rhinoceros. Twenty years ago there were
   about a thousand of them; today there are only 300. Emi fell into a trap when she was a
   baby. Her mother had been killed, probably by poachers, and she was rescued and
   taken to a zoo in Cincinnati. The people in the zoo desperately wanted her to have a
   baby of her own, and Terri Roth, a scientist who works at the zoo, got on the case. A
   male rhinoceros was brought in, and Emi became pregnant a few times—and lost the
   baby every time. This time, in 2000, Terri was determined to do everything she could
   think of to get that baby born! It wasn't easy: the last Sumerian baby birth in captivity
   had happened over a hundred years before.

But Terri had some ideas about what would work. And whether what she did was the cause or not, Emi gave birth to a live, healthy baby boy.

This is Emi's story and the story of her babies (she had another one too!), of the rhinoceros family, and especially of her breed, the Sumatran rhinoceros. The story is filled with interesting information. Here are a few facts:

- Prehistoric rhinos were hairy. Only the Sumatran rhinos are still covered with hair.

- Rhinos are famous for their horns, but their horns are valuable, and they are the main reason so many of them are killed by poachers—hunters who kill them illegally for money. A rhino horn can be worth many thousands of dollars.

- An adult rhino poops about 60 pounds a day.

- Emi's brand-new baby calf, Andalas, weighed 73 pounds. He gained more than 800 pounds in his first year.

The pictures are wonderful. Anyone who likes animals will enjoy this book.

Cerullo, Mary M. *The Truth About Dangerous Sea Creatures.* Photographs by Jeffrey L. Rotman. Illustrations by Michael Wertz. Chronicle Books, 2008. ISBN 978-0811863490. 48 p. Grades 4–8.

So what do you think are the most dangerous animals in the ocean? Take a guess, and then look at this fascinating book to see if you have it right.

The animal that divers fear the most is called the sea urchin. Sea urchins are covered with long, brittle spines, and they break off easily. When a diver accidentally bumps into one, they stick into the diver. They hurt. If the diver tries to pull it out, it breaks easily—into smaller pieces still inside the body. Some are filled with venom! It is not fun.

Here are some amazing facts:

- No one has ever seen a living, healthy, giant squid. We have seen some dead ones. But scientists keep hoping that someday they will find one alive. They are huge!

- The blue-ring octopus is small, but it is full of venom. If it bites, that venom can sometimes kill a human being in a few minutes.

- They used to call them jellyfish, but now they are just called jellies, because they are in no way a fish. Some jellies have venom, even after they are dead. That venom can hurt human beings, even kill them.

- The most dangerous animals in the ocean are in the tropics.

- The stonefish looks like a stone. Most of the time you would never even guess it was a fish! And that's just the beginning. It is also the most poisonous animal in the world. See the photo on page 21

And that's just the beginning. Which of these animals, and a lot of others, would *you* most want to avoid?

Collard, Sneed B., III. *Pocket Babies and Other Amazing Marsupials.* Darby Creek Publishing, 2007. ISBN 1581960468. 72 p. Grades 4–9.

Pocket Babies and Other Amazing Marsupials **by Sneed B. Collard III.**

There are three different kinds of mammals in the world. Most of us (yeah, humans are mammals, too) are "Eutherian" mammals, which give live birth to fully formed babies. A very few are "Monotreme," which lay eggs. The rest—well under 10 percent—are Marsupial or "Matatherian." Those animals give birth to partially formed babies. And this book is about those incredible animals. You probably had no idea that there are so many different kinds of them.

Take a look on page 6 at the kangaroo embryo that has attached itself to its mother to receive food and live inside her pouch. Female kangaroos, this book tells us, are always pregnant. They have one baby, or joey, in their pockets, and another in their bodies.

Here are a few of the many fascinating facts:

- Opossums are marsupials—they are the kind most North Americans are most likely to see in the wild. When the Virginia opossum plays dead, it will roll over and become stiff and even drool. It can stay in this condition for up to four hours!

- A group of kangaroos together is called a mob.

- Pouches do not always open in the same direction. Some pouches open upward, others open downward. Koalas' pouches open downward because the babies need to eat some of their mothers' poop! See the picture on page 29.

- Wombat dung is almost perfectly cube shaped. When the dung hardens, it can be used as a building block.

The facts and pictures in this book are just incredible. You will be astounded at this great information about a lot of animals you probably never heard of—and many that you have.

Collard, Sneed B., III. *Teeth.* Illustrated by Phyllis V. Saroff. Charlesbridge, 2008. ISBN 9781580891202. Unpaged. Grades 2–5.

Teeth **by Sneed B. Collard III.**

Human beings have teeth that do all sorts of things—which is why the teeth in your mouth are not all the same. Many animals have teeth as well, and you will be amazed at some of the things you will learn about them in this book:

- Vampire bats slice the skin of other animals with their teeth and then drink their blood.

- Most frogs and toads don't have teeth at all. When they do have them, they are small teeth, just big enough to hold onto live things before they are swallowed.

- Tusks are teeth. There was an African elephant that had tusks that were more than 11 feet long and weighed more than 200 pounds!

- Sharks have thousands of teeth arranged in rows in their mouths. If they lose a tooth, a new one moves up to replace it.

- Some tongues have teeth, and so do some throats. Read the book to find out which tongues and which throats!

This is really fun information!

Collard, Sneed B., III. *Wings.* Illustrated by Robin Brickman. Charlesbridge, 2008. ISBN 9781570916113. Unpaged. Grades 3–5.

Wings are neat! Sometimes people wish they had them so they could fly wherever they wanted, but only one kind of mammal has wings. Do you know what it is? It is the bat!

And there are a lot of different kinds of bats. The biggest ones are the flying foxes. They can have a wingspan of up to six feet. That is a *huge* bat!

This book has a lot of great information about wings, such as:

- There are about 10,000 species of birds on earth.

- The smallest bird is the bee hummingbird. It weighs less than a penny, and is so tiny that people sometimes think it is a bee.

- Clearwing butterflies have no color at all—they are like glass.

- Peregrine falcons can go as fast as 65 miles an hour.

- Dragonflies and some other insects have four wings instead of two.

- Penguins cannot fly in the air, but they use their wings to fly through the water.

And that is just the beginning.

George, Jean Craighead. *The Wolves Are Back*. Paintings by Wendell Minor. Dutton Children's Books, 2008. ISBN 0525479473. Unpaged. Grades 1–4.

Many years ago, every wolf in Yellowstone Park was gone. Most had been shot. In fact, every wolf in the lower 48 United States was gone—forever, everyone thought. The directors of the national parks decided only gentle animals should be allowed in them. And hardly anyone liked wolves.

But some people did. And they were convinced that our wilderness was not the way it was supposed to be without wolves in it. In 1995 they brought in ten adult wolves from Canada to Yellowstone Park.

The wolves started having babies. They had more babies. They howled. People loved to hear the sound of it.

This beautiful book not only tells us of the return of the wolves to the park, but of the many wonderful things that happened because they were back. You will be amazed at the difference they have made.

Haas, Robert B. *African Critters*. National Geographic, 2008. ISBN 9781426303173. 95 p. Grades 2–6.

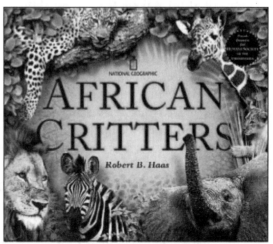

Robert Haas is a famous wildlife photographer, and when you start reading and looking through this book, you will find out why immediately. These are absolutely wonderful photographs of African animals. One thing he particularly loves to photograph is animal babies.

You will also learn a lot of great information, such as:

- Leopards almost always hunt at night—so people do not see them very often. But there are about 100,000 wild leopards in Africa, more than all the lions and cheetahs put together.

African Critters **by Robert B. Haas.**

- Leopards can leap up tall trees while carrying a full-grown antelope in their jaws. This enables them to eat all they want without other animals bothering them.

- Wild dogs are among the most endangered animals in Africa. Take a look at the photo on page 31. People considered them pests and shot them whenever they saw them.

- Hyenas are important to the food chain. They finish off the carcass of an animal that other animals are done with—and thus they recycle a lot of food.

- Oxpeckers are tiny birds that frequently live with buffalos. "They bounce all around the buffalo's hide, inside its ears, and even up its nose in search of tiny insects to feed on" (p. 72). Take a look at the pictures on pages 72–73.

You will not be able to put this book down!

Heuer, Karsten. *Being Caribou: Five Months on Foot with a Caribou Herd.* Walker Books, 2007. ISBN 9780802795656. 48 p. Grades 4–8.

Karsten Heuer was a Canadian park ranger who got a job at Ivvavik National Park, which is right next to the Arctic Ocean and Alaska. It has no roads and no buildings, not even hiking trails. The only trails are made by a huge herd of caribou that goes to its Alaskan calving grounds every year. "It's an amazing migration across four mountain ranges and dozens of rivers that they've been making for the last 27,000 years" (p. 4).

Karsten wanted to go on that migration. He wanted to follow those caribou, and see exactly what they did and how they lived while they migrated.

Being Caribou: Five Months on Foot with a Caribou Herd by **Karsten Heuer.**

He must have married the right woman, for she agreed to follow the caribou with him. It took them five months—and they had to carry all of their food and clothing and their tent on their backs.

This is the story of what they saw, how they lived, and what they learned. It has dozens of amazing color photographs.

They saw caribou predators—hungry animals like bears and wolves.

They saw the caribou actually giving birth—and during that time Karsten and his wife had to stay inside their tiny tent. They even had to go to the bathroom there! They watched the brand-new babies and their mothers learn to communicate with each other. Babies who cannot understand their mother's call will probably die.

They saw the insects come in and drive the caribou and themselves crazy. Fortunately, they had insect-proof clothing, but the caribou were absolutely miserable.

They started having strange visions when they got so tired and hungry that they were barely functioning properly anymore.

If you like animals and adventure, this may be the book for you.

Hodgkins, Fran. *The Whale Scientists: Solving the Mystery of Whale Strandings* (Scientists in the Field). Houghton Mifflin, 2007. ISBN 9780618556731. 64 p. Grades 5–8.

You read about it or see pictures of it in the news every now and then. A whale has gotten up on the beach. The tide has gone out and he or she is just lying there—and will die soon without help. People feel terrible, and many do help. What's even worse is when there is more than one whale—sometimes a whole group of them.

But why does this happen? What is going on? Scientists are not really sure.

In this book we learn about the history of the whale—how millions of years ago it lived like crocodiles do today—it had legs and a tail and a big mouth and it would wait near the edge of the water and grab animals that got too close and gobble them up.

But over the centuries it evolved into the creature we know today, one that can live only in the water.

People have hunted whales for many years. Probably ancient people could only kill the ones that were stranded on a beach, but over a thousand years ago they were being actively hunted. Vikings and Basques started hunting whales in Labrador by the 1500s and hunted so many that they wiped out all of the whales that went near there.

Then serious whale hunting started, especially in the 1800s, and many whales were hunted until they became extinct.

Now people want to know about them more than they want to eat them. Scientists are studying them hard and are still mystified. There are several theories about strandings, such as damaged hearing (caused in part by container ships that make a lot of noise), confusing geography, magnetic forces, bad weather, and illness and injury.

This book has many fine pictures and a great deal of interesting information. By the time you finish reading it, you'll want to know more and you will hope scientists can solve the problem.

Jango-Cohen, Judith. *Real-Life Sea Monsters* (On My Own Science). Illustrated by Ryan Burney. Millbrook Press, 2007. ISBN 9780822567479. 48 p. Grades 1–3.

Have you ever heard stories about huge monsters that live in the ocean? Have you ever wondered if they are true?

Well, so have a lot of people!

This book tells us about three famous monsters that are in lots of stories: the kraken, a horrible huge monster with giant tentacles; the mermaid, half woman and half fish; and the giant sea serpent.

A lot of people—even Christopher Columbus—believed that they had seen sea monsters. Could they have?

We see pictures of real animals that live in the sea that might be mistaken for sea monsters—and some of them are rather monstrous. Oarfish are silvery animals with blue heads. They look like a snake. They can be 50 feet long. In fact, they look a lot like a terrifying sea serpent. Look at the picture on page 37. Would seeing one scare you?

You'll be surprised at what you find out!

Jenkins, Steve. *Down Down Down: A Journey to the Bottom of the Sea.* Houghton Mifflin, 2009. ISBN 9780618966363. Unpaged. Grades 3–5.

"Oceans cover more than two-thirds of the globe's surface, and well over half the planet lies beneath water more than a mile (1½ kilometers) deep. We have explored only a small fraction of the oceans. In fact, more humans have walked on the moon than have visited the deepest spot on in the sea" (from the frontispiece).

Wow! Did you know that the Pacific Ocean is bigger than all of the land on earth put together? There is a lot down there—including lots of life that probably still has not been seen by human beings, and all sorts of interesting activity. Steve Jenkins takes us down to look at some of the creatures that live in all that water.

He starts with some of the beings that leave the water near the top, for a whole variety of reasons. They include sharks, squid, dolphins, and flying squid.

In the first ten feet beneath the surface the water is warm, and there is plenty of sun. That is the top of the Sunlit Zone, which gets darker and darker as we descend. By the time we get to 330 feet below the surface, there is a lot of water pressure and animal bodies are filled with fluid. "Anything containing a hollow air-filled space, such as a human body or a submarine, risks being crushed as it descends."

Then comes the Twilight Zone, where there is not enough light for plants to survive. Only animals live here, and many of them are less familiar to human beings. Look at the pictures of the bioluminescent animals on the two-page spreads—how they really look and how they would look to a human being in the dark, where only the lighted parts show.

The Dark Zone is even lower. Down there are animals most of us have probably never heard of before, like the arrow worm and the pelican eel. Look at the picture of the hairy anglers, which have a strange lifestyle.

Then we get to the Abyssal Plain, where there is a layer of ooze that is sometimes thousands of feet thick. And finally, we get to the hydrothermal vents and the Marianas Trench. Each has different kinds of animals, and all of them are blind.

This is an amazing book with beautiful illustrations and lots more great information at the end.

Jenkins, Steve. *Living Color*. Houghton Mifflin, 2007. ISBN 9780618708970. Unpaged Grades K–4.

We all know that animals are wonderfully colorful creatures. Steve Jenkins tell us on the first page of this beautiful book: "If an animal is very colorful, it is likely that its brilliant skin, scales, or feathers somehow help it stay alive."

Take a look at some of the amazing things you'll read about:

- The male hooded seal has a sac of loose skin hanging from his nose. He blows it up like a red balloon to impress female seals.

- The blue-tongued skink in Australia startles attackers by sticking out its bright blue tongue. That would probably startle anything!

- Crab spiders change their colors in shades of white to yellow to perfectly match flowers. They do not have to build webs. They just wait until a butterfly or bee gets close enough to catch.

- A special kind of algae lives on a three-toed sloth. That sloth has shaggy fur. The algae gives it a greenish tint, which helps hide the sloth from predators in the jungle.

- Maybe the book's most amazing picture is of the long-wattled umbrella bird, which has a huge wattle made up of long purple-black feathers. It looks incredible. It uses its wattle to impress female umbrella birds the way male peacocks impress female peacocks with their tail feathers.

You will not be able to stop looking at these incredible animals.

Jenkins, Steve, and Robin Page. *Sisters & Brothers: Sibling Relationships in the Animal World.* Houghton Mifflin, 2008. ISBN 9780618375967. Unpaged. Grades 1–4.

So how do you get along with your siblings? Do you like them? Hate them? Do you ever help them or take care of them? Do they ever drive you crazy?

How about animals? Do you think they might feel some of those things as well?

With great pictures, the authors of this book tell us about how animal siblings relate to each other. You will learn some fun information, such as:

- Baby elephants are usually born singly, and they spend about twelve years being cared for. Their older sisters help take care of them.

- Nine-banded armadillos always give birth to the same number of babies—four identical brothers and four identical sisters! Each set is absolutely identical to each other.

- New Mexico whiptail lizards are only females—there are no male whiptail lizards. They can reproduce by themselves. But these lizards all look exactly like every other lizard in their community.

- Grizzly bear brothers fight each other a lot for fun, until finally they grow big enough that one of them always wins—and the other one leaves.

- Cheetah brothers stay together and hunt together all of their lives.

And that is just the beginning. This is a fun book.

Markle, Sandra. *Tough, Toothy Baby Sharks.* Walker Books, 2007. ISBN 9780802795939. 32 p. Grades 3–5.

Tough, Toothy Baby Sharks **by Sandra Markle.**

Sharks are fish, not mammals like people and whales. Their skeletons are made of cartilage instead of bone, which makes their skeletons both strong and flexible. Human ears have a cartilage framework.

Some sharks lay eggs. Take a look at the pictures on pages 10 and 11 to see shark eggs.

Others give birth to live babies. On page 16 you will see baby sharks inside their mother's body. The most amazing shark babies, probably, are the sand tiger shark pups. Inside their mother's womb, the babies that develop first eat all the eggs that they find—and then they start eating the other babies! After about nine months, only two babies are left—one in each uterus of its mother. These babies will be about three feet long when they are born.

Baby sharks try to stay safe in several different ways, and there are photographs of them. Look at the baby hammerhead shark on page 25—and at the man holding one on page 24.

If you are interested in sharks, this book is a must-read.

Patent, Dorothy Hinshaw. *When the Wolves Returned: Restoring Nature's Balance in Yellowstone.* Photographs by Dan Hartman and Cassie Hartman. Walker Books, 2008. ISBN 0802796869. 40 p. Grades 3–5.

In 1872 the U.S. government turned the Yellowstone area in northwestern Wyoming into the first national park in the world. It is quite a place. "Yellowstone contains more natural geologic wonders than any other place on Earth—steaming mud pots, boiling hot pools, jetting geysers, and a fabulous, colorful canyon with stunning waterfalls" (p. 5). There was also a lot of wildlife back in 1872.

In the beginning, people were even allowed to hunt the wildlife. After all, not many people came to see the park. It was far away from most of the population. But as time passed, more people came. They loved to look at the elk and deer. But wolves killed elk and deer, and other animals, too.

When the Wolves Returned: Restoring Nature's Balance in Yellowstone **by Dorothy Hinshaw Patent.**

The park authorities decided to kill all of the wolves, and by 1926 there were none left. They had no idea what would happen when they did that. It was a horrible mistake.

Coyotes became the largest predators. All of a sudden other animals were having trouble finding food. There were too many elk without wolves to thin their numbers. They ate the bark of young trees, and all of a sudden the young trees were dying. Now the songbirds who lived in the trees had no place to go. The beavers needed trees, too, and there weren't any.

This is an incredible story, and is a really interesting look at how nature works—and how it is not always a good idea to make changes to it.

Pringle, Laurence. *Penguins! Strange and Wonderful.* Illustrated by Meryl Henderson. Boyds Mills, 2007. ISBN 9781590780909. Unpaged. Grades 3–5.

In 1520 the first European explorers who recorded seeing penguins near the coast of South America called them "strange geese."

As Laurence Pringle tells us, everyone loves penguins. They are an unusual-looking bird, and they are found mainly in cold climates. There are six kinds of them: the crested penguins with orange feathers; the banded penguins, which have a black band—or two black bands—across their chests; the brush-tailed penguins, which have longer tails; the giant penguins (the emperor and the king); and the little blue- and yellow-eyed penguins. Look at the pictures of them early in the book.

You will learn all sorts of interesting things, such as:

- Penguins can swim nine miles an hour, twice as fast as the fastest human.

- Penguins have no teeth, but they have stiff spines in the roof of their mouths and on their tongues. These must look really scary to the animals they hunt—take a look at the picture of the open-mouthed penguin.

- Penguins spend some time every day taking care of their feathers. They spread oil over them to keep them waterproof. The oil comes from a gland at the base of their tails.

- Penguins eat other animals, but other animals eat them, too. The skua, a bird, steals penguin chicks and eggs. Leopard seals and killer whales hunt them as well.

- Lots of penguins were killed in the 1800s because the stored fat in their bodies could be boiled down for oil.

- The animal that treats the penguins the worst is the human being. Read why in the last three pages of the book.

You will learn a lot of neat things about penguins.

Schwartz, David, and Yael M. Schy. *Where in the Wild? Camouflaged Creatures Concealed . . . and Revealed.* Eye-tricking photos by Dwight Kuhn. Tricycle Press, 2007. ISBN 9781582462073. Unpaged. Grades 2–5.

Do you like puzzles and looking for hidden things?

If you do, this may be the book for you. It has puzzles, fun poetry, and great information about animals that camouflage themselves.

Animals change the color of their skin or fur so that other animals cannot find them to eat them. They do this almost automatically. And it works. Because they blend right into the background of the area in which they are hiding right out in the open, predators, or animals who want to eat them, do not see them. Those animals hide in plain sight.

Take a look the poem "Motionless." It gives you a clue to what you will see in the photograph right next to it. But can you see anything in that photo that is blending right in? If you don't find it—or if you want to be sure you got the right thing—open up that page and see what is hidden there. Then, beside that photo, are more pictures and good information about the animal that is hiding.

This is a lot of fun to look through. How many of the animals can you find?

Author Profile: Seymour Simon

Seymour Simon, prolific author of more than 250 books for children, taught junior high science for 20 years. He has written about all aspects of science, but his writing career sprang from his fascination with outer space and astronomy. In his books he hopes to show children how they fit into the vastness of the universe.

Were you a reader when you were a boy? What did you like to read?

I was a voracious reader. As a matter of fact, it's clear to me that my writing is directly related to the books that I read when I was a kid. I was one of those early readers. I was reading because I was being read to by my parents and my older sisters, so I picked up reading before I went to school. We didn't have a lot of books, but we read the same books over and over again. I would follow along with the words and without realizing it I was reading. Very quickly I gravitated toward science fiction. By first and second grade I was reading science fiction magazines. The first book I ever wrote was called *Space Monsters*, which I wrote when I was in second grade. My teacher stapled the pages of the book together and forced the class to listen to me when I read it to them. That was when I started to become an author.

How did you break into publishing?

I wrote magazine articles for many years. Scholastic had a fifth-grade magazine called *News Time*, and for years I was the person who wrote the four-page science supplement every month. So before I wrote my first book, I must have written about 70 or 80 magazine articles. When I wrote books I began writing for other publishers. I was teaching science at that time. I taught science for about 20 years; by the time I left teaching I had already had 60 books published.

How do you choose the topics you want to turn into books?

Almost always they're my topics. I'm coming out with a book on global warming and climate change, and that's my choice. The next book after that is a book on tropical rain forests, and that's my choice. Every once in a while I do a book that my editors would like to do and which I feel I'd like to do as well. I would say that well over 90 percent of the books are really my idea and less than 10 percent are ideas that editors come up with.

How many books do you work on at one time?

I usually work on multiple projects at the same time. I'm doing a number of Internet and CD projects as well as books right now. Currently I'm working on about four or five projects and constantly thinking of other things I'd like to do. Most of the work actually happens before you sit down and write the words. It comes in the planning and the research and the thinking.

What are some of the most exciting research moments you have had while researching a book?

I've written so many books that it would be absolutely impossible to tell you every one of them. I've been in earthquakes. I've photographed mountains all around the world. I've been on whale watching trips and I've seen killer whales. I've photographed icebergs and glaciers in Alaska and volcanoes in Hawaii. I'm continually trying to get out into the field.

Do you write with boys in mind?

No, I absolutely don't. I taught science, of course, to boys and girls, and the girls in my class were as interested in science as the boys. So I don't have any gender-specific kind of science. In fact, if you look at the drawn illustrations in my earliest books, you'll see boys and girls doing the experiments. You'll also see different races and ethnicities and kids in wheelchairs. I've always tried to be as inclusive as possible and not to be exclusive in any way.

Are you going to retire?

I seem to be working faster and harder than ever. I absolutely don't feel any urge to sit back and look at what I've done. The only things that I'm thinking about are things I'd like to do in the future. I'm planning and doing and continuing to write. It's what I love to do. I remember a story about an anthropologist going to talk to a tribe and he asked them what was their word for work. Their response was they have no word for work. Everybody does the things that they do in their life. I love that response. I don't differentiate between work and play. Everything I do is something that I enjoy doing—the writing, the research, and everything else.

Simon, Seymour. *Penguins* (Smithsonian). Collins, 2007. ISBN 9780060283964. 32 p. Grades 2–5.

Penguins are endlessly fascinating, and the information and the pictures here make for a compelling look at them.

Some of the amazing facts are:

- They are great swimmers and divers, and they do not fly—except through the water.

- There are seventeen kinds of penguin species.

- "A penguin's tongue and throat have stiff, backward-facing barbs that help grip slippery food and keep it from sliding out" (p. 6).

- Although most penguins swim at about five or six miles per hour, some can go as fast as fifteen miles per hour!

- They spend most of their lives at sea, but lay their eggs on the land.

Take a look at the photograph of a leopard seal, one of the penguin's most fearsome predators, about to attack a swimming penguin.

If you like penguins, you will love this book.

Singer, Marilyn. *Eggs*. Illustrated by Emma Stevenson. Holiday House, 2008. ISBN 0823417271. 32 p. Grades 3–5.

> It's a quiet crib.
> It's a bobbing boat.
> It's a private pond.
> It's a room with no view.
> It's walls to break through.
> It's breakfast, lunch and dinner.
> It's an egg. (p. 3)

Many kinds of animals, including people, give birth to live babies. But others lay eggs. This includes birds, spiders, most insects, fish, and amphibians—and even some mammals.

But the eggs do not look at all the same. Some are hard eggs. Some are soft. Some are round, and some are oval. An ostrich egg is as big as 19 chicken eggs. The murre's egg (see it on page 9) is sort of cone-shaped. These eggs are laid on cliff edges and are shaped in such a way that they do not roll off!

Pythons stay with their eggs after they lay them. The mother curls herself around them and shivers. Her shivering helps the eggs stay warm. Male penguins incubate their eggs right on their feet!

A lot of animals have an egg tooth—that is a small tooth on top of their beak or snouts. They use that tooth to crack open their shells, which is really hard work. Most have to rest for a long time after they make that first crack in the shell.

This is full of beautiful illustrations and fine information. You will be surprised at what you did not know about eggs.

WORTH READING

Nonfiction books with "boy appeal" that have received positive reviews in *Booklist*, *Horn Book Guide*, and/or *School Library Journal*.

Allen, Judy. *Whales and Dolphins* (I Wonder Why [Flip the Flaps]).Kingfisher, 2008. ISBN 9780753462256. 32 p. Grades 1–3.

Andrekson, Judy. *Fosta: Marathon Master* (True Horse Stories). Tundra Books, 2008. ISBN 9780887768385. 104 p. Grades 5–8.

Apte, Sunita. *Police Horses* (Horse Power). Bearport Publishing, 2007. ISBN 1597164011. 32 p. Grades 1–4.

Armentrout, David, and Patricia Armentrout. *Animals That Fly and Birds That Don't* (Weird and Wonderful Animals). Rourke Publishing, 2008. ISBN 9781604723007. 32 p. Grades 2–4.

Armentrout, David, and Patricia Armentrout. *Crafty Critters* (Weird and Wonderful Animals). Rourke Publishing, 2008. ISBN 9781604723021. 32 p. Grades 2–4.

Armentrout, David, and Patricia Armentrout. *Freaky Faces* (Weird and Wonderful Animals). Rourke Publishing, 2008. ISBN 9781604723038. 32 p. Grades 2–4.

Armentrout, David, and Patricia Armentrout. *Leaps and Bounds* (Weird and Wonderful Animals). Rourke Publishing, 2008. ISBN 9781604723045. 32 p. Grades 2–4.

Armentrout, David, and Patricia Armentrout. *Speed Demons* (Weird and Wonderful Animals). Rourke Publishing, 2008. ISBN 9781604723052. 32 p. Grades 2–4.

Arnold, Caroline. *A Platypus' World* (Caroline Arnold's Animals). Picture Window Books, 2008. ISBN 9781404839854. 24 p. Grades K–2.

Arnold, Caroline. *A Wombat's World* (Caroline Arnold's Animals). Picture Window Books, 2008. ISBN 9781404839861. 24 p. Grades K–2.

Arnosky, Jim. *Whole Days Outdoors: An Autobiographical Album* (Meet the Author). Richard C. Owen, 2006. ISBN 1572748591. 32 p. Grades 2–5.

Arnosky, Jim. *Wild Tracks! A Guide to Nature's Footprint.* Sterling, 2008. ISBN 9781402739859. 32 p. Grades 2–6.

Aronin, Miriam. *Aye-Aye: An Evil Omen* (Uncommon Animals). Bearport Publishing, 2008. ISBN 9781597167314. 32 p. Grades 2–4.

Aronin, Miriam. *Black-footed Ferrets: Back from the Brink* (America's Animal Comebacks). Bearport Publishing, 2007. ISBN 9781597165068. 32 p. Grades 3–5.

Aylmore, Angela. *I Like Cats* (Things I Like). Heinemann, 2007. ISBN 1403492700. 24 p. Grades K–2.

Aylmore, Angela. *I Like Dogs* (Things I Like). Heinemann, 2007. ISBN 1403492697. 24 p. Grades K–2.

Baines, Becky. *A Den Is a Bed for a Bear* (ZigZag). National Geographic, 2008. ISBN 9781426303098. 32 p. Grades K–1.

Baines, Becky. *What Did One Elephant Say to the Other?* (ZigZag). National Geographic, 2008. ISBN 9781426303074. 32 p. Grades K–1.

Barner, Bob. *Penguins, Penguins, Everywhere.* Chronicle Books, 2007. ISBN 9780811856645. 32 p. Grades K–1.

Barnhill, Kelly Regan. *Monsters of the Deep: Deep Sea Adaptation.* Fact Finders, 2008. ISBN 9781429612647. 32 p. Grades K–3.

Bayrock, Fiona. *Bubble Homes and Fish Farts*. Charlesbridge, 2009. ISBN 9781570916694. 48 p. Grades 2–4.

Becker, John E. *Wild Cats: Past and Present*. Darby Creek Publishing, 2008. ISBN 781581960525. 80 p. Grades 5–8.

Bédoyère, Camilla de la. *Are Orangutans So Hairy?* (Why Why Why). Mason Crest Publishers, 2009. ISBN 9781422215708. 32 p. Grades 4–6.

Behrens, Janice. *Let's Find Rain Forest Animals: Up, Down, Around* (Let's Find Out Early Learning Books: The Five Senses/Opposites and Position Words). Children's Press, 2007. ISBN 053-1148742. 24 p. Grades K–1.

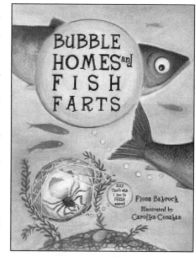

Bubble Homes and Fish Farts by Fiona Bayrock.

Bidner, Jenni. *Is My Cat a Tiger? How Your Cat Compares to Its Wild Cousins*. Lark, 2007. ISBN 1579908152. 64 p. Grades 3–5.

Bjorklund, Ruth. *Rabbits* (Great Pets). Benchmark, 2007. ISBN 9780761427087. 48 p. Grades 2–4.

Blake, Carly. *Do Dolphins Squeak?* (Why Why Why). Mason Crest Publishers, 2009. ISBN 9781422215814. 32 p. Grades 4–6.

Bolan, Sandra. *Caring for Your Mutt* (Our Best Friends). Eldorado Ink, 2008. ISBN 9781932904208. 127 p. Grades 7–12.

Bozzo, Linda. *My First Bird* (My First Pet Library from the American Humane Association). Enslow, 2007. ISBN 076602749X. 32 p. Grades 1–2.

Bozzo, Linda. *My First Cat* (My First Pet Library from the American Humane Association). Enslow, 2007. ISBN 0766027503. 32 p. Grades 1–2.

Bozzo, Linda. *My First Dog* (My First Pet Library from the American Humane Association). Enslow, 2007. ISBN 9780766027541. 32 p. Grades 1–2.

Bozzo, Linda. *My First Fish* (My First Pet Library from the American Humane Association). Enslow, 2007. ISBN 0766027511. 32 p. Grades 1–2.

Bredeson, Carmen. *Giraffes Up Close* (Zoom in on Animals!). Enslow, 2008. ISBN 9780766030817. 24 p. Grades K–3.

Bredeson, Carmen. *Kangaroos Up Close* (Zoom in on Animals!). Enslow, 2008. ISBN 9780766030794. 24 p. Grades 1–3.

Bredeson, Carmen. *Lions Up Close* (Zoom in on Animals!). Enslow, 2008. ISBN 9780766030800. 24 p. Grades K–3.

Bredeson, Carmen. *Orangutans Up Close* (Zoom in on Animals!). Enslow, 2008. ISBN 9780766030787. 24 p. Grades 1–3.

Bruning, Matt. *Zoo Picture Puzzles*. A+, 2009. ISBN 9781429632874. 32 p. Grades K–3.

Buckmaster, Marjorie L. *Freshwater Fishes* (Great Pets). Benchmark, 2007. ISBN 9780761427124. 48 p. Grades 2–4.

Bueche, Shelley. *Dog Scouts of America* (Dog Heroes). Bearport Publishing, 2008. ISBN 9781597166256. 32 p. Grades 3–5.

Calmenson, Stephanie. *May I Pet Your Dog? The How-to Guide for Kids Meeting Dogs (and Dogs Meeting Kids)*. Clarion Books, 2007. ISBN 0618510346. 32 p. Grades K–2.

Camisa, Kathryn. *Hairy Tarantulas* (No Backbone! the World of Invertebrates). Bearport Publishing, 2008. ISBN 9781597167048. 24 p. Grades 1–3.

Caper, William. *American Bison: A Scary Prediction* (America's Animal Comebacks). Bearport Publishing, 2007. ISBN 9781597165044. 32 p. Grades 3–4.

Caper, William. *Platypus: A Century-Long Mystery* (Uncommon Animals). Bearport Publishing, 2008. ISBN 9781597167352. 32 p. Grades 2–4.

Chrustowski, Rick. *Big Brown Bat*. Henry Holt, 2008. ISBN 9780805074994. 32 p. Grades K–3.

Clarke, Penny. *Hippos* (Scary Creatures). Franklin Watts, 2009. ISBN 978-0531216712. 32 p. Grades 3–5.

Coldiron, Deborah. *Eels* (Underwater World). Buddy Books, 2007. ISBN 978-1599288185. 32 p. Grades 2–4.

Coldiron, Deborah. *Manatees* (Underwater World Set II). Buddy Books, 2008. ISBN 9781604531343. 32 p. Grades K–3.

Coldiron, Deborah. *Ocean Sunfish* (Underwater World Set II). Buddy Books, 2008. ISBN 9781604531350. 32 p. Grades K–3.

Coldiron, Deborah. *Octopuses* (Underwater World). Buddy Books, 2007. ISBN 978-1599288154. 32 p. Grades 2–4.

Coldiron, Deborah. *Sea Sponges* (Underwater World). Buddy Books, 2007. ISBN 9781599288123. 32 p. Grades 2–4.

Coldiron, Deborah. *Sharks* (Underwater World Set II). Buddy Books, 2008. ISBN 9781604531381. 32 p. Grades K–3.

Coldiron, Deborah. *Starfish* (Underwater World). Buddy Books, 2007. ISBN 978-1599288130. 32 p. Grades K–3.

Coldiron, Deborah. *Stingrays* (Underwater World). Buddy Books, 2007. ISBN 978-1599288178. 32 p. Grades K–3.

Coldiron, Deborah. *Swordfish* (Underwater World). Buddy Books, 2007. ISBN 978-1599288208. 32 p. Grades 2–4.

Corwin, Jeff. *A Wild Life: the Authorized Biography*. Puffin, 2009. ISBN 9780142414033. 112 p. Grades 4–8.

Craipeau, Jean-lou. *Giants of the Ocean* (Half and Half, Level 3). Treasure Bay, 2009. ISBN 9781601152121. 53 p. Grades 2–5.

Crosby, Jeff. *Little Lions, Bull Baiters & Hunting Hounds: A History of Dog Breeds*. Tundra Books, 2008. ISBN 9780887768156. 72 p. Grades 2–4.

Cusick, Dawn. *Animal Tongues*. EarlyLight Books, 2009. ISBN 978097945515. 36 p. Grades 2–5.

Davis, Rebecca Fjelland. *Woof and Wag: Bringing Home a Dog* (Get a Pet). Picture Window Books, 2008. ISBN 9781404848689. 24 p. Grades K–3.

de Lambilly-Bresson, Elisabeth. *Animals in the Desert* (Animal Show and Tell). Gareth Stevens, 2007. ISBN 9780836882049. 16 p. Grades K–3.

de Lambilly-Bresson, Elisabeth. *Animals in the Jungle* (Animal Show and Tell). Gareth Stevens, 2007. ISBN 978083688206. 16 p. Grades K–3.

de Lambilly-Bresson, Elisabeth. *Animals of the Mountains* (Animal Show and Tell). Gareth Stevens, 2007. ISBN 9780836882070. 16 p. Grades K–3.

Dennis, Major Bruce, Kirby Larson, and Mary Nethery. *Nubs: The True Story of a Mutt, a Marine & a Miracle*. Little, Brown, 2009. ISBN 9780316053181. Unpaged. Grades 2–5.

Doering, Amanda Tourville. *Flutter and Float: Bringing Home Goldfish* (Get a Pet). Picture Window Books, 2008. ISBN 9781404848535. 24 p. Grades K–3.

Doering, Amanda Tourville. *Purr and Pounce: Bringing Home a Cat* (Get a Pet). Picture Window Books, 2008. ISBN 9781404848566. 24 p. Grades K–3.

Doering, Amanda Tourville. *Scurry and Squeak: Bringing Home a Guinea Pig* (Get a Pet). Picture Window Books, 2008. ISBN 9781404848597. 24 p. Grades K–3.

Doering, Amanda Tourville. *Skitter and Scoot: Bringing Home a Hamster* (Get a Pet). Picture Window Books, 2008. ISBN 9781404848627. 24 p. Grades K–3.

Doering, Amanda Tourville. *Twitter and Tweet: Bringing Home a Bird* (Get a Pet). Picture Window Books, 2008. ISBN 9781404848658. 24 p. Grades K–3.

Doubilet, David. *Face to Face with Sharks* (Face to Face with Animals). National Geographic, 2009. ISBN 9781426304040. 32 p. Grades 3–5.

Doudna, Kelly. *Frisky Ferrets* (Perfect Pets). ABDO & Daughters, 2007. ISBN 9781599287485. 24 p. Grades K–2.

Doudna, Kelly. *It's a Baby Kangaroo!* ABDO & Daughters, 2010. ISBN 978-1604535761. 24 p. Grades K–3.

Eason, Sarah. *Save the Orangutan*. PowerKids Press, 2009. ISBN 9781435828117. 32 p. Grades 1–3.

Eason, Sarah. *Save the Panda*. PowerKids Press, 2009. ISBN 9781435828124. 32 p. Grades 1–3.

Eason, Sarah. *Save the Polar Bear*. PowerKids Press, 2009. ISBN 9781435828100. 32 p. Grades 1–3.

Eason, Sarah. *Save the Tiger*. PowerKids Press, 2009. ISBN 9781435828131. 32 p. Grades 1–3.

Ehrlich, Fred. *You Can't Lay an Egg If You're an Elephant*. Blue Apple, 2007. ISBN 1593546068. 32 p. Grades K–3.

Feigenbaum, Aaron. *American Alligators: Freshwater Survivors* (America's Animal Comebacks). Bearport Publishing, 2007. ISBN 9781597165037. 32 p. Grades 3–5.

Feinstein, Stephen. *The Jaguar: Help Save This Endangered Species!* (Saving Endangered Species). Enslow, 2008. ISBN 1598450654. 128 p. Grades 4–7.

Fetty, Margaret. *Fire Horses* (Horse Power). Bearport Publishing, 2008. ISBN 9781597166263. 32 p. Grades 2–4.

Fetty, Margaret. *Show Horses* (Horse Power). Bearport Publishing, 2007. ISBN 1597163996. 32 p. Grades 2–4.

Fetty, Margaret. *Yorkshire Terrier: Tiny but Tough* (Little Dogs Rock!). Bearport Publishing, 2009. ISBN 9781597167482. 32 p. Grades K–3.

Fielding, Beth. *Animal Baths: Wild & Wonderful Ways Animals Get Clean*. EarlyLight Books, 2009. ISBN 9780979745522. 48 p. Grades 2–4.

Fielding, Beth. *Animal Colors: A Rainbow of Colors from Animals Around the World*. EarlyLight Books, 2009. ISBN 9780979745546. 32 p. Grades K–4.

Flowers, Pam. *Douggie: The Playful Pup Who Became a Sled Dog Hero*. Graphic Arts Center, 2008. ISBN 9780882406541. Unpaged. Grades K–3.

Franklin, Carolyn. *Ocean Life!* (World of Wonder). Children's Press, 2008. ISBN 0531204510. 32 p. Grades 1–4.

Franklin, Carolyn. *Rain Forest Animals!* (World of Wonder). Children's Press, 2008. ISBN 9780531204528. 32 p. Grades 1–4.

Gagne, Tammy. *Chihuahuas* (Edge Books). Capstone Press, 2008. ISBN 9781429619479. 32 p. Grades 4–6.

Gaines, Ann. *Top 10 Dogs for Kids* (Top Pets for Kids With American Humane). Enslow, 2008. ISBN 9780766030701. 48 p. Grades 2–5.

Gaines, Ann. *Top 10 Small Mammals for Kids* (Top Pets for Kids With American Humane). Enslow, 2008. ISBN 9780766030756. 48 p. Grades 2–5.

Gaines, Richard M. *When Bears Attack!* (When Wild Animals Attack!) Enslow, 2006. ISBN 0766026698. 48 p. Grades 4–6.

Top 10 Small Mammals for Kids **by Ann Gaines.**

Gaines, Richard M. *When Sharks Attack!* (When Wild Animals Attack!). Enslow, 2006. ISBN 0766026647. 48 p. Grades 4–6.

Gaines, Richard M. *When Tigers Attack!* (When Wild Animals Attack!) Enslow, 2006. ISBN 0766026655. 48 p. Grades 4–6.

Ganeri, Anita. *Africa's Most Amazing Animals.* Raintree, 2008. ISBN 978-1410930835. 32 p. Grades 4–6.

Ganeri, Anita. *Asia's Most Amazing Animals.* Raintree, 2008. ISBN 9781410930842. 32 p. Grades 4–6.

Ganeri, Anita. *Australasia's Most Amazing Animals.* Raintree, 2008. ISBN 978-1410930859. 32 p. Grades 4–6.

Ganeri, Anita. *Europe's Most Amazing Animals* (Perspectives). Raintree, 2008. ISBN 9781410930866. 32 p. Grades 4–6.

Ganeri, Anita. *North America's Most Amazing Animals* (Perspectives). Raintree, 2008. ISBN 9781410930873. 32 p. Grades 4–6.

Ganeri, Anita. *The Ocean's Most Amazing Animals* (Perspectives). Raintree, 2008. ISBN 9781410930880. 32 p. Grades 4–6.

Ganeri, Anita. *The Polar Region's Most Amazing Animals* (Perspectives). Raintree, 2008. ISBN 9781410930897. 32 p. Grades 4–6.

Ganeri, Anita. *Rabbits.* 2nd ed. (A Pet's Life). Heinemann-Raintree, 2009. ISBN 9781432933944. 32 p. Grades 3–5.

Ganeri, Anita *South America's Most Amazing Animals* (Perspectives). Raintree, 2008. ISBN 9781410930903. 32 p. Grades 4–6.

Gibbons, Gail. *Elephants of Africa.* Holiday House, 2008. ISBN 9780823421688. 32 p. Grades 1–4.

Goldish, Meish. *Bald Eagles: A Chemical Nightmare* (America's Animal Comebacks). Bearport Publishing, 2007. ISBN 9781597165051. 32 p. Grades 2–5.

Goldish, Meish. *Disgusting Hagfish* (Gross-Out Defenses). Bearport Publishing, 2008. ISBN 9781597167192. 24 p. Grades 2–3.

Goldish, Meish. *Dogs* (Smart Animals). Bearport Publishing, 2007. ISBN 159-7163686. 32 p. Grades 1–4.

Goldish, Meish. *Florida Manatees: Warm Water Miracles* (America's Animal Comebacks). Bearport Publishing, 2007. ISBN 1597165077. 32 p. Grades 2–5.

Goldish, Meish. *Fossa: A Fearsome Predator* (Uncommon Animals). Bearport Publishing, 2008. ISBN 9781597167321. 32 p. Grades 2–4.

Goldish, Meish. *Giraffe: The World's Tallest Mammal* (Supersized!). Bearport Publishing, 2007. ISBN 1597163740. 24 p. Grades 1–3.

Goldish, Meish. *Gorillas* (Smart Animals). Bearport Publishing, 2007. ISBN 1597163694. 32 p. Grades 1–4.

Goldish, Meish. *Gray Wolves: Return to Yellowstone* (America's Animal Comebacks). Bearport Publishing, 2007. ISBN 9781597165020. 32 p. Grades 2–5.

Goldish, Meish. *Hollywood Dogs* (Dog Heroes). Bearport Publishing, 2007. ISBN 1597164046. 32 p. Grades 1–5.

Goldish, Meish. *Hollywood Horses* (Horse Power). Bearport Publishing, 2008. ISBN 9781597166270. 32 p. Grades 2–4.

Goldish, Meish. *Moray Eel: Dangerous Teeth* (Afraid of the Water). Bearport Publishing, 2009. ISBN 9781597169417. 24 p. Grades 2–4.

Goldish, Meish. *Red Wolves: And Then There Were Almost None* (America's Animal Comebacks). Bearport Publishing, 2009. ISBN 9781597167420. 32 p. Grades 3–6.

Goldish, Meish. *Stonefish: Needles of Pain* (Afraid of the Water). Bearport Publishing, 2009. ISBN 9781597169431. 24 p. Grades 2–4.

Goldish, Meish. *Toy Poodle: Oodles of Fun* (Little Dogs Rock!). Bearport Publishing, 2009. ISBN 9781597167468. 32 p. Grades K–3.

Goodbody, Slim. *Birds* (Slim Goodbody's Inside Guide to Pets). Gareth Stevens, 2007. ISBN 9780836889536. 32 p. Grades 3–6.

Goodbody, Slim. *Cats* (Slim Goodbody's Inside Guide to Pets). Gareth Stevens, 2007. ISBN 9780836889543. 32 p. Grades 3–6.

Goodbody, Slim. *Dogs* (Slim Goodbody's Inside Guide to Pets). Gareth Stevens, 2007. ISBN 9780836889550. 32 p. Grades 3–6.

Greene, Jacqueline Dembar. *Grizzly Bears: Saving the Silvertip* (America's Animal Comebacks). Bearport Publishing, 2007. ISBN 9781597165334. 32 p. Grades 3–4.

Guiberson, Brenda Z. *Ice Bears*. Illustrated by Ilya Spirin. Henry Holt, 2008. ISBN 9780805076073. Unpaged. Grades 1–4.

Guiberson, Brenda Z. *Life in the Boreal Forest*. Henry Holt, 2009. ISBN 9780805077186. 40 p. Grades 3–5.

Hall, Becky. *Morris and Buddy: The Story of the First Seeing Eye Dog*. Albert Whitman, 2007. ISBN 0807552844. 40 p. Grades 2–5.

Hall, Howard. *A Charm of Dolphins: The Threatened Life of a Flippered Friend* (Jean-Michel Cousteau Presents). London Town, 2007. ISBN 9780976613480. 48 p. Grades 5–8.

Hall, Kirsten. *African Elephant: The World's Biggest Land Mammal* (Supersized!). Bearport Publishing, 2007. ISBN 9781597163873. 24 p. Grades K–2.

Hall, Kirsten. *Great Bustard: The World's Heaviest Flying Bird* (Supersized!). Bearport Publishing, 2007. ISBN 1597163902. 24 p. Grades 1–3.

Halls, Kelly Milner. *Wild Horses: Galloping Through Time* (Darby Creek Exceptional Titles). Darby Creek Publishing, 2008. ISBN 9781581960655. 72 p. Grades 4–6.

Hanel, Rachael. *Tigers* (Living Wild). Creative Education, 2008. ISBN 978-1583416600. 48 p. Grades 3–5.

Hansen, Rosanna. *Caring for Cheetahs*. Boyds Mills, 2007. ISBN 1590783875. 32 p. Grades 4–7.

Hansen, Sarah. *When Mountain Lions Attack!* (When Wild Animals Attack!). Enslow, 2006. ISBN 076602668X. 48 p. Grades 4–7.

Hart, Joyce. *Big Dogs* (Great Pets). Benchmark, 2007. ISBN 9780761427070. 48 p. Grades 2–4.

Hart, Joyce. *Cats* (Great Pets). Benchmark, 2007. ISBN 9780761427100. 48 p. Grades 2–4.

Hatkoff, Craig. *Knut: How One Little Polar Bear Captivated the World*. Scholastic Press, 2007. ISBN 9780545047166. 40 p. Grades K–3.

Hatkoff, Juliana, Isabella Hatkoff, and Craig Hatkoff. *Winter's Tail: How One Little Dolphin Learned to Swim Again*. Scholastic Press, 2009. ISBN 9780545123358. 32 p. Grades 1–3.

Hatkoff, Juliana, Isabella Hatkoff, Craig Hatkoff, and Paula Kahumbu. *Looking For Miza*. Scholastic Press, 2008. ISBN 9780545085403. 40 p. Grades 2–5.

Head, Honor. *Amazing Fish* (Amazing Life Cycles). Gareth Stevens, 2007. ISBN 9780836888959. 32 p. Grades 3–5.

Head, Honor. *Amazing Mammals* (Amazing Life Cycles). Gareth Stevens, 2007. ISBN 9780836888966. 32 p. Grades 3–5.

Helget, Nicole. *Giraffes* (Living Wild). Creative Education, 2008. ISBN 9781583416549. 48 p. Grades 4–6.

Helman, Andrea. *Hide and Seek: Nature's Best Vanishing Acts*. Walker Books, 2008. ISBN 0802796907. 40 p. Grades 2–4.

Hengel, Katherine. *It's a Baby Australian Fur Seal!* (Baby Australian Animals). SandCastle, 2009. ISBN 9781604535747. 24 p. Grades K–3.

Hengel, Katherine. *It's a Baby Flying Fox!* (Baby Australian Animals). SandCastle, 2009. ISBN 9781604535754. 24 p. Grades K–3.

Hengel, Katherine. *It's a Baby Spiny Anteater!* (Baby Australian Animals). ABDO & Daughters, 2009. ISBN 9781604535785. 24 p. Grades K–3.

Hengel, Katherine. *It's a Baby Tasmanian Devil!* (Baby Australian Animals). ABDO & Daughters, 2009. ISBN 9781604535792. 24 p. Grades K–3.

Hirschi, Ron. *Lions, Tigers, and Bears: Why Are Big Predators So Rare?* Boyds Mills, 2007. ISBN 9781590784358. 40 p. Grades 3–5.

Hirschi, Ron. *Our Three Bears*. Boyds Mills, 2008. ISBN 9781590780152. 48 p. Grades 3–5.

Hodge, Susie. *Ocean Survival* (Extreme Habitats). Gareth Stevens, 2007. ISBN 9780836882476. 32 p. Grades 4–6.

Hodgkins, Fran. *The House of a Million Pets*. Henry Holt, 2007. ISBN 97808050797462 63 p. Grades 3–6.

Houran, Lori Haskins. *Pug: What a Mug!* (Little Dogs Rock!). Bearport Publishing, 2009. ISBN 9781597167405. 32 p. Grades K–3.

Hudak, Heather C. *Thumbelina: The World's Smallest Horse* (Inspiring Animals). Weigl Publishers, 2008. ISBN 9781590368541. 24 p. Grades 2–3.

Huggins-Cooper, Lynn. *Amazing Creatures* (QEB Awesome Animals). QEB Publishing, 2008. ISBN 9781595665638. 32 p. Grades 4–7.

Huggins-Cooper, Lynn. *Beastly Birds and Bats* (QEB Awesome Animals). QEB Publishing, 2009. ISBN 9781595665621. 32 p. Grades 4–7.

Huggins-Cooper, Lynn. *Freaky Fish* (QEB Awesome Animals). QEB Publishing, 2008. ISBN 9781595665607. 32 p. Grades 4–7.

Hunt, Joni Phelps. *A Band of Bears: The Rambling Life of a Lovable Loner* (Jean-Michel Cousteau Presents). London Town, 2006. ISBN 9780976613459. 48 p. Grades 5–8.

Jackson, Emma. *A Home for Dixie: The True Story of a Rescued Puppy*. Collins, 2008. ISBN 9780061449628. 40 p. Grades 2–4.

Jango-Cohen, Judith. *Hippopotamuses* (Animals Animals). Benchmark, 2007. ISBN 9780761422389. 48 p. Grades 3–5.

Jenkins, Martin. *Ape*. Candlewick Press, 2007. ISBN 9780763634711. 45 p. Grades K–3.

Jenkins, Steve. *Dogs and Cats*. Houghton Mifflin, 2007. ISBN 0618507671. 40 p. Grades 2–5.

Jenkins, Steve. *Never Smile at a Monkey: And 17 Other Important Things to Remember*. Houghton Mifflin, 2009. ISBN 9780618966202. 32 p. Grades 1–4.

Johnson, Jinny. *Cats and Kittens* (Get to Know Your Pet). Smart Apple Media, 2008. ISBN 9781599200880. 32 p. Grades 3–6.

Johnson, Jinny. *Dogs and Puppies* (Get to Know Your Pet). Smart Apple Media, 2008. ISBN 9781599200897. 32 p. Grades 3–5.

Johnson, Jinny. *Guinea Pigs* (Get to Know Your Pet). Black Rabbit Books, 2009. ISBN 9781599202112. 24 p. Grades 2–4.

Johnson, Jinny. *Hamsters and Gerbils* (Get to Know Your Pet). Smart Apple Media, 2009. ISBN 9781897563311. 32 p. Grades 3–6.

Johnson, Jinny. *Rabbits* (Get to Know Your Pet). Smart Apple Media, 2009. ISBN 9781897563328. 32 p. Grades 3–6.

Johnson, Jinny. *Rats and Mice* (Get to Know Your Pet). Smart Apple Media, 2009. ISBN 9781897563335. 32 p. Grades 3–6.

Jones, Charlotte Foltz. *The King Who Barked: Real Animals Who Ruled.* Holiday House, 2009. ISBN 9780823419258. 40 p. Grades 3–5.

Joubert, Dereck, and Beverly Joubert. *Face to Face with Lions* (Face to Face with Animals). National Geographic, 2008. ISBN 9781426302077. 32 p. Grades 4–8.

Keenan, Sheila. *Animals in the House: A History of Pets and People.* Scholastic Press, 2007. ISBN 0439692865. 112 p. Grades 3–6.

Kelly, Irene. *Even an Ostrich Needs a Nest: Where Birds Begin.* Holiday House, 2009. ISBN 9780823421022. 20 p. Grades K–3.

Kennedy, Marge. *Pets at the White House* (Scholastic News Nonfiction Readers). Children's Press, 2009. ISBN 978-0531224335. 24 p. Grades K–1.

Face to Face with Lions **by Dereck Joubert and Beverly Joubert.**

KIDSLABEL. *Spot 7 Animals* (Seek & Find). Chronicle Books, 2007. ISBN 0811857220. 40 p. All ages.

Komiyam, Teruyuki. *Life-Size Zoo: From Tiny Rodents to Gigantic Elephants, an Actual Size Animal Encyclopedia.* Seven Footer Press, 2009. ISBN 978-1934734209. 48 p. Grades K–3.

Krensky, Stephen. *Creatures from the Deep* (Monster Chronicles). Lerner Publications, 2007. ISBN 9780822567615. 48 p. Grades 4–7.

Laidlaw, Rob. *Wild Animals in Captivity.* Fitzhenry and Whiteside, 2008. ISBN 978-1554550258. 48 p. Grades 5–8.

Laman, Tim. *Face to Face with Orangutans* (Face to Face with Animals). National Geographic, 2009. ISBN 9781426304644. 32 p. Grades 3–5.

Landau, Elaine. *Bats: Hunters of the Night* (Animals After Dark). Enslow, 2007. ISBN 9780766027725. 32 p. Grades 2–3.

Landau, Elaine. *Big Cats: Hunters of the Night* (Animals After Dark) Enslow, 2007. ISBN 9780766027701. 32 p. Grades 2–3.

Landau, Elaine. *Owls: Hunters of the Night* (Animals After Dark). Enslow, 2007. ISBN 9780766027688. 32 p. Grades 2–3.

Landau, Elaine. *Raccoons: Scavengers of the Night* (Animals After Dark). Enslow, 2007. ISBN 9780766027671. 32 p. Grades 2–3.

Lang, Aubrey. *Baby Mountain Sheep* (Nature Babies). Fitzhenry and Whiteside, 2007. ISBN 9781554550425. 36 p. Grades K–3.

Lang, Aubrey. *Baby Polar Bear* (Nature Babies). Fitzhenry and Whiteside, 2008. ISBN 9781554551019. 36 p. Grades K–2.

Larrew, Brekka Hervey. *Labradoodles* (Edge Books). Capstone Press, 2008. ISBN 9781429620093. 32 p. Grades 4–6.

Two Bobbies: A True Story of Hurricane Katrina, Friendship, and Survival by Kirby Larson and Mary Nethery.

Larson, Kirby, and Mary Nethery. *Two Bobbies: A True Story of Hurricane Katrina, Friendship, and Survival.* Walker Books, 2008. ISBN 9780802797544. 32 p. Grades K–3.

Leardi, Jeanette. *Southern Sea Otters: Fur-tastrophe Avoided* (America's Animal Comebacks). Bearport Publishing, 2007. ISBN 9781597165341. 32 p. Grades 3–4.

Leavitt, Amie Jane. *Care for a Pet Chimpanzee* (How to Convince Your Parents You Can . . .) (Robbie Readers). Mitchell Lane, 2007. ISBN 9781584156079. 32 p. Grades 2–4.

Leavitt, Amie Jane. *Care for a Pet Mouse* (How to Convince Your Parents You Can . . .) (Robbie Readers). Mitchell Lane, 2007. ISBN 978-1584156062. 32 p. Grades 2–4.

Leon, Vicki. *A Pod of Killer Whales: The Mysterious Life of the Intelligent Orca* (Jean-Michel Cousteau Presents). London Town, 2006. ISBN 9780976613473. 48 p. Grades 5–8.

Lewin, Ted, and Betsy Lewin. *Balarama: A Royal Elephant.* Lee & Low Books, 2009. ISBN 9781600602658. 56 p. Grades 2–5.

Llewellyn, Claire. *Killer Creatures* (Navigators). Kingfisher, 2008. ISBN 978-0753462270. 48 p. Grades 4–7.

Lockwood, Sophie. *Bats* (The World of Mammals). Child's World, 2008. ISBN 978-1592969265. 40 p. Grades 4–6.

Lockwood, Sophie. *Lions* (The World of Mammals). Child's World, 2008. ISBN 978-1592969333. 40 p. Grades 4–6.

Lockwood, Sophie. *Skunks* (The World of Mammals). Child's World, 2008. ISBN 978-1592969296. 40 p. Grades 4–6.

Lockwood, Sophie. *Whales* (World of Mammals). Child's World, 2008. ISBN 978-1592969302. 40 p. Grades 4–6.

London, Jonathan. *Flamingo Sunset.* Marshall Cavendish, 2008. ISBN 0761453849. 30 p. Grades K–3.

Long, John. *A Moose's Morning*. Down East Books, 2007. ISBN 9780892727339. 32 p. Grades K–3.

Lourie, Peter. *Whaling Season: A Year in the Life of an Arctic Whale Scientist*. Houghton Mifflin, 2009. ISBN 9780618777099. 80 p. Grades 4–8.

Love, Pamela. *Crawling Crabs* (No Backbone! the World of Invertebrates). Bearport Publishing, 2007. ISBN 9781597165099. 24 p. Grades 1–3.

Lumry, Amanda, and Laura Hurwitz. *Safari in South Africa* (Adventures Of Riley). Scholastic Press, 2008. ISBN 9780545068277. 40 p. Grades 1–4.

Lunis, Natalie. *Chihuahua: Senor Tiny* (Little Dogs Rock!). Bearport Publishing, 2009. ISBN 9781597167437. 32 p. Grades K–3.

Lunis, Natalie. *Dachshund: The Hot Dogger*(Little Dogs Rock!). Bearport Publishing, 2009. ISBN 9781597167444. 32 p. Grades K–3.

Lunis, Natalie. *Gooey Jellyfish* (No Backbone! the World of Invertebrates). Bearport Publishing, 2007. ISBN 9781597165105. 24 p. Grades 1–3.

Lunis, Natalie. *Jack Russell Terrier: Bundle of Energy* (Little Dogs Rock!). Bearport Publishing, 2009. ISBN 9781597167475. 32 p. Grades K–3.

Lunis, Natalie. *Ostrich: The World's Biggest Bird* (Supersized!). Bearport Publishing, 2007. ISBN 1597163945. 24 p. Grades K–2.

Lunis, Natalie. *Portuguese Man-of-War: Floating Misery* (Afraid of the Water). Bearport Publishing, 2009. ISBN 9781597169462. 24 p. Grades 2–4.

Lunis, Natalie. *Prickly Sea Stars* (No Backbone! the World of Invertebrates). Bearport Publishing, 2007. ISBN 9781597165082. 24 p. Grades 1–3.

MacLeod, Elizabeth. *Why Do Cats Have Whiskers?* Kids Can, 2008. ISBN 9781554531967. 64 p. Grades 3–5.

MacLeod, Elizabeth. *Why Do Horses Have Manes?* Kids Can, 2009. ISBN 9781554533121. 64 p. Grades 3–5.

Malam, John. *Pinnipeds* (Scary Creatures). Scholastic Press, 2009. ISBN 9780531216729. 32 p. Grades 3–5.

Mara, Wil. *Beavers* (Animals Animals). Benchmark, 2007. ISBN 9780761425243. 48 p. Grades 3–4.

Mara, Wil. *Coyotes* (Animals Animals). Benchmark, 2008. ISBN 9780761429289. 48 p. Grades 4–6.

Mara, Wil. *Ducks* (Animals Animals). Benchmark, 2008. ISBN 9780761429272. 47 p. Grades 4–6.

Markert, Jenny. *Penguins* (New Naturebooks). Child's World, 2007. ISBN 1592968503. 32 p. Grades 1–3.

Markle, Sandra. *Animal Heroes: True Rescue Stories* (Exceptional Social Studies Titles for Intermediate Grades). Millbrook Press, 2008. ISBN 9780822578840. 64 p. Grades 3–6.

Markle, Sandra. *A Baby Lobster Grows Up* (Scholastic News Nonfiction Readers). Children's Press, 2007. ISBN 0531174751. 24 p. Grades 1–2.

Finding Home by **Sandra Markle.**

Markle, Sandra. *Finding Home.* Charlesbridge, 2008. ISBN 9781580891226. 32 p. Grades K–3.

Markle, Sandra. *How Many Baby Pandas?* Walker Books, 2009. ISBN 9780802797841. 32 p. Grades K–4.

Markle, Sandra. *Insects: Biggest! Littlest!* Boyds Mills, 2009. ISBN 9781590785126. 32 p. Grades 1–3.

Markle, Sandra. *Musk Oxen* (Animal Prey). Lerner Publications, 2006. ISBN 082256064X. 39 p. Grades 2–5.

Markle, Sandra. *Octopuses* (Animal Prey). Lerner Publications, 2006. ISBN 082-2560631. 40 p. Grades 2–5.

Markle, Sandra. *Outside and Inside Woolly Mammoths* (Outside and Inside). Walker Books, 2007. ISBN 9780802795892. 40 p. Grades 4–8.

Markle, Sandra. *Porcupines* (Animal Prey). Lerner Publications, 2006. ISBN 978-0822564393. 40 p. Grades 3–5.

Markle, Sandra. *Sharks: Biggest! Littlest!* Boyds Mills, 2008. ISBN 9781590785133. 32 p. Grades 3–4.

Markovics, Joyce L. *Tasmanian Devil: Nighttime Scavenger* (Uncommon Animals). Bearport Publishing, 2008. ISBN 978-1597167338. 32 p. Grades 2–4.

How Many Baby Pandas? by **Sandra Markle.**

Markovics, Joyce L. *Weddell Seal: Fat and Happy* (Uncommon Animals). Bearport Publishing, 2008. ISBN 9781597167345. 32 p. Grades 2–4.

Marsico, Katie. *A Kangaroo Joey Grows Up* (Scholastic News Nonfiction Readers). Children's Press, 2007. ISBN 053-117476X. 24 p. Grades 1–2.

Marsico, Katie. *A Manatee Calf Grows Up* (Scholastic News Nonfiction Readers). Children's Press, 2007. ISBN 978-0531174791. 24 p. Grades 1–2.

Marsico, Katie. *A Peachick Grows Up* (Scholastic News Nonfiction Readers). Children's Press, 2007. ISBN 978-0531174807. 24 p. Grades 1–2.

Weddell Seal: Fat and Happy by Joyce L. Markovics.

Mason, Paul. *Animal Spies* (Atomic Series). Raintree, 2007. ISBN 9781410929754. 32 p. Grades 3–6.

Mataya, Marybeth. *Are You My Cat?* (Are You My Pet?). Magic Wagon, 2008. ISBN 9781602702424. 32 p. Grades K–3.

Mataya, Marybeth. *Are You My Dog?* (Are You My Pet?). Magic Wagon, 2008. ISBN 9781602702431. 32 p. Grades K–3.

Mayo, Margaret. *Roar!* Carolrhoda Books, 2007. ISBN 9780761394730. Unpaged. Grades K–1.

McCarthy, Meghan. *Seabiscuit the Wonder Horse*. Simon & Schuster, 2008. ISBN 9781416933601. 40 p. Grades 1–3.

McDonald, Mary Ann. *Foxes*. Child's World, 2007. ISBN 9781592968459. 32 p. Grades 2–4.

McMillan, Beverly, and John A. Musick. *Sharks* (Insiders). Simon & Schuster, 2008. ISBN 9781416938675. 64 p. Grades 4–6.

Mead, Wendy. *Top 10 Birds for Kids* (Top Pets for Kids With American Humane). Enslow, 2008. ISBN 9780766030725. 48 p. Grades 2–5.

Mehus-Roe, Kristin. *Dogs for Kids: Everything You Need to Know About Dogs*. BowTie Press, 2007. ISBN 1931993831. 384 p. Grades 4–7.

Meltzer Kleinhenz, Sydnie. *Elephants* (Pebble Plus). Capstone Press, 2008. ISBN 9781429612456. 24 p. Grades K–2.

Miller, Debbie S. *Survival at 40 Below*. Illustrated by Jon Van Zyle. Walker Books, 2009. ISBN 9780802798169. 40 p. Grades 2–4.

Miller, Marie-Therese. *Helping Dogs* (Dog Tales: True Stories About Amazing Dogs). Chelsea House, 2007. ISBN 0791090353. 72 p. Grades 3–5.

Miller, Marie-Therese. *Hunting and Herding Dogs* (Dog Tales: True Stories About Amazing Dogs). Chelsea House, 2007. ISBN 0791090388. 72 p. Grades 3–5.

Miller, Sara Swan. *Eyes* (All Kinds Of). Marshall Cavendish, 2007. ISBN 978-0761425199. 48 p. Grades 4–8.

Miller, Sara Swan. *Feet* (All Kinds Of). Marshall Cavendish, 2007. ISBN 978-0761425205. 48 p. Grades 4–8.

Miller, Sara Swan. *Mouths* (All Kinds Of). Marshall Cavendish, 2007. ISBN 978-0761425212. 48 p. Grades 4–8.

Miller, Sara Swan. *Noses* (All Kinds Of). Marshall Cavendish, 2007. ISBN 978-0761425229. 48 p. Grades 4–8.

Mitchell, Susan K. *Animal Body-part Regenerators: Growing New Heads, Tails, and Legs* (Amazing Animal Defenses). Enslow, 2008. ISBN 9780766032958. 48 p. Grades 2–4.

Mitchell, Susan K. *Animal Chemical Combat: Poisons, Smells, and Slime* (Amazing Animal Defenses). Enslow, 2008. ISBN 9780766032941. 48 p. Grades 2–4.

Mitchell, Susan K. *Animal Mimics: Look-alikes and Copycats* (Amazing Animal Defenses). Enslow, 2008. ISBN 9780766032934. 48 p. Grades 2–4.

Mitchell, Susan K. *Animals with Awesome Armor: Shells, Scales, and Exoskeletons* (Amazing Animal Defenses). Enslow, 2008. ISBN 9780766032965. 48 p. Grades 2–4.

Mitchell, Susan K. *Animals with Crafty Camouflage: Hiding in Plain Sight* (Amazing Animal Defenses). Enslow, 2008. ISBN 9780766032910. 48 p. Grades 2–4.

Animals with Wicked Weapons: Stingers, Barbs, and Quills **by Susan K. Mitchell.**

Mitchell, Susan K. *Animals with Wicked Weapons: Stingers, Barbs, and Quills* (Amazing Animal Defenses). Enslow, 2008. ISBN 9780766032927. 48 p. Grades 2–4.

Momatiuk, Yva. *Face to Face with Wild Horses* (Face to Face with Animals). National Geographic, 2009. ISBN 9781426304668. 32 p. Grades 3–5.

Monahan, Erin. *Arabian Horses* (Pebble Books: Horses). Capstone Press, 2009. ISBN 9781429622332. 24 p. Grades K–3.

Morgan, Sally. *Clown Fish and Other Coral Reef Life* (Under the Sea). QEB Publishing, 2009. ISBN 9781595665669. 24 p. Grades 2–4.

Morgan, Sally. *Hermit Crabs and Other Shallow Water Creatures* (QEB Under the Sea) Black Rabbit Books, 2009. ISBN 9781595665690. 24 p. Grades 2–4.

Morgan, Sally. *Mega Mouth Sharks and Other Deep Sea Dwellers* (QEB Under the Sea). Black Rabbit Books, 2009. ISBN 9781595665683. 24 p. Grades 2–4.

Morgan, Sally. *Orcas and Other Cold-Ocean Life* (QEB Under the Sea). QEB Publishing, 2009. ISBN 9781595665676. 24 p. Grades 2–4.

Mortensen, Lori. *Killer Sharks* (Monsters). KidHaven Press, 2008. ISBN 978-0737740448. 48 p. Grades 4–6.

Murray, Julie. *Acting Animals* (Going to Work: Animal Edition). Buddy Books, 2009. ISBN 9781604535600. 32 p. Grades 1–3.

Murray, Julie. *Crime-Fighting Animals* (Going to Work: Animal Edition). Buddy Books, 2009. ISBN 9781604535617. 32 p. Grades 1–3.

Murray, Julie. *Military Animals* (Going to Work: Animal Edition). Buddy Books, 2009. ISBN 9781604535624. 32 p. Grades 1–3.

Murray, Julie. *Search-and-Rescue Animals* (Going to Work: Animal Edition). Buddy Books, 2009. ISBN 9781604535631. 32 p. Grades 1–3.

Murray, Julie. *Service Animals* (Going to Work: Animal Edition). Buddy Books, 2009. ISBN 9781604535648. 32 p. Grades 1–3.

Murray, Julie. *Therapy Animals* (Going to Work: Animal Edition). Buddy Books, 2009. ISBN 9781604535655. 32 p. Grades 1–3.

Myers, Jack. *The Puzzle of the Platypus: And Other Explorations of Science in Action* (Scientists Probe 11 Animal Mysteries). Boyds Mills, 2008. ISBN 978-1590785560. 64 p. Grades 3–5.

Nagda, Ann Whitehead. *Cheetah Math: Learning About Division from Baby Cheetahs*. Henry Holt, 2007. ISBN 9780805076455. 32 p. Grades 3–5.

Neuman, Pearl. *Bloodsucking Leeches* (No Backbone! the World of Invertebrates!). Bearport Publishing, 2009. ISBN 9781597167550. 24 p. Grades K–3.

Newcomb, Rain, and Rose McLarney. *Is My Hamster Wild? The Secret Lives of Hamsters, Gerbils & Guinea Pigs*. Lark, 2008. ISBN 9781600592423. 48 p. Grades 4–6.

Nichols, Catherine. *Prickly Porcupines* (Gross-Out Defenses). Bearport Publishing, 2008. ISBN 9781597167215. 24 p. Grades 2–3.

Nichols, Catherine. *Smelly Skunks* (Gross-Out Defenses). Bearport Publishing, 2008. ISBN 9781597167161. 24 p. Grades 2–3.

Nichols, Catherine. *Therapy Horses* (Horse Power). Bearport Publishing, 2007. ISBN 1597164003. 32 p. Grades 1–4.

Nichols, Catherine. *Tricky Opossums* (Gross-Out Defenses). Bearport Publishing, 2008. ISBN 9781597167185. 24 p. Grades K–3.

Face to Face with Gorillas
by Michael Nichols.

Nichols, Michael. *Face to Face with Gorillas* (Face to Face with Animals). National Geographic, 2009. ISBN 9781426304064. 32 p. Grades 3–5.

Nicklin, Flip. *Face to Face with Whales.* National Geographic, 2008. ISBN 978-1426302442. 32 p. Grades 4–6.

Nicklin, Flip, and Linda Nicklin. *Face to Face with Dolphins* (Face to Face with Animals). National Geographic, 2007. ISBN 9781426301414. 32 p. Grades 3–6.

Nuzzolo, Deborah. *Bull Shark* (Pebble Plus). Capstone Press, 2008. ISBN 9781429617260. 24 p. Grades K–2.

Nuzzolo, Deborah. *Cheetahs* (Pebble Plus). Capstone Press, 2008. ISBN 9781429612449. 24 p. Grades K–2.

Nuzzolo, Deborah. *Great White Shark* (Pebble Plus). Capstone Press, 2008. ISBN 9781429617277. 24 p. Grades K–2.

Nuzzolo, Deborah. *Hammerhead Shark* (Pebble Plus). Capstone Press, 2008. ISBN 9781429617284. 24 p. Grades K–2.

Nuzzolo, Deborah. *Mako Shark* (Pebble Plus). Capstone Press, 2008. ISBN 9781429617291. 24 p. Grades K–2.

Nuzzolo, Deborah. *Tiger Shark* (Pebble Plus). Capstone Press, 2008. ISBN 9781429617307. 24 p. Grades K–2.

Nuzzolo, Deborah. *Whale Shark* (Pebble Plus). Capstone Press, 2008. ISBN 9781429617314. 24 p. Grades K–2.

Hammerhead Shark by Deborah Nuzzolo.

Olmstead, Kathleen. *Jacques Cousteau: A Life Under the Sea* (Sterling Biographies). Sterling, 2008. ISBN 9781402744402. 128 p. Grades 7–9.

O'Neill, Michael Patrick. *Ocean Magic.* Batfish Books, 2008. ISBN 9780972865357. 45 p. Grades 1–4.

O'Neill, Michael Patrick. *Shark Encounters.* Batfish Books, 2008. ISBN 978-0972865340. 45 p. Grades 1–4.

Osborne, Mary Pope, and Natalie Pope Boyce. *Sea Monsters: A Nonfiction Companion to "Dark Day in the Deep Sea"* (Magic Tree House Research Guides). Random House, 2008. ISBN 9780375946639. 128 p. Grades 1–4.

O'Sullivan, Robyn. *More Than Man's Best Friend: The Story of Working Dogs* (Science Chapters). National Geographic, 2006. ISBN 0792259408. 48 p. Grades 2–4.

Otfinoski, Steven. *Koalas* (Animals Animals). Benchmark, 2007. ISBN 978-0761425267. 48 p. Grades 2–5.

Otfinoski, Steven. *Seahorses* (Animals Animals). Benchmark, 2007. ISBN 978-0761425298. 48 p. Grades 3–4.

Otfinoski, Steven. *Skunks* (Animals Animals). Benchmark, 2008. ISBN 978-0761429296. 47 p. Grades 4–6.

Packard, Mary. *Working Horses* (Horse Power). Bearport Publishing, 2007. ISBN 1597164038. 32 p. Grades 1–4.

Patkau, Karen. *Creatures Yesterday and Today.* Tundra Books, 2008. ISBN 9780887768330. 32 p. Grades K–3.

Pearl, Norman. *Sharks: Ocean Hunters* (Powerful Predators). PowerKids Press, 2008. ISBN 9781404245099. 24 p. Grades 3–4.

Pearl, Norman. *Tigers: Hunters of Asia* (Powerful Predators). PowerKids Press, 2008. ISBN 9781404245075. 24 p. Grades 3–4.

Perkins, Wendy. *American Shorthair Cats* (Pebble Books). Capstone Press, 2008. ISBN 9781429612159. 24 p. Grades K–3.

Perkins, Wendy. *Maine Coon Cats* (Pebble Books). Capstone Press, 2008. ISBN 9781429612166. 24 p. Grades K–3.

Person, Stephen. *Arctic Fox: Very Cool!* (Uncommon Animals). Bearport Publishing, 2008. ISBN 9781597167307. 32 p. Grades 2–4.

Peterson, Cris. *Clarabelle: Making Milk and So Much More.* Boyds Mills, 2007. ISBN 9781590783108. 32 p. Grades 2–4.

Pipe, Jim. *Swarms* (Scary Creatures). Scholastic Press, 2009. ISBN 9780531216743. 32 p. Grades 3–5.

Pitts, Zachary. *The Pebble First Guide to Horses* (Pebble Books). Capstone Press, 2008. ISBN 9781429617086. 32 p. Grades K–3.

Pitts, Zachary. *The Pebble First Guide to Wildcats* (Pebble Books). Capstone Press, 2008. ISBN 9781429617093. 32 p. Grades K–1.

Pohl, Kathleen. *Animals of the Ocean* (Animal Show and Tell). Gareth Stevens, 2007. ISBN 9780836882087. 16 p. Grades K–3.

Polydoros, Lori. *Grizzly Bears: On the Hunt* (Blazers). Capstone Press, 2009. ISBN 9781429623162. 32 p. Grades 1–4.

Polydoros, Lori. *Lions: On the Hunt* (Blazers). Capstone Press, 2009. ISBN 9781429623193. 32 p. Grades 1–4.

Posada, Mia. *Guess What Is Growing Inside This Egg.* Millbrook Press, 2006. ISBN 9780822561927. Unpaged. Grades K–2.

Rake, Jody Sullivan. *The Aye-Aye* (Pebble Plus). Capstone Press, 2008. ISBN 9781429617376. 24 p. Grades 1–2.

Rake, Jody Sullivan. *The Frogfish* (Pebble Plus). Capstone Press, 2008. ISBN 9781429617383. 24 p. Grades 1–2.

Rake, Jody Sullivan. *Killer Whales Up Close* (First Facts: Whales and Dolphins Up Close). Capstone Press, 2009. ISBN 9781429622653. 24 p. Grades K–3.

Rake, Jody Sullivan. *Meerkats* (Pebble Plus). Capstone Press, 2008. ISBN 9781429612494. 24 p. Grades K–2.

Rake, Jody Sullivan. *The Naked Mole-Rat* (Pebble Plus). Capstone Press, 2008. ISBN 9781429617390. 24 p. Grades 1–2.

Rake, Jody Sullivan. *The Proboscis Monkey* (Pebble Plus). Capstone Press, 2008. ISBN 9781429617406. 24 p. Grades 1–2.

Rau, Dana Meachen. *Top 10 Cats for Kids* (Top Pets for Kids With American Humane Society). Enslow, 2008. ISBN 9780766030718. 48 p. Grades 2–5.

Rau, Dana Meachen. *Top 10 Fish for Kids* (Top Pets for Kids With American Humane Society). Enslow, 2008. ISBN 9780766030732. 48 p. Grades 2–5.

Riehecky, Janet. *Great White Sharks: On the Hunt* (Blazers). Capstone Press, 2009. ISBN 9781429623155. 32 p. Grades 1–4.

Rodriguez, Ana María. *Secret of the Bloody Hippo . . . and More!* (Animal Secrets Revealed!). Enslow, 2008. ISBN 9780766029583. 48 p. Grades 4–6.

Rodriguez, Ana María. *Secret of the Plant-killing Ants. . . and More!* (Animal Secrets Revealed!). Enslow, 2008. ISBN 9780766029538. 48 p. Grades 4–6.

Secret of the Puking Penguins . . . and More! **by Ana María Rodriguez.**

Rodriguez, Ana María. *Secret of the Puking Penguins . . . and More!* (Animal Secrets Revealed!). Enslow, 2008. ISBN 9780766029552. 48 p. Grades 4–6.

Rodriguez, Ana María. *Secret of the Singing Mice . . . and More!* (Animal Secrets Revealed!). Enslow, 2008. ISBN 9780766029569. 48 p. Grades 4–6.

Rodriguez, Ana María. *Secret of the Sleepless Whales . . . and More!* (Animal Secrets Revealed!). Enslow, 2008. ISBN 9780766029576. 48 p. Grades 4–6.

Rodriguez, Ana María. *Secret of the Suffocating Slime Trap . . . and More!* (Animal Secrets Revealed!). Enslow, 2008. ISBN 9780766029545. 48 p. Grades 4–6.

Rosing, Norbert. *Face to Face with Polar Bears* (Face to Face with Animals). National Geographic, 2007. ISBN 9781426301391. 32 p. Grades 3–6.

Rustad, Martha E. H. *Parrotfish* (Blastoff! Readers: Oceans Alive). Children's Press, 2007. ISBN 9780531147399. 24 p. Grades K–3.

Rustad, Martha E. H. *Sea Urchins* (Blastoff! Readers: Oceans Alive). Children's Press, 2007. ISBN 9780531147412. 24 p. Grades K–3.

Rustad, Martha E. H. *Stingrays* (Blastoff Readers: Oceans Alive). Children's Press, 2007. ISBN 9780531175705. 24 p. Grades K–1.

Ryder, Joanne. *Panda Kindergarten*. Collins, 2009. ISBN 9780060578503. 32 p. Grades K–1.

Salzmann, Mary Elizabeth. *Brilliant Birds* (Perfect Pets). ABDO & Daughters, 2007. ISBN 9781599287447. 23 p. Grades K–2.

Salzmann, Mary Elizabeth. *Flashy Fish* (Perfect Pets). ABDO & Daughters, 2007. ISBN 9781599287478. 24 p. Grades K–2.

Salzmann, Mary Elizabeth. *Goofy Guinea Pigs* (Perfect Pets). ABDO & Daughters, 2007. ISBN 9781599287492. 24 p. Grades K–2.

Sandler, Michael. *Military Horses* (Horse Power). Bearport Publishing, 2007. ISBN 159716402X. 32 p. Grades 1–4.

Sandler, Michael. *Race Horses* (Horse Power). Bearport Publishing, 2007. ISBN 1597163988. 32 p. Grades 1–4.

Sartore, Joel. *Face to Face with Grizzlies* (Face to Face with Animals). National Geographic, 2007. ISBN 9781426300516. 32 p. Grades 3–6.

Savage, Stephen. *Duck* (Animal Neighbors). PowerKids Press, 2008. ISBN 978-1435849884. 32 p. Grades 3–6.

Savage, Stephen. *Mouse* (Animal Neighbors). PowerKids Press, 2008. ISBN 9781435849907. 32 p. Grades 3–6.

Savage, Stephen. *Rat* (Animal Neighbors). PowerKids Press, 2008. ISBN 978-1435849914. 32 p. Grades 3–6.

Sayre, April Pulley. *Trout Are Made of Trees*. Charlesbridge, 2008. ISBN 9781580891370. 32 p. Grades K–3.

Schach, David. *Sea Dragons* (Blastoff! Readers: Oceans Alive). Children's Press 2007. ISBN 9780531175637. 24 p. Grades K–1.

Schaefer, Lola M. *Look Behind! Tales of Animal Ends*. Greenwillow, 2008. ISBN 9780060883935. 32 p. Grades K–3.

Schreiber, Anne. *Sharks!* (National Geographic Readers). National Geographic, 2008. ISBN 9781426302886. 32 p. Grades K–3.

Searl, Duncan. *Beagle: A Howling Good Time* (Little Dogs Rock!). Bearport Publishing, 2009. ISBN 9781597167499. 32 p. Grades K–3.

Searl, Duncan. *Wolves* (Smart Animals). Bearport Publishing, 2007. ISBN 159-7163708. 32 p. Grades 1–4.

Seidensticker, John. *Predators* (Insiders). Simon & Schuster, 2008. ISBN 9781416938637. 64 p. Grades 4–8.

Sengupta, Monalisa. *Discover Big Cats* (Discover Animals). Enslow, 2009. ISBN 9780766034730. 48 p. Grades 4–6.

Sengupta, Monalisa. *Discover Sharks* (Discover Animals). Enslow, 2009. ISBN 9780766034747. 48 p. Grades 4–6.

Seuling, Barbara. *Some Porcupines Wrestle: And Other Freaky Facts About Animal Antics and Families* (Freaky Facts). Picture Window Books, 2008. ISBN 9781404841147. 40 p. Grades 3–5.

Sexton, Colleen. *Clown Fish* (Blastoff! Readers: Oceans Alive). Children's Press, 2007. ISBN 9780531175620. 24 p. Grades K–3.

Sexton, Colleen. *Frogfish* (Blastoff! Readers: Oceans Alive). Children's Press, 2009. ISBN 9780531217122. 24 p. Grades K–3.

Sexton, Colleen. *Lionfish* (Blastoff! Readers: Oceans Alive). Children's Press, 2009. ISBN 9780531217139. 24 p. Grades K–3.

Sexton, Colleen. *Puffins* (Blastoff! Readers: Oceans Alive). Children's Press, 2009. ISBN 9780531217153. 24 p. Grades K–3.

Sexton, Colleen. *Sharks* (Blastoff! Readers: Oceans Alive). Children's Press, 2007. ISBN 9780531175651. 24 p. Grades K–3.

Sexton, Colleen. *Shrimp* (Blastoff! Readers: Oceans Alive). Children's Press, 2009. ISBN 9780531217160. 24 p. Grades K–3.

Sexton, Colleen. *Swordfish* (Blastoff! Readers: Oceans Alive). Children's Press, 2009. ISBN 9780531217146. 24 p. Grades K–3.

Sexton, Colleen. *Walruses* (Blastoff! Readers: Oceans Alive). Children's Press, 2007. ISBN 9780531147429. 24 p. Grades K–3.

Shores, Erika L. *The Pebble First Guide to Whales* (Pebble Books). Capstone Press, 2008. ISBN 9781429617130. 32 p. Grades K–1.

Sill, Cathryn. *About Penguins: A Guide for Children* (About . . .). Peachtree Publishers, 2009. ISBN 9781561454884. 48 p. Grades K–3.

Sill, Cathryn. *About Rodents: A Guide for Children* (About . . .). Peachtree Publishers, 2008. ISBN 9781561454549. 48 p. Grades 1–4.

Simon, Seymour. *Dolphins* (Smithsonian). Collins, 2009. ISBN 9780060283940. 32 p. Grades 2–5.

Simon, Seymour. *Gorillas* (Smithsonian). Collins, 2009. ISBN 9780060891022. 32 p. Grades K–3.

Sitarski, Anita. *Cold Light: Creatures, Discoveries, and Inventions That Glow*. Boyds Mills, 2007. ISBN 1590784685. 48 p. Grades 4–7.

Sivertsen, Linda. *Generation Green: The Ultimate Teen Guide to Living an Eco-Friendly Life*. Simon Pulse, 2008. ISBN 9781416961222. 272 p. Grades 9–up.

Siwanowicz, Igor. *Animals Up Close*. DK, 2009. ISBN 9780756645137. 96 p. Grades 4–6.

Smith, Miranda. *Sharks* (Kingfisher Knowledge). Kingfisher, 2008. ISBN 978-0753461945. 64 p. Grades 4–6.

Smith, Molly. *Blue Whale: The World's Biggest Mammal* (Supersized!). Bearport Publishing, 2007. ISBN 1597163856. 24 p. Grades K–3.

Sobol, Richard. *Breakfast in the Rainforest: A Visit with Mountain Gorillas* (Traveling Photographer). Candlewick Press, 2008. ISBN 9780763622817. 48 p. Grades 2–4.

Somervill, Barbara A. *Wildlife Photographer* (Cool Careers). Cherry Lake, 2008. ISBN 9781602793002. 32 p. Grades 4–7.

Sommers, Michael A. *Antarctic Melting: The Disappearing Antarctic Ice Cap* (Extreme Environmental Events). Rosen, 2006. ISBN 1404207414. 64 p. Grades 4–8.

Souza, D. M. *Look What Feet Can Do* (Look What Animals Can Do). Lerner Publications, 2006. ISBN 0761394605. 48 p. Grades 2–4.

Spada, Ada. *Fangs, Claws & Talons: Animal Predators*. Lark, 2007. ISBN 978-1600591501. 48 p. Grades 3–6.

St. George, Judith. *Zarafa: The Giraffe Who Walked to the King*. Philomel Books, 2009. ISBN 9780399250491. 40 p. Grades 1–3.

Staub, Frank J. *Running Free: America's Wild Horses* (Prime). Enslow, 2007. ISBN 0766026701. 48 p. Grades 2–4.

Stefoff, Rebecca. *Deer* (Animalways). Benchmark, 2007. ISBN 9780761425342. 108 p. Grades 3–6.

Stevens, Kathryn. *Camels*. Child's World, 2007. ISBN 9781592968442. 32 p. Grades 2–4.

Stevens, Kathryn. *Cats* (Pet Care for Kids). Child's World, 2009. ISBN 978-1602531802. 24 p. Grades K–2.

Stevens, Kathryn. *Dogs* (Pet Care for Kids). Child's World, 2009. ISBN 978-1602531819. 24 p. Grades K–2.

Stevens, Kathryn. *Fish* (Pet Care for Kids). Child's World, 2009. ISBN 978-1602531826. 24 p. Grades K–2.

Stevens, Kathryn. *Hamsters* (Pet Care for Kids). Child's World, 2009. ISBN 978-1602531833. 24 p. Grades K–2.

Stevens, Kathryn. *Hermit Crabs* (Pet Care for Kids). Child's World, 2009. ISBN 978-1602531840. 24 p. Grades K–2.

Stevens, Kathryn. *Parakeets* (Pet Care for Kids). Child's World, 2009. ISBN 9781602531864. 24 p. Grades K–2.

Stewart, Melissa. *Rabbits* (Animals Animals). Benchmark, 2007. ISBN 978-0761425281. 48 p. Grades 3–4.

Stewart, Melissa. *Why Are Animals Blue?* (Rainbow of Animals). Enslow, 2009. ISBN 9780766032514. 32 p. Grades K–2.

Stewart, Melissa. *Why Are Animals Green*? (Rainbow of Animals). Enslow, 2009. ISBN 9780766032521. 32 p. Grades K–2.

Stewart, Melissa. *Why Are Animals Orange?* (Rainbow of Animals). Enslow, 2009. ISBN 9780766032507. 32 p. Grades K–3.

Stewart, Melissa. *Why Are Animals Purple?* (Rainbow of Animals). Enslow, 2009. ISBN 9780766032545. 32 p. Grades K–2.

Stewart, Melissa. *Why Are Animals Red*? (Rainbow of Animals). Enslow, 2009. ISBN 9780766032491. 32 p. Grades K–2.

Stewart, Melissa. *Why Are Animals Yellow?* (Rainbow of Animals). Enslow, 2009. ISBN 9780766032538. 32 p. Grades K–2.

Stockdale, Susan. *Fabulous Fishes*. Peachtree Publishers, 2008. ISBN 978-1561454297. 32 p. Grades K–3.

Sullivant, Holly J. *Hamsters* (Our Best Friends). Eldorado Ink, 2008. ISBN 978-1932904307. 112 p. Grades 7–12.

Swanson, Diane. *Animal Aha! Thrilling Discoveries in Wildlife Science*. Annick Press, 2009. ISBN 9781554511655. 48 p. Grades 4–6.

Swanson, Diane. *A Crash of Rhinos, A Party of Jays: The Wacky Ways We Name Animal Groups*. Annick Press, 2006. ISBN 1554510481. 24 p. Grades K–2.

Swinburne, Stephen R. *Armadillo Trail: The Northward Journey of the Armadillo*. Boyds Mills, 2009. ISBN 9781590784631. 32 p. Grades K–4.

Tait, Leia. *Emi Saving Her Rhino Species* (Inspiring Animals). Weigl Publishers, 2008. ISBN 9781590368565. 24 p. Grades 2–3.

Tait, Leia. *Little Draggin' Bear* (Inspiring Animals). Weigl Publishers, 2008. ISBN 9781590368619. 24 p. Grades 2–3.

Tait, Leia. *Pecorino: Posing Worldwide* (Inspiring Animals). Weigl Publishers, 2008. ISBN 9781590368589. 24 p. Grades 2–3.

Talbott, Hudson. *United Tweets of America: 50 State Birds: Their Stories, Their Glories*. Putnam, 2008. ISBN 9780399245206. Unpaged. Grades 2–5.

Taschek, Karen. *Hanging with Bats: Ecobats, Vampires, and Movie Stars* (Worlds of Wonder). University of New Mexico Press, 2008. ISBN 9780826344038. 96 p. Grades 4–6.

Tate, Nikki. *Behind the Scenes at the Racetrack: The Racehorse*. Fitzhenry and Whiteside, 2007. ISBN 9781554550180. 88 p. Grades 5–8.

Taylor, Barbara. *Planet Animal*. Barron's Educational Series, 2009. ISBN 978-0764162053. 32 p. Grades 3–5.

Thomas, William David. *Veterinarian*. (Cool Careers). Gareth Stevens, 2008. ISBN 9780836891973. 32 p. Grades 4–7.

Thomson, Ruth. *The Life Cycle of a Crab* (Learning About Life Cycles). PowerKids Press, 2009. ISBN 9781435828346. 24 p. Grades K–2.

Thomson, Ruth. *The Life Cycle of an Owl* (Learning About Life Cycles). Rosen, 2009. ISBN 9781435828339. 24 p. Grades K–2.

Thomson, Sarah L. *Extreme Stars! Q&A* (Smithsonian Q & A). Collins, 2006. ISBN 0060899336. 48 p. Grades 3–5.

Townsend, John. *Bone Detective* (Crabtree Contact). Crabtree Publishing, 2008. ISBN 9780778738060. 32 p. Grades 4–6.

Turner, Pamela S. *A Life in the Wild: George Schaller's Struggle to Save the Last Great Beasts*. Farrar, Straus and Giroux, 2008. ISBN 9780374345785. 112 p. Grades 5–8.

Turner, Pamela S. *Prowling the Seas: Exploring the Hidden World of Ocean Predators*. Walker Books, 2009. ISBN 9780802797483. 48 p. Grades 3–6.

Vadon, Catherine. *Meet the Shark*. Two-Can Publishing, 2007. ISBN 978-1587285981. 45 p. Grades 1–4.

Vogel, Julia. *Bats* (Our Wild World). NorthWord, 2007. ISBN 9781559719698. 48 p. Grades 4–7.

Wahman, Wendy. *Don't Lick the Dog: Making Friends with Dogs*. Henry Holt, 2009. ISBN 9780805087338. 32 p. Grades K–2.

Walker, Richard. *Animal Life* (One Million Things). DK, 2009. ISBN 978-0756652340. 128 p. Grades 5–8.

Warhol, Tom. *Owls* (Animalways). Benchmark, 2007. ISBN 9780761425373. 111 p. Grades 3–6.

Wearing, Judy. *Jellyfish* (Wow World of Wonder). Weigl Publishers, 2009. ISBN 9781605961002. 24 p. Grades K–3.

Wearing, Judy. *Manta Rays* (World of Wonder: Underwater Life). Weigl Publishers, 2009. ISBN 9781605961057. 24 p. Grades K–3.

Wearing, Judy. *Sea Horses* (World of Wonder: Underwater Life). Weigl Publishers, 2009. ISBN 9781605961033. 24 p. Grades K–3.

Webster, Dennis. *Absolutely Wild*. David R Godine, 2008. ISBN 9781567923759. 32 p. Grades K–3.

Wells, Robert B. *Polar Bear, Why Is Your World Melting?* Albert Whitman, 2008. ISBN 9780807565995. 32 p. Grades 1–4.

Wheeler, Jill C. *Cockapoos* (Designer Dogs Set 7). Checkerboard Books, 2008. ISBN 9781599289625. 24 p. Grades 4–6.

Wheeler, Jill C. *Goldendoodles* (Designer Dogs Set 7). Checkerboard Books, 2008. ISBN 9781599289632. 24 p. Grades 4–6.

Wheeler, Jill C. *Labradoodles* (Designer Dogs Set 7). Checkerboard Books, 2008. ISBN 9781599289649. 24 p. Grades 4–6.

Wheeler, Jill C. *Puggles* (Designer Dogs Set 7). Checkerboard Books, 2008. ISBN 9781599289656. 24 p. Grades 4–6.

Wheeler, Jill C. *Schnoodles* (Designer Dogs Set 7). Checkerboard Books, 2008. ISBN 9781599289663. 24 p. Grades 4–6.

Whitehead, Sarah. *How to Speak Cat*. Scholastic Press, 2008. ISBN 9780545020794. 96 p. Grades 4–8.

Whitehead, Sarah. *How to Speak Dog*. Scholastic Press, 2008. ISBN 9780545020787. 96 p. Grades 4–8.

Winner, Cherie. *Everything Bird: What Kids Really Want to Know about Birds* (Kids Faqs). NorthWord, 2007. ISBN 9781559719629. 64 p. Grades 3–4.

Wood, Selina. *Owning a Pet Dog* (Owning a Pet). Sea to Sea Publications, 2008. ISBN 9781597710565. 32 p. Grades 4–6.

Zabludoff, Marc. *Monkeys* (Animalways). Benchmark, 2007. ISBN 9780761425359. 108 p. Grades 3–6.

Zecca, Katherine. *A Puffin's Year*. Down East Books, 2007. ISBN 9780892727421. 32 p. Grades 2–4.

Chapter 8

Science

Science can cover many topics of particular interest to boys. In this chapter you will find books about space travel, experiments, inventions, bodily functions, global warming, illegal drugs, and even explosions. It's easy to see how these topics could capture the interest of inquisitive readers with the right encouragement. One surefire topic for the CSI generation is crime solving through forensic science. These books provide the perfect combination of crime, grossness, and a heavy dose of science. There are so many new titles in this category that there is a separate booklist at the end of the chapter just dealing with forensic science.

BOOKTALKS

Chaikin, Andrew, with Victoria Kohl. *Mission Control, This Is Apollo: The Story of the First Voyages to the Moon*. Illustrated by Alan Bean. Viking, 2009. ISBN 9780670011568. 114 p. Grades 5–8.

When Andrew Chaikin was a kid, he knew he wanted to be an astronaut. He was lucky. He got to meet a real one when he was 12 years old. The astronaut was Alan Bean, who ended up being one of the few people to go to the moon and walk around on it.

Now the two men are working together! Andrew never got to be an astronaut, but he knew what he loved the most—learning about space and the space program. Together he and Alan, who became an artist after he stopped being an astronaut, have created this wonderful book that describes the first voyages to the moon.

Going to the moon became a matter of national pride for the United States. The Soviet Union became the first country in space in 1957 when it launched Sputnik, the first artificial satellite. This made Americans really scared that anyone could do space exploration better than their country. The U.S. government got with the program and launched its own artificial satellite a few months later. But it was a day late and a dollar short, for by then the Soviets had already put a dog into space. Then they put an astronaut into space.

The new American president, John F. Kennedy, felt we had to win the space race. By May 1961, the U.S. sent astronaut Alan Shepard up and down. It only lasted 15 minutes, but they had put a man into space. America had proved it could do it. The president then said the United States needed to get a man to the moon by the end of the decade.

This book is the story of how that happened. Sometimes it is a happy story, sometimes it is a story of great suspense, sometimes it's a tragic story, but ultimately it is an exciting, fantastic ride through the history of the Apollo program, loaded with Alan Bean's wonderful paintings and lots of photographs. You will be startled at some of the things you read.

- The computers on the spaceships had less memory than your cell phone does.

- The terrible accident that killed three astronauts on January 27, 1967, caused all sorts of changes to be made to the command module. Their chamber was full of oxygen, and the door to it was so heavy that they could not budge it when the chamber caught on fire. The oxygen they were breathing through tubes quickly turned to fire.

- Read about going to the bathroom in space on page 17. Originally, there were no space toilets, and, believe me, you would not want to go through what the astronauts had to go through!

- Some of the original space flights had no backup engine. If something happened to the rocket engine, that was it. The astronauts would stay in space, probably forever.

This is a great read.

Cherry, Lynne, and Gary Braasch. *How We Know What We Know About Our Changing Climate: Scientists and Kids Explore Global Warming*. Dawn, 2008. ISBN 1584691034. 66 p. Grades 5–8.

Right off the bat, Professor David Sobel of Antioch University tells us there is a lot more good news than bad in this book. Yes, scientists all agree that the earth is warming up much more quickly than it ever has before. And bad things can happen and are happening because of that. But we can make a difference. Kids can make a difference!

Kids 100 years ago in Nova Scotia kept track of what was happening in nature near their schools—over 1,700 schools. They recorded when birds arrived, when the first ice thawed or froze on the water, when the trees started blooming, and much, much more.

Today that information is a treasure, for we can compare when these things happen now to when they happened 100 years before. And we are finding that everything is happening much, much sooner than it used to in the spring—and later in the fall and winter.

Scientists are studying what is happening, and kids are helping them and making huge contributions. You will learn things like:

- Many animals are no longer living in the same areas where they used to live. They are moving further north, because the weather is warmer. Sometimes it is difficult for them to find the kind of food they need in a different area.

- Bristlecone pine trees can live for almost 5,000 years. Their growth rings show the conditions in which they lived every year of their lives. Scientists are able to take cores from trees so they do not get damaged—take a look at the picture on page 23.

- Glaciers are melting—look at the pictures of the Athabasca Glacier in British Columbia, one taken in 1917 and one in 2005.

- Students in Siberia are helping scientists to see if more fresh water is flowing into the Arctic Ocean—read all about it on page 34.

- Read about what you can do to help starting on page 54.

It's an amazing book full of interesting information.

Floca, Brian. *Moonshot: The Flight of Apollo 11.* A Richard Jackson Book: Atheneum, 2009. ISBN 9781416950462. Unpaged. Grades 1–4.

On May 20, 1969, the crew of Apollo 11 boldly took off to a place where no one had gone before: to the moon!

Their two small spaceships sat atop a rocket that launched them into space, and they lay squeezed together in seats, all on their backs. First they orbited the earth, then they left it behind—as well as the rocket.

Now they could float around. In fact, everything in the space ship floated around. There was a lot of Velcro to keep everything in its proper place. They had no pillows and no beds, no day and no night. It was always dark outside. And using the bathroom was another skill they had to develop—think pipes and hoses and bags—and a really smelly place!

Finally they arrived at their destination. Neil Armstrong and Buzz Aldrin took off in the tiniest spaceship, the *Eagle*, to land on the moon, and Michael Collins stayed in the other, the *Columbia*, to be the loneliest human being in existence for a few hours—he orbited the moon, completely by himself.

Did they make it? Did they make it back? Brian Floca's spare, simple, riveting text and wonderful illustrations tell the glorious story. It's a winner!

Jackson, Donna M. *Extreme Scientists: Exploring Nature's Mysteries from Perilous Places.* Houghton Mifflin, 2009. ISBN 978061877068. 80 p. Grades 4–8.

The three scientists you'll meet in this book have amazing adventures. They go up high, down deep, and even into the eye of a hurricane. And to do those things is their job!

Paul Flaherty is the hurricane guy. By the time he was in second grade, he knew he wanted to be a meteorologist. He was always interested in how and why weather happened. He followed his dream.

He went to college and studied meteorology, the science of weather, and then he started teaching that to military students. One day he saw a job posting for a hurricane hunter and he applied for it.

Hurricanes are powerful, deadly storms, typically about 300 miles across. In the center there is an eye, which is a relatively calm place compared to everything else. Paul and the team of hurricane hunters fly directly through the storm and into the eye. And there they measure and they observe and they predict what the hurricane is going to do next. What they do saves many lives.

Hazel Barton is a cave woman. Really! She searches caves looking for microbes, including bacteria and fungi. They are considered the oldest form of life on earth. "Scientists refer to these super-resilient creatures as 'extremophiles.' They believe the microbes' ability to flourish under extreme conditions may provide insights to everything from life on Mars to cleaning the environment" (p. 29). Hazel studies the extremophiles that live in caves, and she has to find them! This means going deep underground, swimming in underwater lakes, going anywhere the extremophiles might live. The photographs are incredible—and Hazel has hurt herself in her explorations.

Stephen Sillett is a skywalker, who goes to the tops of the tallest living things on earth—the tall redwoods in old-growth forests. He admits he loved to climb trees when he was a kid in Pennsylvania, but he never got to climb up any as tall as the California and Oregon trees he climbs today.

Redwood trees can live to be more than 2,000 years old. Scientists are interested in how they survive and what kind of life is at the top of the trees. Getting to the top is not easy. They shoot a fishing line up over a branch with a bow and arrow, hoping it will go over a strong, safe branch. Then they pull the line down and climb up. The lowest branches are sometimes over 100 feet from the ground.

What they find surprises them. There is an entire ecosystem at the top of the tree—new trees, not just redwood trees, are growing on the original tree. Animals they do not expect to see live up there. Some never see the ground. Steve sometimes spends the night near the top of the tree.

All of the stories in this book are incredible. Take a look at some of the fantastic, exciting jobs some scientists get to do!

McCarthy, Meghan. *Astronaut Handbook.* Alfred A. Knopf, 2008. ISBN 9780375844591 Unpaged. Grades 1–3.

So what do you think it would be like to go to astronaut school? Fun? Exciting? Hard? Sometimes yucky?

You would be right. It is all of those things and more!

You will have to decide what kind of astronaut you want to be before you start training. You had better be fit and healthy and be willing to work as part of a team. You will have to go through survival training.

You will learn what you eat on a space ship (does it look good?) and what a space toilet looks like—it is sort of surprising. You will learn what to wear, too.

This is a fun way to learn what it is like to be an astronaut.

O'Brien, Patrick. *You Are the First Kid on Mars*. G. P. Putnam's Sons, 2009. ISBN 9780399246340. Unpaged. Grades 2–5.

Have you ever wanted to live on another planet? If you ever do, it will probably be Mars, because Mars is the most like Earth—although it is not much at all like Earth. How would you get there? What would you do?

This book has interesting illustrations that describe what it would be like. You would probably have to go at a time when Mars and Earth are closest together—about 35 million miles apart. Even then it will take four months for a rocket to get there. You would probably take an elevator on Earth. It would be attached to a cable that would take you to a space station where the Mars rocket would be waiting for you. On that, you would travel about 75,000 miles an hour. You would not have a lot of room, and it would be crowded.

When you arrived at your destination, you would get into a lander to take you to the planet. And there you would put on your space suit and walk, with big bouncing steps, on Mars.

You would walk to a Mars habitat, a structure in which scientists and others live and work. They would be exploring and always trying to find out if there is life on this planet.

You will learn about what the weather and the landscape of Mars are like—and maybe make up your own mind about whether this is a place you would like to be able to visit someday.

Turner, Pamela S. *Life on Earth—and Beyond: An Astrobiologist's Quest*. Charlesbridge, 2008. ISBN 9781580891349. 111 p. Grades 5–9.

Not that long ago, people believed in Martians—aliens who lived on Mars. When exploratory vehicles were sent to Mars to take pictures, scientists discovered there was no way that any kind of a being existed there, except maybe, just maybe, microbes, which are so small they can only be seen with a microscope. There did seem to be evidence that at least at one time there was water on Mars, and where water exists there is often life.

But how could it be proven that microbes exist in dry, extremely hot, or extremely cold places like Mars?

A scientist like Chris McKay is the guy you need to ask. And that is what Pamela Turner, who wrote this book, did.

Chris is fascinated by this topic. He realized that if he went to extremely cold or hot places that were also almost completely dry, he could test to see if microbes could exist in those places. And off he

Life on Earth—and Beyond: An Astrobiologist's Quest by **Pamela S. Turner.**

went, to places like the Dry Valleys in Antarctica, the Sahara Desert in Africa, and the Atacama Desert in Chile. Then he went to places that were cold and had water to see whether microbes could live in frozen areas.

He discovered astounding things. In Siberia, the members of the expedition drilled holes into the permafrost, ground that had been frozen solid for millions of years. They pulled up soil samples. There were frozen bacteria in those samples, and not all of those frozen bacteria stayed frozen. Some of them defrost and began eating and reproducing! They had been frozen for three and a half million years, but they were doing just fine!

One of the most incredible things Chris did was dive into a lake in Antarctica, one that was covered with ice 16 feet thick. His team had to cut out a hole in the ice so he could get to the lake and take samples of the water. Read about what he wore and how it all worked.

And then read about what they found out on all of these research trips, in this amazing book.

WORTH READING

Nonfiction books with "boy appeal" that have received positive reviews in *Booklist*, *Horn Book Guide*, and/or *School Library Journal*.

Aguilar, David A. *11 Planets: A New View of the Solar System.* National Geographic, 2008. ISBN 9781426302367. 48 p. Grades 4–6.

Aguilar, David A. *Planets, Stars, and Galaxies: A Visual Encyclopedia of Our Universe.* National Geographic, 2007. ISBN 9781426301704. 192 p. Grades 4–6.

Allman, Toney. *Jaws of Life* (Great Idea). Norwood House Press, 2008. ISBN 9781599531915. 48 p. Grades 4–6.

Aronson, Marc. *Bill Gates* (Up Close). Viking, 2008. ISBN 9780670063482. 192 p. Grades 6–10.

11 Planets: A New View of the Solar System **by David A. Aguilar.**

Bailey, Diane. *Brain Surgeons* (Extreme Careers). Rosen, 2008. ISBN 9781404217874. 64 p. Grades 5–8.

Baines, Becky. *Your Skin Holds You In: A Book About Your Skin* (ZigZag). National Geographic, 2008. ISBN 9781426303111. 32 p. Grades K–2.

Beck, Esther. *Cool Odor Decoders: Fun Science Projects About Smells* (Cool Science). Checkerboard Library, 2007. ISBN 9781599289090. 32 p. Grades 4–6.

Your Skin Holds You In: A Book About Your Skin **by Becky Baines.**

Beyond: A Solar System Voyage **by Michael Benson.**

Benson, Michael. *Beyond: A Solar System Voyage*. Abrams Books for Young Readers, 2009. ISBN 9780810983229. 128 p. Grades 6–9.

Bodden, Valerie. *The Story of Coca-Cola* (Built for Success). Creative Education, 2008. ISBN 9781583416020. 48 p. Grades 4–6.

Bourgeois, Paulette. *The Dirt on Dirt*. Kids Can, 2008. ISBN 9781554531011. 48 p. Grades 3–6.

Bredeson, Carmen. *What Do Astronauts Do?* (I Like Space!). Enslow, 2008. ISBN 978-0766029422. 32 p. Grades 1–3.

Bredeson, Carmen. *What Is the Solar System?* (I Like Space!). Enslow, 2008. ISBN 978-0766029446. 32 p. Grades 1–3.

Breguet, Amy E. *Vicodin, OxyContin, and Other Pain Relievers* (Junior Drug Awareness). Chelsea House, 2008. ISBN 9780791097007. 112 p. Grades 7–10.

Brynie, Faith Hickman. *101 Questions About Muscles: To Stretch Your Mind and Flex Your Brain* (101 Questions). Twenty-First Century Books, 2007. ISBN 9780822563808. 176 p. Grades 7–up.

Bryson, Bill. *A Really Short History of Nearly Everything*. Delacorte, 2009. ISBN 9780385738101. 176 p. Grades 5–8.

Calabresi, Linda. *Human Body* (Insiders). Simon & Schuster, 2008. ISBN 141-6938613. 64 p. Grades 4–7.

Carson, Mary Kay. *Extreme Planets Q&A* (Smithsonian Q&A Series). Collins, 2008. ISBN 9780060899752. 48 p. Grades 2–4.

Claybourne, Anna. *Electricity* (Why It Works). QEB Publishing, 2008. ISBN 978-1595665591. 24 p. Grades K–2.

Cobb, Vicki. *We Dare You! Hundreds of Science Bets, Challenges, and Experiments You Can Do at Home.* Skyhorse Publishing, 2008. ISBN 9781602392250. 321 p. Grades 3–7.

Collard, Sneed B., III. *Science Warriors: The Battle Against Invasive Species* (Scientists in the Field). Houghton Mifflin, 2008. ISBN 9780618756360. 48 p. Grades 5–8.

Cooper, Sharon Katz. *Learning from Fossils* (Heinemann, Read and Learn). Heinemann, 2007. ISBN 1403493170. 24 p. Grades K–2.

Corrigan, Jim. *Steve Jobs* (Business Leaders). Morgan Reynolds, 2008. ISBN 978-1599350769. 128 p. Grades 7–up.

DiConsiglio, John. *When Birds Get Flu and Cows Go Mad! How Safe Are We?* (24/7: Science Behind the Scenes). Franklin Watts, 2007. ISBN 0531175286. 64 p. Grades 5–7.

Dixon-Engel, Tara. *Neil Armstrong: One Giant Leap for Mankind* (Sterling Biographies). Sterling, 2008. ISBN 9781402744969. 128 p. Grades 4–6.

Drake, Jane. *Alien Invaders: Species That Threaten Our World.* Tundra Books, 2008. ISBN 9780887767982. 56 p. Grades 4–6.

Dreier, David. *Electrical Circuits: Harnessing Electricity* (Exploring Science). Compass Point Books, 2007. ISBN 0756532671. 48 p. Grades 5–7.

Dumont-Le Cornec, Elisabeth. *Wonders of the World: Natural and Man-Made Majesties.* Abrams Books for Young Readers, 2007. ISBN 0810994178. 150 p. Grades 5–9.

Earth Matters. DK, 2008. ISBN 9780756634353. 256 p. Grades 5–up.

Feinstein, Stephen. *Alexander Graham Bell: The Genius Behind the Phone* (Inventors Who Changed the World). Enslow, 2008. ISBN 9781598450552. 128 p. Grades 4–6.

Feinstein, Stephen. *Louis Pasteur: The Father of Microbiology* (Inventors Who Changed the World). Enslow, 2008. ISBN 9781598450781. 128 p. Grades 4–6.

Fortey, Jacqueline. *Great Scientists* (DK Eyewitness Books). DK, 2007. ISBN 9780756629748. 72 p. Grades 5–8.

Fox, Tom. *Snowball Launchers, Giant-Pumpkin Growers, and Other Cool Contraptions.* Sterling, 2006. ISBN 0806955155. 128 p. Grades 4–7.

Friedman, Lauri S. *Michael Dell* (Business Leaders). Morgan Reynolds, 2008. ISBN 9781599350837. 128 p. Grades 6–up.

Frisch-Schmoll, Joy. *Gravity* (Simple Science). Creative Education, 2008. ISBN 9781583415764. 24 p. Grades K–3.

Gardner, Robert. *Forensic Science Projects with a Crime Lab You Can Build.* (Build-a-Lab! Science Experiments). Enslow, 2007. ISBN 076602806. 128 p. Grades 6–9.

Gardner, Robert. *Meteorology Projects with a Weather Station You Can Build* (Build-a-Lab! Science Experiments). Enslow, 2008. ISBN 9780766028074. 128 p. Grades 4–6.

***Sound Projects with a Music Lab You Can Build* by Robert Gardner.**

Gardner, Robert. *Sound Projects with a Music Lab You Can Build* (Build-a-Lab! Science Experiments). Enslow, 2008. ISBN 9780766028098. 128 p. Grades 4–6.

Gass, Justin T. *Quaaludes* (Drugs: The Straight Facts). Chelsea House, 2008. ISBN 9780791085462. 96 p. Grades 7–10.

Giddens, Sandra. *Obsessive-Compulsive Disorder* (Teen Mental Health). Rosen, 2008. ISBN 9781404218017. 48 p. Grades 7–10.

Goldsmith, Connie. *Superbugs Strike Back: When Antibiotics Fail* (Discovery!). Twenty-First Century, 2006. ISBN 9780822566076. 112 p. Grades 7–up.

Goldsmith, Mike. *Stars and Planets* (Navigators). Kingfisher, 2008. ISBN 9780753462300. 48 p. Grades 3–5.

Graham, Ian. *Fighting Crime* (Why Science Matters). Heinemann, 2008. ISBN 978-1432918323. 56 p. Grades 7–10.

Graham, Ian. *Microscopic Scary Creatures* (Scary Creatures). Franklin Watts, 2009. ISBN 9780531216736. 32 p. Grades 3–5.

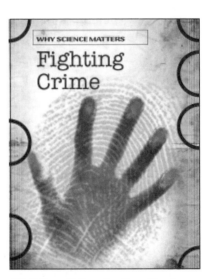

***Fighting Crime* by Ian Graham.**

Guillain, Charlotte. *Magnets* (Investigate). Heinemann, 2008. ISBN 978-1432913915. 32 p. Grades K–3.

Harrow, Jeremy. *Crystal Meth* (Incredibly Disgusting Drugs). Rosen, 2007. ISBN 9781404219533. 48 p. Grades 5–8.

Hilliard, Richard. *Lucky 13: Survival in Space.* Boyds Mills, 2008. ISBN 9781590785577. 32 p. Grades 4–6.

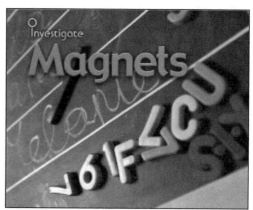

Magnets by Charlotte Guillain.

Hopwood, James. *Cool Dry Ice Devices: Fun Science Projects with Dry Ice* (Cool Science). Checkerboard Library, 2007. ISBN 9781599289076. 32 p. Grades 4–6.

Hopwood, James. *Cool Gravity Activities: Fun Science Projects About Balance* (Cool Science). Checkerboard Library, 2007. ISBN 9781599289083. 32 p. Grades 4–6.

Horn, Geoffrey M. *Meteorologist* (Cool Careers). Gareth Stevens, 2008. ISBN 9780836891942. 32 p. Grades 3–5.

Hyland, Tony. *Astronauts* (Extreme Jobs). Smart Apple Media, 2007. ISBN 978-1583407431. 32 p. Grades 4–6.

Jackson, Donna M. *Phenomena: Secrets of the Senses.* Little, Brown, 2008. ISBN 97803161664921. 76 p. Grades 4–6.

Jackson, Ellen. *Mysterious Universe: Supernovae, Dark Energy, and Black Holes* (Scientists in the Field). Houghton Mifflin, 2008. ISBN 9780618563258. 64 p. Grades 5–8.

Juzwiak, Rich. *Addictive Personality* (Teen Mental Health). Rosen, 2008. ISBN 9781404218024. 48 p. Grades 7–10.

Kafka, Tina. *Cloning* (Hot Topics). Lucent Books, 2007. ISBN 9781590189795. 111 p. Grades 7–up.

Kant, Jared, Martin Franklin, and Linda Wasmer Andrews. *The Thought That Counts: A Firsthand Account of One Teenager's Experience with Obsessive-Compulsive Disorder* (The Annenberg Foundation Trust at Sunnylands' Adolescent Mental Health Initiative). Oxford University Press, 2008. ISBN 9780195316889. 192 p. Grades 8–up.

Keegan, Kyle. *Chasing the High: A Firsthand Account of One Young Person's Experience with Substance Abuse.* Oxford University Press, 2008. ISBN 9780195314717. 192 p. Grades 8–up.

Kenda, Margaret, and Phyllis S. Williams. *Science Wizardry for Kids.* 2nd ed. Illustrated by Deborah Gross. Barron's Educational Series, 2009. ISBN 9780764141775. 242 p. Grades 3–6.

Kirkland, Kyle. *Electricity and Magnetism* (Physics in Our World). Facts on File, 2007. ISBN 9780816061129. 148p. Grades 8–12.

Knowles, Johanna. *Over-the-Counter Drugs* (Junior Drug Awareness). Chelsea House, 2008. ISBN 9780791097595. 112 p. Grades 7–10.

Koellhoffer, Tara. *Prozac and Other Antidepressants* (Junior Drug Awareness). Chelsea House, 2008. ISBN 9780791097472. 112 p. Grades 7–10.

Kompelien, Tracy. *Cool Rocks: Creating Fun and Fascinating Collections!* (Cool Collections). Checkerboard Library, 2006. ISBN 1596797711. 32 p. Grades 2–4.

Kreske, Damian. P. *How to Say No to Drugs* (Junior Drug Awareness). Chelsea House, 2008. ISBN 9780791096994. 112 p. Grades 7–10.

Landau, Elaine. *Bites and Stings* (Head-to-Toe Health). Marshall Cavendish, 2008. ISBN 9780761428503. 32 p. Grades K–3.

Latta, Sara L. *The Good, the Bad, the Slimy: The Secret Life of Microbes* (Prime). Enslow, 2006. ISBN 9780766012943. 128 p. Grades 5–8.

Lemke, Donald B. *Steve Jobs, Steven Wozniak, and the Personal Computer* (Graphic Library). Capstone Press, 2006. ISBN 0736864881. 32 p. Grades 4–6.

Lesinski, Jeanne M. *Bill Gates: Entrepreneur and Philanthropist* (Lifeline Biographies). Twenty-First Century Books, 2008. ISBN 9781580135702. 112 p. Grades 5–9.

Levinson, Nancy Smiler. *Rain Forests* (Holiday House Reader). Holiday House, 2008. ISBN 9780823418992. 40 p. Grades K–3.

Llewellyn, Claire. *Ask Dr. K. Fisher about Planet Earth.* Illustrated by Kate Shepherd. Kingfisher, 2009. ISBN 9780753463048. 32 p. Grades K–4.

Lockwood, Brad. *Bill Gates: Profile of a Digital Entrepreneur* (Career Profiles). Rosen, 2007. ISBN 9781404219069. 112 p. Grades 5–8.

Macaulay, David, with Richard Walker. *The Way We Work: Getting to Know the Amazing Human Body.* Houghton Mifflin, 2008. ISBN 97806182337866. 336 p. Grades 6–up.

Macdonald, Guy. *My Brilliant Body: Everything You Ever Wanted to Know About Your Own Body.* Barron's Educational Series, 2008. ISBN 9780764161728. 128 p. Grades 4–6.

Madaras, Lynda. *On Your Mark, Get Set, Grow! A "What's Happening to My Body?" Book for Younger Boys* (What's Happening to My Body?). Newmarket, 2008. ISBN 1557047804. 119 p. Grades 4–6.

Manning, Mick. *Under Your Skin: Your Amazing Body.* Albert Whitman, 2007. ISBN 9780807583135. 23 p. Grades 1–3.

Manson, Ainslie. *Boy in Motion: Rick Hansen's Story.* Greystone Books, 2008. ISBN 9781553652526. 48 p. Grades 1–3.

McCarthy, Meghan. *Astronaut Handbook*. Alfred A. Knopf, 2008. ISBN 978-0375844591. 40 p. Grades K–3.

McGowen, Tom. *Space Race: The Mission, the Men, the Moon* (America's Living History). Enslow, 2008. ISBN 9780766029101. 128 p. Grades 4–6.

McKay, Kim. *True Green Kids: 100 Things You Can Do to Save the Planet*. National Geographic, 2008. ISBN 9781426304422. 144 p. Grades 4–6.

Meltzer, Milton. *Albert Einstein: A Biography*. Holiday House, 2007. ISBN 978-0823419661. 32 p. Grades 3–6.

Menzel, Peter. *What the World Eats*. Tricycle Press, 2008. ISBN 9781582462462. 160 p. Grades 4–8.

Miller, Edward. *The Tooth Book: A Guide to Healthy Teeth and Gums*. Holiday House, 2008. ISBN 9780823420926. 32 p. Grades K–4.

Musolf, Nell. *The Story of Microsoft* (Built for Success). Creative Education, 2008. ISBN 9781583416075. 48 p. Grades 4–6.

Olien, Rebecca. *Kids Care! 75 Ways to Make a Difference for People, Animals & the Environment* (A Williamson Kids Can Book). Williamson Books, 2007. ISBN 9780824967932. 128 p. Grades 3–6.

Olive, M. Foster. *Crack* (Drugs: The Straight Facts). Chelsea House, 2008. ISBN 9780791097106. 85 p. Grades 7–10.

Olive, M. Foster . *LSD* (Drugs: The Straight Facts). Chelsea House, 2008. ISBN 9780791097090. 103 p. Grades 7–10.

O'Shei, Tim. *Marconi and Tesla: Pioneers of Radio Communication* (Inventors Who Changed the World). Enslow, 2008. ISBN 9781598450767. 128 p. Grades 4–6.

O'Shei, Tim. *Philo T. Farnsworth: Visionary Inventor of Television* (Inventors Who Changed the World). Enslow, 2008. ISBN 9781598450750. 128 p. Grades K–3.

Oxlade, Chris. *Electricity* (Investigate). Heinemann, 2008. ISBN 9781432913892. 32 p. Grades K–3.

Parker, Steve. *Human Body: An Interactive Guide to the Inner Workings of the Body* (Discoverology Series). Barron's Educational Series, 2008. ISBN 978-0764160837. 32 p. Grades 4–7.

Pellant, Chris. *Fossils* (Rock Stars). Gareth Stevens, 2008. ISBN 9780836892232. 24 p. Grades 2–4.

Pellant, Chris. *Crystals and Gemstones* (Rock Stars). Gareth Stevens, 2008. ISBN 9780836892222. 24 p. Grades 2–4.

Pellant, Chris, and Helen Pellant. *Minerals* (Rock Stars). Gareth Stevens, 2008. ISBN 9780836892246. 24 p. Grades 2–4.

Pellant, Chris, and Helen Pellant. *Rocks* (Rock Stars). Gareth Stevens, 2008. ISBN 9780836892253. 24 p. Grades 2–4.

Peterson, Judy Monroe. *Exploring Space: Astronauts & Astronomers* (Extreme Scientists). PowerKids Press, 2008. ISBN 9781404245280. 24 p. Grades 3–5.

Peterson, Judy Monroe. *Weather Watchers: Climate Scientists* (Extreme Scientists). PowerKids Press, 2008. ISBN 9781404245273. 24 p. Grades 3–5.

Piehl, Janet. *Forest Fires* (Pull Ahead Books). Lerner Publications, 2007. ISBN 9780822579076. 32 p. Grades K–3.

Pipe, Jim. *Desert Survival* (Extreme Habitats). Gareth Stevens, 2007. ISBN 0836882458. 32 p. Grades 4–6.

Pipe, Jim. *Polar Region Survival* (Extreme Habitats). Gareth Stevens, 2007. ISBN 9780836882483 . 32 p. Grades 4–6.

Pitts, Zachary. *The Pebble First Guide to Rocks and Minerals* (Pebble Books). Capstone Press, 2008. ISBN 9781429617116. 32 p. Grades K–1.

Porterfield, Jason. *Downers: Depressant Abuse* (Incredibly Disgusting Drugs). Rosen, 2007. ISBN 9781404219571. 48 p. Grades 5–8.

Price, Sean. *Nicotine* (Junior Drug Awareness). Chelsea House, 2008. ISBN 9780791096963. 120 p. Grades 7–10.

Richardson, Gillian. *Kaboom! Explosions of All Kinds*. Annick Press, 2009. ISBN 9781554512041. 88 p. Grades 4–7.

Robinson, Matthew. *Inhalant Abuse* (Incredibly Disgusting Drugs). Rosen, 2007. ISBN 9781404219588. 48 p. Grades 5–8.

Robinson, Tom. *Jeff Bezos: Amazon.com Architect* (Publishing Pioneers). ABDO & Daughters, 2009. ISBN 9781604537598. 112 p. Grades 5–8.

Ross, Stewart. *Moon: Science, History, and Mystery*. Scholastic Press, 2009. ISBN 9780545127325. 128 p. Grades 4–6.

Salzmann, Mary Elizabeth. *Accordion to Zeppelin: Inventions from A to Z* (Let's Look A to Z). Super Sandcastle, 2008. ISBN 9781604530087. 32 p. Grades K–3.

Sawyer, Sarah. *Career Building Through Podcasting.* (Digital Career Building). Rosen, 2007. ISBN 1404219447. 64 p. Grades 7–10.

Schuh, Mari. *Loose Tooth* (Pebble Plus). Capstone Press, 2008. ISBN 978-1429612432. 24 p. Grades K–3.

Schuman, Michael A. *Bill Gates: Computer Mogul and Philanthropist* (People to Know Today). Enslow, 2008. ISBN 9780766026933. 128 p. Grades 5–8.

Scott, Elaine. *All About Sleep From A to Zzzz*. Viking, 2008. ISBN 9780670061884. 48 p. Grades 4–6.

Scott, Elaine. *Mars and the Search for Life*. Clarion Books, 2008. ISBN 978-0618766956. 64 p. Grades 5–8.

Serafini, Frank. *Looking Closely along the Shore*. Kids Can, 2008. ISBN 978-1554531417 40 p. Grades K–3.

Serafini, Frank. *Looking Closely through the Forest.* Kids Can, 2008. ISBN 9781554532124. 40 p. Grades K–3.

Seuling, Barbara. *It Never Rains in Antarctica: and Other Freaky Facts About Climate, Land, and Nature.* Picture Window Books, 2008. ISBN 9781404841178. 40 p. Grades 2–5.

Seuling, Barbara. *You Blink Twelve Times a Minute: And Other Freaky Facts About the Human Body.* Picture Window Books, 2008. ISBN 9781404841161. 40 p. Grades 2–5.

Sheff, Nic. *Tweak: Growing Up on Methamphetamines.* Ginee Seo Books, 2008. ISBN 9781416913627. 336 p. Grades 9–up.

Shuster, Kate. *Is There Other Life in the Universe?* (What Do You Think?). Heinemann, 2008. ISBN 9781432916725. 56 p. Grades 6–up.

Silverstein, Alvin, and Virginia B. Silverstein. *The Food Poisoning Update* (Disease Update). Enslow, 2007. ISBN 0766027481. 128 p. Grades 5–8.

Simon, Seymour. *The Human Body.* Collins, 2008. ISBN 9780060555429. 64 p. Grades 4–7.

Simon, Seymour. *Lungs: Your Respiratory System.* Collins, 2007. ISBN 0060546549. 32 p. Grades 2–5.

Simpson, Kathleen. *The Human Brain: Inside Your Body's Control Room* (National Geographic Investigates). National Geographic, 2009. ISBN 9781426304200. 64 p. Grades 4–8.

Smith, Miranda. *Human Body* (Navigators). Kingfisher, 2008. ISBN 9780753462294. 48 p. Grades 4–7.

Smith, Terri Peterson. *Alcohol* (Junior Drug Awareness). Chelsea House, 2008. ISBN 9780791097649. 119 p. Grades 7–10.

Sohn, Emily. *The Illuminating World of Light with Max Axiom, Super Scientist* (Graphic Science Graphic Novels). Capstone Press, 2007. ISBN 142960140X. 32 p. Grades 5–8.

Spilsbury, Louise, and Richard Spilsbury. *Space Pioneers: Astronauts* (Scientists at Work). Heinemann, 2007. ISBN 9781403499516. 32 p. Grades 4–6.

Stewart, David. *How Your Body Works* (Amaze). Franklin Watts, 2008. ISBN 9780531204559. 32 p. Grades 1–3.

Stewart, Melissa. *Extreme Coral Reef! Q&A* (Smithsonian Q & A). Collins, 2008. ISBN 9780061115776. 48 p. Grades K–3.

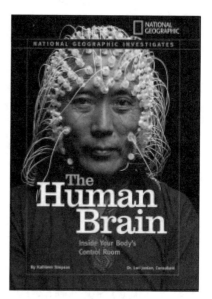

The Human Brain: Inside Your Body's Control Room **by Kathleen Simpson.**

Stewart, Melissa. *Extreme Nature! Q&A* (Smithsonian Q & A). Collins, 2006. ISBN 0060899360. 48 p. Grades K–3.

Stewart, Melissa. *Extreme Rocks & Minerals! Q&A* (Smithsonian Q & A). Collins, 2007. ISBN 9780060899820. 48 p. Grades K–3.

Strother, Ruth. *Bill Gates* (Essential Lives). ABDO & Daughters, 2007. ISBN 9781599288413. 112 p. Grades 5–8.

Swanson, Diane. *You Are Weird: Your Body's Peculiar Parts and Funny Functions.* Illustrated by Kathy Boake. Kids Can, 2009. ISBN 9781554532827. 40 p. Grades 3–6.

Secrets of the Deep: Marine Biologists **by Mike Unwin.**

Unwin, Mike. *Secrets of the Deep: Marine Biologists* (Scientists at Work). Heinemann, 2007. ISBN 9781403499523. 32 p. Grades 4–6.

Viegas, Jennifer. *Pierre Omidyar: The Founder of Ebay* (Internet Career Bios). Rosen, 2006. ISBN 1404207155. 112 p. Grades 5–8.

Walker, Richard. *How the Incredible Human Body Works. . . by the Brainwaves.* DK, 2007. ISBN 9780756631451. 64 p. Grades 2–4.

West, Krista. *Steroids and Other Performance-Enhancing Drugs* (Junior Drug Awareness). Chelsea House, 2008. ISBN 9780791097489. 112 p. Grades 7–10.

Winchester, Elizabeth Siris. *The Right Bite: Dentists as Detectives.* Franklin Watts, 2007. ISBN 0531187340. 64 p. Grades 4–8.

Woods, Michael, and Mary B. Woods. *Space Disasters* (Disasters Up Close). Lerner Publications, 2007. ISBN 9780822567752. 64 p. Grades 4–6.

Wyckoff, Edwin Brit. *Stopping Bullets with a Thread: Stephanie Kwolek and Her Incredible Invention* (Genius at Work! Great Inventor Biographies). Enslow, 2008. ISBN 9780766028500. 32 p. Grades K–3.

Young, Karen Romano. *Across the Wide Ocean: The Why, How, and Where of Navigation for Humans and Animals at Sea.* Collins, 2007. ISBN 9780060090869. 80 p. Grades 5–7.

Forensic Science

Adams, Bradley. *Forensic Anthropology* (Inside Forensic Science). Chelsea House, 2006. ISBN 0791091988. 128 p. Grades 9–up.

Adelman, Howard C., M.D. *Forensic Medicine* (Inside Forensic Science). Chelsea House, 2006. ISBN 0791089266. 128 p. Grades 9–up.

Allman, Toney. *Poisoning* (Crime Scene Investigations). Lucent Books, 2008. ISBN 9781420500646. 104 p. Grades 7–10.

Barnes, D. K., and D. B. Beres. *Killer at Large: Criminal Profilers and the Cases They Solve!* (24/7: Science Behind the Scenes: Forensic Files). Franklin Watts, 2007. ISBN 9780531175262. 64 p. Grades 4–8.

Beck, Esther. *Cool Biological Clues: What Hair, Bones, and Bugs Tell Us* (Checkerboard How-To Library: Cool CSI). ABDO & Daughters, 2009. ISBN 9781604534832. 32 p. Grades 4–6.

Beck, Esther. *Cool Crime Scene Basics* (Checkerboard How-To Library: Cool CSI). ABDO & Daughters, 2009. ISBN 9781604534849. 32 p. Grades 4–6.

Beck, Esther. *Cool Eyewitness Encounters: How's Your Memory?* (Checkerboard How-To Library: Cool CSI). ABDO & Daughters, 2009. ISBN 9781604534856. 32 p. Grades 4–6.

Bell, Suzanne. *Fakes and Forgeries* (Essentials of Forensic Science). Facts on File, 2008. ISBN 9780816055142. 108 p. Grades 7–12.

Beres, D. B. *Dusted and Busted! The Science of Fingerprinting* (24/7: Science Behind the Scenes: Forensic Files). Franklin Watts, 2007. ISBN 9780531154571. 64 p. Grades 4–8.

Blohm, Craig E. *The O. J. Simpson Murder Trial* (Crime Scene Investigations). Lucent Books, 2008. ISBN 9781420500387. 104 p. Grades 7–10.

Burns, Jan. *Kidnapping* (Crime Scene Investigations). Lucent Books, 2007. ISBN 9781590189894. 104 p. Grades 4–8.

Denega, Danielle. *Gut-Eating Bugs: Maggots Reveal the Time of Death!* (24/7: Science Behind the Scenes: Forensic Files). Franklin Watts, 2007. ISBN 0531175251. 64 p. Grades 4–8.

Denega, Danielle. *Have You Seen This Face? The Work of Forensic Artists* (24/7: Science Behind the Scenes: Forensic Files). Franklin Watts, 2007. ISBN 9780531154588. 64 p. Grades 4–8.

Denega, Danielle. *Skulls and Skeletons: True-Life Stories of Bone Detectives* (24/7: Science Behind the Scenes: Forensic Files). Franklin Watts, 2007. ISBN 0531120643. 64 p. Grades 4–8.

Gordon, Olivia. *Cold Case File: Murder in the Mountains* (Crime Solvers). Bearport Publishing, 2007. ISBN 9781597165471. 32 p. Grades 3–6.

Hamilton, Sue. *DNA Analysis: Forensic Fluids & Follicles* (Crime Scene Investigation). ABDO & Daughters, 2008. ISBN 9781599289878. 32 p. Grades 3–6.

Hamilton, Sue. *Fingerprint Analysis: Hints from Prints* (Crime Scene Investigation). ABDO & Daughters, 2008. ISBN 9781599289885. 32 p. Grades 3–6.

Hamilton, Sue. *Forensic Artist: Solving the Case with a Face* (Crime Scene Investigation). ABDO & Daughters, 2008. ISBN 9781599289892. 32 p. Grades 3–6.

Hamilton, Sue. *Forensic Ballistics: Styles of Projectiles* (Crime Scene Investigation). ABDO & Daughters, 2008. ISBN 9781599289908. 32 p. Grades 3–6.

Hamilton, Sue. *Forensic Entomology: Bugs & Bodies* (Crime Scene Investigation). ABDO & Daughters, 2008. ISBN 9781599289915. 32 p. Grades 3–6.

Hamilton, Sue. *How to Become a Crime Scene Investigator* (Crime Scene Investigation). ABDO & Daughters, 2008. ISBN 9781599289922. 32 p. Grades 3–6.

Innes, Brian. *DNA and Body Evidence* (Forensic Evidence). M.E. Sharpe, 2007. ISBN 9780765681157. 96 p. Grades 9–12.

Joyce, Jaime. *Bullet Proof! The Evidence That Guns Leave Behind* (24/7: Science Behind the Scenes: Forensic Files). Franklin Watts, 2007. ISBN 0531118207. 64 p. Grades 5–up.

Levine, Louis. *Forensic DNA Analysis* (Inside Forensic Science). Chelsea House, 2007. ISBN 0791089231. 128 p. Grades 8–12.

Mackay, Jenny. *Fingerprints and Impression Evidence* (Crime Scene Investigations). Lucent Books, 2007. ISBN 9781420500370. 104 p. Grades 4–8.

Morrison, Yvonne. *The DNA Gave It Away! Teens Solve Crime* (Shockwave: Science in Practice). Franklin Watts, 2008. ISBN 9780531188422. 32 p. Grades 5–9.

Murray, Julie. *Crime-Fighting Animals* (Going to Work: Animal Edition). Buddy Books, 2009. ISBN 9781604535617. 32 p. Grades 1–3.

Nardo, Don. *DNA Evidence* (Crime Scene Investigations). Gale Cengage, 2007. ISBN 9781590189511. 104 p. Grades 4–8.

Newton, Michael. *Celebrities and Crime* (Criminal Investigations). Chelsea House, 2008. ISBN 9780791094020. 112 p. Grades 7–10.

Newton, Michael. *Serial Killers* (Criminal Investigations). Chelsea House, 2008. ISBN 9780791094112. 120 p. Grades 7–up.

O'Brien, Susan. *Child Abduction and Kidnapping*. Chelsea House, 2008. ISBN 9780791094037. 135 p. Grades 7–10.

Parks, Peggy J. *Computer Hacking* (Crime Scene Investigations). Lucent Books, 2008. ISBN 9781420500356. 104 p. Grades 7–10.

Prokos, Anna. *Guilty by a Hair! Real-life DNA Matches!* (24/7: Science Behind the Scenes: Forensic Files). Franklin Watts, 2007. ISBN 0531118215. 64 p. Grades 4–8.

Rainis, Kenneth G. *Blood and DNA Evidence: Crime-Solving Science Experiments* (Forensic Science Projects). Enslow, 2006. ISBN 0766019586. 104 p. Grades 8–11.

Rainis, Kenneth G. *Fingerprints: Crime-Solving Science Experiments* (Forensic Science Projects). Enslow, 2006. ISBN 0766019608. 128 p. Grades 8–11.

Rainis, Kenneth G. *Hair, Clothing, and Tire Track Evidence: Crime-Solving Science Experiments* (Forensic Science Projects). Enslow, 2006. ISBN 0766027295. 128 p. Grades 7–up.

Stewart, Gail. *The Crime Scene Photographer* (Crime Scene Investigations). Lucent Books, 2008. ISBN 9781420500363. 104 p. Grades 7–up.

Stripp, Richard. *The Forensic Aspects of Poisons* (Inside Forensic Science). Chelsea House, 2007. ISBN 079109197X. 128 p. Grades 7–up.

Townsend, John. *Bone Detective* (Crabtree Contact). Crabtree Publishing, 2008. ISBN 9780778738060. 32 p. Grades 4–6.

Townsend, John. *Forensic Evidence: Prints* (Crabtree Contact). Crabtree Publishing, 2008. ISBN 9780778738336. 32 p. Grades 4–6.

West, David. *Detective Work with Ballistics* (Graphic Forensic Science). Rosen, 2008. ISBN 9781404214347. 48 p. Grades 4–7.

Yancey, Diane. *The Case of the Green River Killer* (Crime Scene Investigations). Lucent Books, 2007. ISBN 9781590189559. 104 p. Grades 7–10.

Yancey, Diane. *Tracking Serial Killers* (Crime Scene Investigations). Lucent Books, 2007. ISBN 9781590189856. 104 p. Grades 7–10.

Yancey, Diane. *The Zodiac Killer* (Crime Scene Investigations). Lucent Books, 2008. ISBN 9781420500639. 112 p. Grades 7–10.

Yount, Lisa. *Forensic Science: From Fibers to Fingerprints* (Milestones in Discovery and Invention). Chelsea House, 2006. ISBN 0816057516. 176 p. Grades 5–up.

Zedeck, Beth E. *Forensic Pharmacology* (Inside Forensic Science). Chelsea House, 2006. ISBN 0791089207. 128 p. Grades 9–12.

Chapter ———————— 9

Machines and the Military

Many boys (and you know which ones they are) can't get enough of books about vehicles, machines, and aspects of the military. Have these books on your shelves and you don't need to do booktalks—just put them in the hands of the right boys and let the reading begin.

BOOKTALKS

Gifford, Clive *Robots: Uncover the World of Artificial Intelligence through Fun Facts and Easy Projects* (Science Kids). Kingfisher, 2007. ISBN 9780753461259. 48 p. Grades 3–5.

This book has pictures of many robots that are good at doing many different things. Most of them are controlled by computers, and you will not believe what they can do!

- Check out the jet wash, the giant robot arm that can clean jumbo jets in about three hours. It would take a bunch of people about twelve hours to do the same work. Its picture is on page 11.

- Look at the robot snake on page 16—it can slide through pipes. Or, on the same page, the robot dog! Would you like one for a pet? There are guard dog robots on page 31, too.

- Robots are often used in the movies. Check out some famous ones on pages 40 and 41.

- Then there are projects you can do—like build your own model robot.

It is a fun book to look through and to learn from.

Sandler, Michael. *Pararescuemen in Action* (Special Ops). Bearport Publishing, 2008. ISBN 9781597166331. 32 p. Grades 3–7.

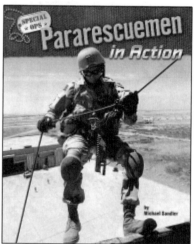

Pararescuemen are parachute jumpers and are part of the U.S. Air Force. They perform the world's toughest rescues. This is a job that is for men only—women are not allowed to join. A lot of their missions happen during wartime. If a plane goes down, pararescuemen search for it.

This special operations squad started in World War II, when an army plane flying on a top secret mission crashed. Almost everyone parachuted in time, but they were in a jungle in enemy territory and needed help. Three airmen went in and rescued them. The Air Force decided to create six permanent teams of PJs—which stands for pararescue jumpers.

So what do you have to do to be a PJ? The training is really tough. Guys in training may have to do as many as 1,000 sit-ups a day! They may have to eat bugs and collect dew so they have water to drink. And they have to learn to use a lot of special equipment.

Pararescuemen in Action by Michael Sandler.

Take a look at this neat book. Would you like to join the pararescuemen?

Spradlin, Michael. *Texas Rangers: Legendary Lawmen*. Illustrations by Roxie Munro. Walker Books, 2008. ISBN 9780802780966. Unpaged. Grades 3–5.

When American settlers started moving to Texas in the 1820s, they realized they

Texas Rangers: Legendary Lawmen by Michael Spradlin.

needed protection from bandits and Indian attacks. Their governor, Stephen Austin, started a group of volunteers to defend Texas and the "Texians" who lived there whenever danger arose. They called them Ranger Companies —and there have been Texas Rangers ever since.

Read all about these adventurous, valiant men. Some of the facts you'll learn include:

- Thirty-two Rangers went into the Alamo to help out during its attack. They all were killed.

- "Big Foot" Wallace's real name was William. He was tall and had big feet! His group of Rangers chased the Mexican army back to Mexico in 1841, but got lost going back—and were captured by their enemies and taken back into Mexico. Their attempts to escape made the president of Mexico order that every tenth ranger should be shot by a firing squad. The jailers passed around a jar of beans. If a Ranger got a black one, he was safe. If he got a white one, they shot him.

- A Texas Ranger named John B. Armstrong captured John Wesley Hardin, who had killed more than 20 men by the time he was 22 years old. It was a daring and dangerous arrest.

- Texas Rangers caught the famous bank robbers Bonnie Parker and Clyde Barrow.

This is an interesting book!

WORTH READING

Nonfiction books with "boy appeal" that have received positive reviews in *Booklist*, *Horn Book Guide*, and/or *School Library Journal*.

Abramson, Andra Serlin. *Fighter Planes* (Up Close). Sterling, 2008. ISBN 978-1402747960. 28 p. Grades 2–6.

Abramson, Andra Serlin. *Fire Engines* (Up Close). Sterling, 2008. ISBN 978-1402747984. 28 p. Grades 2–6.

Abramson, Andra Serlin. *Heavy Equipment* (Up Close). Sterling, 2008. ISBN 140-2747993. 24 p. Grades 2–4.

Abramson, Andra Serlin. *Race Cars* (Up Close). Sterling, 2008. ISBN 978-1402756412. 28 p. Grades 4–6.

Adams, Simon. *Artillery* (War Machines). Smart Apple Media, 2008. ISBN 978-1599202266. 32 p. Grades 4–6.

Adams, Simon. *Tanks* (War Machines). Smart Apple Media, 2008. ISBN 978-1599202242. 32 p. Grades 4–6.

Adams, Simon. *Warplanes* (War Machines). Smart Apple Media, 2008. ISBN 978-1599202235. 32 p. Grades 4–6.

Adams, Simon. *Warships* (War Machines). Smart Apple Media, 2008. ISBN 978-1599202259. 32 p. Grades 4–6.

Allman, Toney. *The Nexo Robot*. Norwood House, 2009. ISBN 9781599533421. 48 p. Grades 4–6.

Angelo, Joseph A. *Robot Spacecraft* (Frontiers in Space). Facts on File, 2006. ISBN 0816057737. 32 p. Grades 9–12.

Angelo, Joseph A. *Rockets* (Frontiers in Space). Facts on File, 2006. ISBN 081-6057710. 208 p. Grades 9–12.

Angelo, Joseph A. *Satellites* (Frontiers in Space). Facts on File, 2006. ISBN 081-6057729. 336 p. Grades 9–12.

Aylmore, Angela. *I Like Cars* (Things I Like). Heinemann, 2007. ISBN 1403492689. 24 p. Grades K–2.

Aylmore, Angela. *I Like Planes* (Things I Like). Heinemann, 2007. ISBN 1403492670. 24 p. Grades K–2.

Balmer, Alden J. *Doc Fizzix Mousetrap Racers: The Complete Builder's Manual*. Fox Chapel Publishing, 2008. ISBN 9781565233591. 144 p. Grades 6–up.

Bearce, Stephanie. *All About Electric and Hybrid Cars and Who's Driving Them* (Tell Your Parents). Mitchell Lane, 2009. ISBN 9781584157632. 48 p. Grades 4–7.

Bledsoe, Karen, and Glen Bledsoe. *Fighter Planes: Fearless Fliers* (Mighty Military Machines). Enslow, 2006. ISBN 0766026604. 48 p. Grades 4–9.

Bledsoe, Karen, and Glen Bledsoe. *Helicopters: High-flying Heroes* (Mighty Military Machines). Enslow, 2006. ISBN 0766026639. 48 p. Grades 4–9.

Bos, Samone. *Super Structures*. DK, 2008. ISBN 9780756640880. 80 p. Grades 5–8.

Bradley, Michael. *Corvette* (Cars). Marshall Cavendish, 2008. ISBN 978-0761429760. 32 p. Grades 4–5.

Bradley, Michael. *Ferrari* (Cars). Marshall Cavendish, 2008. ISBN 9780761429784. 32 p. Grades 4–5.

Bradley, Michael. *Ford Truck* (Cars). Marshall Cavendish, 2008. ISBN 978-0761429791. 32 p. Grades 4–5.

Bradley, Michael. *Hummer* (Cars). Marshall Cavendish, 2008. ISBN 978-0761429814. 32 p. Grades 4–5.

Bradley, Michael. *Mustang* (Cars). Marshall Cavendish, 2008. ISBN 978-0761429821. 32 p. Grades 4–5.

Bradley, Michael. *T-Bird* (Cars). Marshall Cavendish, 2008. ISBN 9780761429838. 32 p. Grades 4–5.

Brennan, Kristine. *Danica Patrick* (Modern Role Models). Mason Crest Publishers, 2008. ISBN 9781422204870. 64 p. Grades 6–up.

Brinster, Dick. *Jeff Gordon* (Race Car Legends). Chelsea House, 2007. ISBN 9780791087602. 80 p. Grades 4–6.

Camelo, Wilson. *The U.S. Air Force and Military Careers* (The U.S. Armed Forces and Military Careers). Enslow, 2006. ISBN 0766025241. 128 p. Grades 7–10.

Chapman, Caroline S. *Battles & Weapons* (Picture That). Two-Can Publishing, 2007. ISBN 1587285886. 64 p. Grades 3–6.

Clausen-Grace, Nicki. *Demolition Derbies* (The Thrill of Racing). Rourke Publishing, 2008. ISBN 9781604723687. 24 p. Grades 3–4.

Clausen-Grace, Nicki. *Sprint Car Racing* (The Thrill of Racing). Rourke Publishing, 2008. ISBN 9781604723779. 24 p. Grades 3–4.

Cooper, Wade. *On the Road* (Scholastic Reader Level 1). Cartwheel Books, 2008. ISBN 9780545007207. 32 p. Grades K–3.

Coppendale, Jean, and Ian Graham. *The Great Big Book of Mighty Machines*. Firefly Books, 2009. ISBN 9781554075218. 160 p. Grades K–3.

Curlee, Lynn. *Train*. Atheneum, 2009. ISBN 9781416948483. 48 p. Grades 4–6.

David, Jack. *Choppers* (Torque: Motorcycles). Children's Press, 2007. ISBN 978-0531184769. 24 p. Grades 3–5.

David, Jack. *Cruisers* (Torque: Motorcycles). Children's Press, 2007. ISBN 978-0531184783. 24 p. Grades 3–5.

David, Jack. *Enduro Motorcycles* (Torque: Motorcycles). Children's Press, 2007. ISBN 9780531184790. 24 p. Grades 3–5.

David, Jack. *F-14 Tomcats* (Torque: Military Machines). Children's Press, 2008. ISBN 9780531216439.. 24 p. Grades 3–7.

David, Jack. *F-15 Eagles* (Torque: Military Machines). Children's Press, 2008. ISBN 9780531216446.. 24 p. Grades 3–7.

David, Jack. *HH-60 Pave Hawk Helicopters* (Torque: Military Machines). Children's Press, 2008. ISBN 9780531210529. 24 p. Grades 3–7.

David, Jack. *Motocross Racing* (Torque: Action Sports). Children's Press, 2007. ISBN 9780531184912. 24 p. Grades 3–5.

Dawson, Dylan. *Lincoln Logs Building Manual: Graphic Instructions for 37 World-Famous Designs*. Sterling, 2007. ISBN 9781402750779. 144 p. Grades 3–8.

Dawson, Dylan. *Tinkertoy Building Manual: Graphic Instructions for 37 World-Famous Designs*. Sterling, 2007. ISBN 9781402750786. 144 p. Grades 3–8.

Dayton, Connor. *Greg Biffle* (Nascar Champions). Rosen, 2007. ISBN 1404238166. 24 p. Grades 2–5.

Dayton, Connor. *Jamie McMurray* (Nascar Champions). Rosen, 2007. ISBN 1404238131. 24 p. Grades 2–5.

Dayton, Connor. *Jeff Burton* (Nascar Champions). Rosen, 2007. ISBN 1404238123. 24 p. Grades 2–5.

Doeden, Matt. *The U.S. Air Force* (Pebble Plus). Capstone Press, 2008. ISBN 9781429617321. 24 p. Grades 1–2.

Doeden, Matt. *The U.S. Army* (Pebble Plus). Capstone Press, 2008. ISBN 9781429617338. 24 p. Grades 1–2.

Doeden, Matt. *The U.S. Coast Guard* (Pebble Plus). Capstone Press, 2008. ISBN 9781429617345. 24 p. Grades 1–2.

The U.S. Air Force by Matt Doeden.

Doeden, Matt. *Weapons of Ancient Times* (Weapons of War). Capstone Press, 2008. ISBN 9781429619677. 32 p. Grades K–3.

Doeden, Matt. *Weapons of the Middle Ages* (Weapons of War). Capstone Press, 2008. ISBN 9781429619691. 32 p. Grades K–3.

Egan, Erin. *Hottest Race Cars* (Wild Wheels!). Enslow, 2007. ISBN 0766028712. 48 p. Grades 4–6.

Fleischman, John. *Black and White Airmen: Their True History.* Houghton Mifflin, 2007. ISBN 0618562974. 16 p. Grades 6–up.

Franks, Katie. *I Want to Be a Race Car Driver* (Dream Jobs). PowerKids Press, 2007. ISBN 9781404236233. 24 p. Grades 2–4.

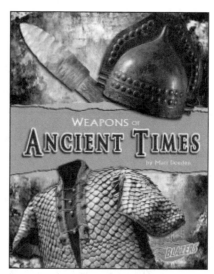

Weapons of Ancient Times by Matt Doeden.

Gifford, Clive. *Ducati* (Red-Hot Bikes). Sea to Sea Publications, 2008. ISBN 9781597711357. 32 p. Grades 3–6.

Gifford, Clive. *Honda* (Red-Hot Bikes). Sea to Sea Publications, 2008. ISBN 9781597711364. 32 p. Grades 3–6.

Gifford, Clive. *Robots.* Atheneum, 2008. ISBN 9781416964148. 32 p. Grades 4–6.

Gilpin, Daniel. *BMW* (Red-Hot Bikes). Sea to Sea Publications, 2008. ISBN 9781597711340. 32 p. Grades 3–6.

Gilpin, Daniel. *Triumph* (Red-Hot Bikes). Sea to Sea Publications, 2008. ISBN 9781597711371. 32 p. Grades 3–6.

Gitlin, Marty. *Jeff Gordon: Racing's Brightest Star* (Heroes of Racing). Enslow, 2008. ISBN 9780766029972. 128 p. Grades 4–6.

Gitlin, Marty. *Jimmie Johnson: Racing Champ* (Heroes of Racing). Enslow, 2008. ISBN 9780766029996. 128 p. Grades 4–6.

Golden, Erin. *Big Bigger Biggest Trucks and Diggers—With DVD* (Caterpillar). Chronicle Books, 2008. ISBN 9780811864329. 33 p. Grades K–3.

Goldish, Meish. *Freaky-Big Airplanes* (World's Biggest). Bearport Publishing, 2009. ISBN 9781597169592. 24 p. Grades 2–3.

Goodman, Michael E. *Montreal Canadiens* (The NHL: History and Heroes). Creative Education, 2008. ISBN 9781583416181. 42 p. Grades 4–6.

Goodman, Michael E. *The Story of the New York Rangers* (The NHL: History and Heroes). Creative Education, 2008. ISBN 9781583416198. 48 p. Grades 4–6.

Goodman, Susan E. *Motorcycles!* (Step into Reading). Random House, 2007. ISBN 9780375941160. 48 p. Grades 1–3.

Goodstein, Madeline. *Wheels! Science Projects with Bicycles, Skateboards, and Skates* (Score! Sports Science Projects). Enslow, 2009. ISBN 9780766031074. 104 p. Grades 4–7.

Graham, Ian. *Aircraft* (How Machines Work). Smart Apple Media, 2008. ISBN 9781599202921. 32 p. Grades 3–5.

Graham, Ian. *Attack Fighters* (Designed for Success). Heinemann, 2008. ISBN 9781432916442. 32 p. Grades 4–6.

Graham, Ian. *Emergency Vehicles* (How Machines Work). Smart Apple Media, 2008. ISBN 9781599202945. 32 p. Grades 3–6.

Graham, Ian. *Fast Cars* (How Machines Work). Smart Apple Media, 2008. ISBN 9781599202891. 32 p. Grades 3–6.

Graham, Ian. *Machines and Inventions* (World of Wonder). Children's Press, 2008. ISBN 9780531204274. 32 p. Grades 1–4.

Graham, Ian. *Military Technology*. Smart Apple Media, 2008. ISBN 9781599201658. 46 p. Grades 7–10.

Graham, Ian. *Military Vehicles* (Designed for Success). Heinemann, 2008. ISBN 9781432916459. 32 p. Grades 4–6.

Off-Road Vehicles by **Ian Graham.**

Graham, Ian. *Off-Road Vehicles* (Designed for Success). Heinemann, 2008. ISBN 978-1432916466. 32 p. Grades 4–6.

Graham, Ian. *Race Cars* (Designed for Success). Heinemann, 2008. ISBN 9781432916473. 32 p. Grades 4–6.

Graham, Ian. *Sports Cars* (Designed for Success). Heinemann, 2008. ISBN 9781432916480. 32 p. Grades 4–6.

Graham, Ian. *Superbikes* (Designed for Success). Heinemann, 2008. ISBN 9781432916503. 32 p. Grades 4–6.

Graham, Ian. *Superboats* (Designed for Success). Heinemann, 2008. ISBN 9781432916497. 32 p. Grades 4–6.

Graham, Ian. *You Wouldn't Want to Be in the First Submarine! An Undersea Expedition You'd Rather Avoid* (You Wouldn't Want to . . .). Franklin Watts, 2008. ISBN 9780531219126. 32 p. Grades 3–5.

Greve, Tom. *Formula One Racing* (The Thrill of Racing). Rourke Publishing, 2008. ISBN 9781604723700. 24 p. Grades 3–4.

Greve, Tom. *Indy Racing* (The Thrill of Racing). Rourke Publishing, 2008. ISBN 9781604723724. 24 p. Grades 3–4.

Greve, Tom. *Stock Car Racing* (The Thrill of Racing). Rourke Publishing, 2008. ISBN 9781604723755. 24 p. Grades 3–4.

Harmon, Daniel E. *First Car Smarts* (Get $mart With Your Money). Rosen, 2009. ISBN 9781435852693. 64 p. Grades 8–12.

Harris, Nicholas. *A Year at a Construction Site* (Time Goes By). Millbrook Press, 2008. ISBN 9781580135498. 24 p. Grades K–3.

Hinman, Bonnie. *Extreme Cycling with Dale Holmes* (Robbie Readers). Mitchell Lane, 2006. ISBN 158415487X. 32 p. Grades 2–4.

Hodgkins, Fran. *How People Learned to Fly* (Let's-Read-and-Find-Out Science 2). Collins, 2007. ISBN 9780060295585. 33 p. Grades 1–3.

Hopwood, James. *Cool Distance Assistants: Fun Science Projects to Propel Things* (Cool Science). Checkerboard Library, 2007. ISBN 9781599289069. 32 p. Grades 4–6.

Hudak, Heather C. *Extreme BMX* (Extreme). Weigl Publishers, 2008. ISBN 978-1590369104. 32 p. Grades 4–8.

Hudak, Heather C. *Extreme MotoX* (Extreme). Weigl Publishers, 2008. ISBN 978-1590369189. 32 p. Grades 4–8.

Jacobs, Paul DuBois. *NASCAR ABCs*. Gibbs Smith, 2007. ISBN 9781423601197. 32 p. Grades K–2.

Jennings, Terry. *Construction Vehicles* (How Machines Work). Smart Apple Media, 2008. ISBN 9781599202938. 32 p. Grades 3–6.

Jennings, Terry. *Trucks* (How Machines Work). Smart Apple Media, 2008. ISBN 9781599202914. 32 p. Grades 3–6.

Juettner, Bonnie. *Hybrid Cars* (A Great Idea Series). Norwood House Press, 2009. ISBN 9781599531939. 48 p. Grades 4–7.

Kenney, Sean. *Cool Cars and Trucks*. Henry Holt, 2009. ISBN 9780805087611. 32 p. Grades K–3.

Kortenkamp, Steve. *Space Robots* (Blazers). Capstone Press, 2009. ISBN 978-1429623223. 32 p. Grades 2–3.

Levine, Shar, and Leslie Johnstone. *The Ultimate Guide to Your Microscope*. Sterling, 2008. ISBN 9781402743290. 144 p. Grades 5–9.

Lindeen, Mary. *Ships* (Blastoff Readers: Mighty Machines). Bellwether, 2007. ISBN 9781600140600. 24 p. Grades K–3.

Lindeen, Mary. *Tractors* (Blastoff Readers: Mighty Machines) Bellwether, 2007. ISBN 9781600140617. 24 p. Grades K–3.

Lindeen, Mary. *Trains* (Blastoff Readers: Mighty Machines). Bellwether, 2007. ISBN 9781600140624. 24 p. Grades K–3.

Lindeen, Mary. *Trucks* (Blastoff Readers: Mighty Machines). Bellwether, 2007. ISBN 9781600140631. 24 p. Grades K–3.

Low, William. *Machines Go to Work*. Henry Holt, 2009. ISBN 9780805087598. 42 p. Grades K–1.

Maass, Robert. *Little Trucks with Big Jobs*. Henry Holt, 2007. ISBN 9780805077483. 32 p. Grades K–1.

MacDonald, James. *Dale Earnhardt, Jr.: Racing's Living Legacy* (Heroes of Racing). Enslow, 2008. ISBN 9780766029965. 128 p. Grades 4–6.

Manning, Mick. *Viking Longship* (Fly on the Wall). Frances Lincoln, 2006. ISBN 1845074653. 40 p. Grades 3–5.

Marks, Jennifer L. *Mean Machines: A Spot-it Challenge* (A+ Books). Capstone Press, 2009. ISBN 9781429622219. 32 p. Grades K–2.

Mello, Tara Baukus. *Danica Patrick* (Race Car Legends). Chelsea House, 2007. ISBN 9780791091265. 71 p. Grades 4–6.

Mello, Tara Baukus. *Mark Martin* (Race Car Legends). Chelsea House, 2007. ISBN 9780791086643. 72 p. Grades 4–6.

Mello, Tara Baukus. *The Need for Speed* (Race Car Legends: Collector's Edition). Chelsea House, 2007. ISBN 9780791086674. 64 p. Grades 4–6.

Morganelli, Adrianna. *Formula One* (Automania!). Crabtree Publishing, 2006. ISBN 9780778730316. 32 p. Grades 4–6.

Morris, Neil. *Should Substance-using Athletes Be Banned for Life?* (What Do You Think?). Heinemann, 2008. ISBN 9781432916763. 56 p. Grades 7–up.

Nardo, Don. *Robots* (Monsters). KidHaven Press, 2007. ISBN 9780737737790. 48 p. Grades 4–6.

Nielsen, L. Michelle. *Vintage Cars 1919–1930* (Automania!). Crabtree Publishing, 2006. ISBN 9780778730118. 32 p. Grades 4–6.

***Green Berets in Action* by Marc Tyler Nobleman.**

Nobleman, Marc Tyler. *Green Berets in Action* (Special Ops). Bearport Publishing, 2008. ISBN 9781597166317. 32 p. Grades 4–6.

Oxlade, Chris. *Motorcycles* (How Machines Work). Smart Apple Media, 2008. ISBN 9781599202907. 32 p. Grades 3–6.

Parr, Ann. *The Allisons* (Race Car Legends). Chelsea House, 2007. ISBN 9780791086940. 77 p. Grades 4–6.

Poolos, J. *Wild About ATVs* (Wild Rides). PowerKids Press, 2007. ISBN 1404237933. 24 p. Grades 2–6.

Poolos, J. *Wild About Hot Rods* (Wild Rides). PowerKids Press, 2007. ISBN 1404237909. 24 p. Grades 2–6.

Poolos, J. *Wild About Monster Trucks* (Wild Rides). PowerKids Press, 2007. ISBN 1404237917. 24 p. Grades 2–6.

Reed, Jennifer. *The U.S. Marine Corps* (Pebble Plus). Capstone Press, 2008. ISBN 9781429617352. 24 p. Grades 1–2.

Reed, Jennifer. *The U.S. Navy* (Pebble Plus). Capstone Press, 2008. ISBN 9781429617369. 24 p. Grades 1–2.

Rice, Earle, Jr. *The U.S. Army and Military Careers* (The U.S. Armed Forces and Military Careers). Enslow, 2007. ISBN 076602699X. 128 p. Grades 5–up.

Rigsby, Mike. *Amazing Rubber Band Cars: Easy-to-Build Wind-up Racers, Models, and Toys*. Chicago Review Press, 2007. ISBN 9781556527364. 128 p. Grades 4–8.

Riley, Gail Blasser. *Delta Force in Action* (Special Ops). Bearport Publishing, 2008. ISBN 9781597166355. 32 p. Grades 4–6.

Roberts, Cynthia. *Rescue Helicopters* (Machines at Work). Child's World, 2007. ISBN 9781592968350. 24 p. Grades 2–4.

Roberts, Cynthia. *Tow Trucks* (Machines at Work). Child's World, 2007. ISBN 9781592968367. 24 p. Grades 2–4.

Rogers, Hal. *Trains* (Machines at Work). Child's Word, 2008. ISBN 9781592969609. 24 p. Grades K–1.

Roselius, J. Chris. *Matt Kenseth: Speeding to Victory* (Heroes of Racing). Enslow, 2008. ISBN 9780766030008. 128 p. Grades 4–6.

Sandler, Michael. *Army Rangers in Action* (Special Ops). Bearport Publishing, 2008. ISBN 9781597166324. 32 p. Grades 4–6.

Sandler, Michael. *Marine Force Recon in Action* (Special Ops). Bearport Publishing, 2008. ISBN 9781597166348. 32 p. Grades 4–6.

Scholastic. *Mega Trucks*. Scholastic Press, 2008. ISBN 9780439850568. 32 p. Grades K–3.

Siy, Alexandra. *Cars on Mars: Roving the Red Planet*. Charlesbridge, 2009. ISBN 9781570914621. 64 p. Grades 5–8.

Smedman, Lisa. *From Boneshakers to Choppers: The Rip-Roaring History of Motorcycles*. Annick Press, 2007. ISBN 1554510163. 120 p. Grades 5–8.

Smith, Miranda. *Speed Machines and Other Record-Breaking Vehicles*. Kingfisher, 2009. ISBN 9780753462874. 64 p. Grades 4–6.

***Delta Force in Action* by Gail Blasser Riley.**

Smithsonian Institution. *Extreme Aircraft! Q&A*. Collins, 2007. ISBN 0060899433. 48 p. Grades K–2.

Sneed, Dani. *Ferris Wheel! George Ferris and His Amazing Invention* (Genius at Work! Great Inventor Biographies). Enslow, 2008. ISBN 9780766028340. 32 p. Grades K–3.

Souter, Gerry. *Military Rifles: Fierce Firepower* (Mighty Military Machines). Enslow, 2006. ISBN 0766026620. 48 p. Grades 3–9.

Spalding, Lee-Anne Trimble. *Off-Road Racing* (The Thrill of Racing). Rourke Publishing, 2008. ISBN 9781604723762. 24 p. Grades 3–4.

Spalding, Lee-Anne Trimble. *Sport Bike Racing* (The Thrill of Racing). Rourke Publishing, 2008. ISBN 9781604723748. 24 p. Grades 3–4.

Spalding, Lee-Anne Trimble. *GoKart Racing (*The Thrill of Racing). Rourke Publishing, 2008. ISBN 9781604723717. 24 p. Grades 3–4.

Spalding, Lee-Anne Trimble. *Monster Truck Racing* (The Thrill of Racing. Rourke Publishing, 2008. ISBN 9781604723731. 24 p. Grades 3–4.

Spilsbury, Richard. *At the Construction Site* (Perspectives). Raintree, 2008. ISBN 9781410931771. 32 p. Grades 4–6.

Stein, R. Conrad. *The U.S. Marine Corps and Military Careers* (The U.S. Armed Forces and Military Careers). Enslow, 2006. ISBN 0766025217. 128 p. Grades 5–8.

Stewart, Mark. *NASCAR at the Track* (The Science of Nascar). Lerner Publications, 2007. ISBN 9780822587415. 48 p. Grades 4–6.

NASCAR Designed to Win **by Mark Stewart and Mike Kennedy.**

Stewart, Mark, and Mike Kennedy. *NASCAR Designed to Win* (The Science of Nascar). Lerner Publications, 2007. ISBN 978-0822590064. 48 p. Grades 4–6.

Stewart, Mark. *NASCAR in the Driver's Seat* (The Science of Nascar). Lerner Publications, 2008. ISBN 9780822587378. 48 p. Grades 4–6.

Stewart, Mark. *NASCAR in the Pits* (The Science of Nascar). Lerner Publications, 2007. ISBN 9780822587385. 48 p. Grades 4–6.

Sutherland, Jonathan, and Diane Canwell. *Aircraft Carriers* (Amazing Ships). Gareth Stevens, 2007. ISBN 9780836883763. 32 p. Grades 4–6.

Sutherland, Jonathan, and Diane Canwell. *Container Ships and Oil Tankers* (Amazing Ships). Gareth Stevens, 2007. ISBN 9780836883770. 32 p. Grades 4–6.

Sutherland, Jonathan, and Diane Canwell. *Cruise Ships* (Amazing Ships). Gareth Stevens, 2007. ISBN 9780836883787. 32 p. Grades 4–6.

Sutherland, Jonathan, and Diane Canwell. *Submarines* (Amazing Ships). Gareth Stevens, 2007. ISBN 9780836883794. 32 p. Grades 4–6.

Teitelbaum, Michael. *Humvees: High Mobility in the Field* (Mighty Military Machines). Enslow, 2006. ISBN 0766026612. 48 p. Grades 4–10.

Teitelbaum, Michael. *Submarines: Underwater Stealth* (Mighty Military Machines). Enslow, 2006. ISBN 0766026590. 48 p. Grades 4–10.

Todd, Traci N. *C Is for Caboose.* Chronicle Books, 2007. ISBN 9780811856430 40 p. Grades K–4.

Todd, Traci N. *T Is for Tugboat: Navigating the Seas from A to Z.* Chronicle Books, 2008. ISBN 9780811860949. 40 p. Grades 2–4.

Tourville, Amanda Doering. *Bulldozers* (Mighty Machines). Magic Wagon, 2009. ISBN 9781602706217. 32 p. Grades K–2.

Tourville, Amanda Doering. *Cranes* (Mighty Machines). Magic Wagon, 2009. ISBN 9781602706224. 32 p. Grades K–3.

Tourville, Amanda Doering. *Dump Trucks* (Mighty Machines). Magic Wagon, 2009. ISBN 9781602706231. 32 p. Grades K–3.

Wilker, Josh, and G. S. Prentzas. *A. J. Foyt* (Race Car Legends: Collector's Edition). Chelsea House, 2007. ISBN 9780791087596. 72 p. Grades 4–6.

Wolny, Philip. *High-Risk Construction Work: Life Building Skyscrapers, Bridges, and Tunnels* (Extreme Careers). Rosen, 2008. ISBN 9781404217898. 64 p. Grades 5–8.

Woods, Bob. *Hottest Motorcycles* (Wild Wheels!). Enslow, 2007. ISBN 0766028747. 48 p. Grades 4–7.

Woods, Bob. *Hottest Muscle Cars* (Wild Wheels!). Enslow, 2007. ISBN 978-0766028722. 48 p. Grades 4–7.

Woods, Bob. *Hottest Sports Cars* (Wild Wheels!). Enslow, 2007. ISBN 978-0766028739. 48 p. Grades 4–7.

Woods, Bob. *NASCAR Tech* (The World of Nascar). Child's World, 2008. ISBN 9781602530782. 32 p. Grades 4–6.

YES Magazine Editors. *Robots: From Everyday to Out of This World.* Kids Can, 2008. ISBN 9781554532032. 48 p. Grades 3–6.

Yomtov, Nel. *Navy SEALs in Action* (Special Ops). Bearport Publishing, 2008. ISBN 9781597166300. 32 p. Grades 3–6.

Zimmermann, Karl. *Ocean Liners: Crossing and Cruising the Seven Seas.* Boyds Mills, 2008. ISBN 9781590785522. 48 p. Grades 4–6.

Zobel, Derek. *F-22 Raptors* (Torque: Military Machines). Children's Press, 2008. ISBN 9780531216453. 24 p. Grades 3–7.

Zronik, John. *Street Cred* (Automania!). Crabtree Publishing, 2006. ISBN 978-0778730064. 32 p. Grades 4–6.

Chapter 10

Around the World

Human history is full of action-packed stories and fascinating time periods. Play up the aspects of these books that boys love—the action, the blood-and-guts, and the heroic deeds. For boys who dream of adventure, these books about pirates, castles, Vikings, gladiators, Aztecs, and mummies will send them on a trip around the world and throughout history.

BOOKTALKS

Bruce, Julia. *Conquest! Can You Build a Roman City?* (Step into History). Illustrated by Peter Dennis. Enslow, 2009. ISBN 9780766034785. 32 p. Grades 3–6.

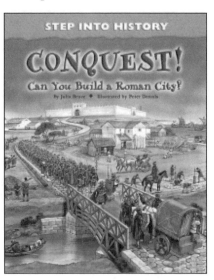

Conquest! Can You Build a Roman City? by Julia Bruce.

You are a general in the Roman army in the first century AD. Rome has a special assignment for you. Rome has been conquering the people all around it and building the size and territory of its empire. Its leaders want you to conquer a barbarian region and establish it as a colony. If you succeed, you will be the governor. You must build a fort and a city and be fair and honest.

Exactly how are you going to do this?

This book tells us how the Romans conquered new territory and built cities. First the army came into a region, set up camp, and then had a battle with the barbarians. The Roman army was really a great fighting unit. The barbarians were usually defeated fairly quickly.

The Romans knew that more resistance was likely to take place, so next they built a fort—and inside the fort they built living and working spaces for the army and the people who traveled with the army. They needed to build aqueducts to bring in water, and eventually all sorts of public and private buildings.

The drawings here are great fun to look at. They really show us how the Romans were so efficient 2,000 years ago.

Bruce, Julia. *Siege! Can You Capture a Castle?* (Step into History). Illustrated by Peter Dennis. Enslow, 2009. ISBN 9780766034754. 32 p. Grades 3–6.

Siege! Can You Capture a Castle? by Julia Bruce.

It is the year 1300, and it's up to you. Your king has commanded you, a loyal troop commander, to put down a rebellion of the nobles. You know which one to go for: the leader of the rebels.

You talk to him, you try to come to an agreement. Nothing seems to be working. Now it is time to try force. You are going to have to storm his castle, conduct a siege! That means that no one can go in or out of the castle, and, with time and luck, the people in the castle may surrender —if they do not starve to death first.

So how exactly are you going to make this happen?

This book gives us a grand look at how it all works, and some of the weapons and attack strategies that might get you to your goal.

Take a look at the pictures in the book, then notice a few interesting things:

- Spies are good things to have on both sides. You want to know what the enemy is going to do next.

- Try to cut off the fresh water supply in the castle. The defenders cannot last long at all without it.

- The weapons in 1300 were mostly bows and arrows, swords, and spears for personal combat, not to mention axes, maces, and something called a glaive. Find out what it is on page 11.

- Look at the attack camp—what do you need, and how can you hide what you are doing from the enemy?

- And inside, what can the defenders of the castle do? Learn what an oubliette is (and try not to get put in one) and a murder hole.

If you are at all interested in military strategy and warfare, this is the book for you.

Malam, John. *You Wouldn't Want to Live in Pompeii! A Volcanic Eruption You'd Rather Avoid* (You Wouldn't Want to . . .). Illustrated by David Antram. Franklin Watts, 2008. ISBN 9780531187487. 32 p. Grades 4–8.

It is almost 2,000 years ago, AD 79 to be exact, and you live in a town in southern Italy called Pompeii. The bad news is that you are a slave. Once you dreamt about being a writer or a poet or a philosopher, but your luck turned bad when you were captured by pirates and sold as a slave. Now you live with a family and take care of and help teach their son. Your life isn't *too* bad.

But that is about to change. A big mountain near Pompeii called Mount Vesuvius has been doing some strange things. Smoke and steam come out the top, and things rumble quite a bit. No one seems to be too worried until the day when light gray ash starts raining down on everything and everybody. By noon Vesuvius is erupting, and ash and pumice (small stones) are raining down. The streets are filling up with rocks. Roofs cave in from the weight. You may not be able to open the door to get out of the house. You have trouble breathing if you go outside.

Outside things are not good. There are earthquakes. There is a tsunami. There is sulfur gas, which smells like rotten eggs and makes it even harder to breathe. And then boiling ash and pumice start raining down. And you are in the middle of it.

What will you do? Where will you go to save yourself?

This has a lot of great information on what life was like on one of the worst days in history. Read all about it!

WORTH READING

Nonfiction books with "boy appeal" that have received positive reviews in *Booklist*, *Horn Book Guide*, and/or *School Library Journal*.

Augarde, Steve. *Leonardo Da Vinci* (Lifelines). Illustrated by Leo Brown. Kingfisher, 2009. ISBN 9780753461747. 64 p. Grades 4–6.

Beller, Susan Provost. *Roman Legions on the March: Soldiering in the Ancient Roman Army* (Soldiers on the Battlefront). Twenty-First Century Books, 2007. ISBN 9780822567813. 112 p. Grades 5–8.

Bingham, Jane. *The Aztec Empire* (Time Travel Guide). Raintree, 2007. ISBN 9781410930392. 64 p. Grades 4–6.

Bingham, Jane. *How People Lived in Ancient Egypt*. PowerKids Press, 2008. ISBN 9781404244337. 30 p. Grades 2–4.

Bingham, Jane. *How People Lived in Ancient Rome*. PowerKids Press, 2008. ISBN 9781404244320. 30 p. Grades 2–4.

Bingham, Jane. *The Inca Empire* (Time Travel Guide). Raintree, 2008. ISBN 9781410930408. 64 p. Grades 4–6.

Bordessa, Kris. *Great Medieval Projects You Can Build Yourself* (Build It Yourself). Nomad Press, 2008. ISBN 9781934670262. 128 p. Grades 4–7.

Buller, Laura. *Vikings* (History Dudes). DK, 2007. ISBN 9780756629403. 64 p. Grades 4–up.

Butterfield, Moira. *Knight* (Medieval Lives). Smart Apple Media, 2008. ISBN 9781599201689. 45 p. Grades 5–8.

Cando, Rich, and Laura Buller. *Ancient Egyptians* (History Dudes). DK, 2007. ISBN 9780756629410. 64 p. Grades 4–up.

Christie, Peter *The Curse of Akkad: Climate Upheavals That Rocked Human History*. Annick Press, 2008. ISBN 9781554511198. 144 p. Grades 5–8.

Claybourne, Anna. *Ancient Greece* (Time Travel Guide). Raintree, 2007. ISBN 9781410930354. 64 p. Grades 4–6.

Clifford, Barry. *Real Pirates: The Untold Story of* The Whydah *from Slave Ship to Pirate Ship*. National Geographic, 2008. ISBN 9781426302794. 32 p. Grades 4–7.

Coleman, Janet Wyman, and International Spy Museum. *Secrets, Lies, Gizmos, and Spies: A History of Spies and Espionage*. Abrams Books for Young Readers, 2006. ISBN 0810957566. 128 p. Grades 3–8.

Coombs, Rachel. *A Year in a Castle* (Time Goes By). Millbrook Press, 2008. ISBN 9781580135504. 24 p. Grades K–3.

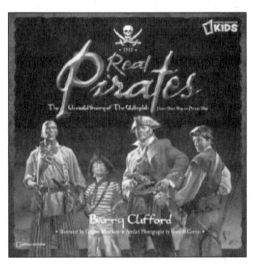

Real Pirates: The Untold Story of The Whydah *from Slave Ship to Pirate Ship* **by Barry Clifford.**

Coulter, Laurie. *Ballplayers and Bone Setters: One Hundred Ancient Aztec and Maya Jobs You Might Have Adored or Abhorred*. Annick Press, 2008. ISBN 9781554511419 96 p. Grades 4–6.

Deckker, Zilah. *Ancient Rome: Archaeology Unlocks the Secrets of Rome's Past* (National Geographic Investigates). National Geographic, 2007. ISBN 978-1426301285. 64 p. Grades 4–6.

DiConsiglio, John. *Master of the Guillotine* (A Wicked History). Franklin Watts, 2008. ISBN 9780531205037. 128 p. Grades 6–8.

Dixon, Philip. *Knights & Castles* (Insiders). Simon & Schuster, 2007. ISBN 9781416938644. 64 p. Grades 2–5.

Dougherty, Terri. *Raising the Flag: The Battle of Iwo Jima* (Edge Books). Capstone Press, 2008. ISBN 9781429619394. 32 p. Grades 4–6.

Eamer, Claire. *Traitors' Gate: and Other Doorways to the Past*. Annick Press, 2008. ISBN 9781554511457 112 p. Grades 6–8.

Galford, Ellen. *Julius Caesar: The Boy Who Conquered an Empire* (National Geographic World History Biographies). National Geographic, 2007. ISBN 9781426300653. 64 p. Grades 5–8.

Gifford, Clive. *Spies Revealed*. Atheneum, 2008. ISBN 9781416971139. 32 p. Grades 4–6.

Gilbert, Adrian. *Secret Agents* (QEB Spy Files). Black Rabbit Books, 2008. ISBN 978- 1595665928. 32 p. Grades 3–6.

Gilkerson, William. *A Thousand Years of Pirates*. Tundra Books, 2009. ISBN 978-0887769245. 96 p. Grades 6–10.

Gogerly, Liz. *Ancient Egypt* (Time Travel Guide). Raintree, 2007. ISBN 978-1410930378. 64 p. Grades 4–6.

Goldberg, Enid A., and Norman Itzkowitz. *Genghis Khan: 13th Century Mongolian Tyrant* (A Wicked History). Franklin Watts, 2007. ISBN 9780531125960. 128 p. Grades 6–8.

Goldberg, Enid A., and Norman Itzkowitz. *Grigory Rasputin: Holy Man or Mad Monk?* (A Wicked History). Franklin Watts, 2007. ISBN 9780531125946. 128 p. Grades 6–8.

Goldberg, Enid A., and Norman Itzkowitz. *Tomas de Torquemada: Architect of Torture During the Spanish Inquisition* (A Wicked History). Franklin Watts, 2007. ISBN 053112598. 128 p. Grades 6–8.

Goldberg, Enid A., and Norman Itzkowitz. *Vlad the Impaler: The Real Count Dracula* (A Wicked History). Franklin Watts, 2007. ISBN 0531125998. 128 p. Grades 6–8.

Grant, Reg. *World War II*. DK, 2008. ISBN 9780756638306. 192 p. Grades 7–up.

Gruber, Beth. *Ancient Inca: Archaeology Unlocks the Secrets of Inca's Past* (National Geographic Investigates). National Geographic, 2006. ISBN 0792278275. 64 p. Grades 4–8.

Gruber, Beth. *Ancient Iraq: Archaeology Unlocks the Secrets of Iraq's Past* (National Geographic Investigates). National Geographic, 2007. ISBN 0792253825. 64 p. Grades 4–8.

Hall, Kirsten. *A History of Pirates* (Pirates!). ABDO & Daughters, 2007. ISBN 599287617. 32 p. Grades 4–8.

Hamilton, John. *Bartholomew Roberts* (Pirates!). ABDO & Daughters, 2007. ISBN 1599287579. 32 p. Grades 4–7.

Hamilton, John. *A Pirate's Life* (Pirates!). ABDO & Daughters, 2007. ISBN 1599287625. 32 p. Grades 4–7.

Hamilton, Sue. *Blackbeard* (Pirates!). ABDO & Daughters, 2007. ISBN 1599287587. 32 p. Grades 4–7.

Hamilton, Sue. *Captain Kidd* (Pirates!). ABDO & Daughters, 2007. ISBN 159-9287595. 32 p. Grades 4–7.

Hamilton, Sue. *Henry Morgan* (Pirates!). ABDO & Daughters, 2007. ISBN 599-287609. 32 p. Grades 4–7.

Hampton, Wilborn. *Gladiators* (Fearsome Fighters). Creative Education, 2007. ISBN 9781583415351. 48 p. Grades 5–8.

Hanel, Rachel. *Knights* (Fearsome Fighters). Creative Education, 2007. ISBN 9781583415368. 48 p. Grades 5–8.

Hanel, Rachel. *Pirates* (Fearsome Fighters). Creative Education, 2007. ISBN 9781583415375. 48 p. Grades 4–7.

Harrison, David L. *Pirates.* Wordsong, 2008. ISBN 9781590784556. 32 p. Grades 3–6.

Howe, John. *Lost Worlds.* Kingfisher, 2009. ISBN 9780753461075. 96 p. Grades 4–6.

Howitt, Carolyn. *500 Things to Know About the Ancient World.* Barron's Educational Series, 2007. ISBN 9780764138638. 152 p. Grades 5–8.

Hull, Robert. *Peasant* (Medieval Lives). Smart Apple Media, 2008. ISBN 9781599201726. 44 p. Grades 5–8.

Hynson, Colin. *How People Lived in Ancient Greece.* PowerKids Press, 2008. ISBN 9781404244313. 30 p. Grades 2–4.

Lassieur, Allison. *The History of Pirates: From Privateers to Outlaws* (Edge Books). Capstone Press, 2006. ISBN 0736864237. 32 p. Grades 2–4.

Lassieur, Allison. *Vikings* (Edge Books). Capstone Press, 2006. ISBN 0736864342. 32 p. Grades 3–5.

Lewin, Ted. *Horse Song: The Naadam of Mongolia.* Lee & Low Books, 2008. ISBN 9781584302773. 56 p. Grades K–3.

Malam, John. *Ancient Rome* (Time Travel Guide). Raintree, 2007. ISBN 9781410930361. 64 p. Grades 4–6.

Malam, John. *You Wouldn't Want to Be a Victorian Mill Worker! A Grueling Job You'd Rather Not Have* (You Wouldn't Want to). Franklin Watts, 2007. ISBN 0531187470. 32 p. Grades 4–8.

Malam, John. *You Wouldn't Want to Live in Pompeii! A Volcanic Eruption You'd Rather Avoid* (You Wouldn't Want to). Franklin Watts, 2008. ISBN 078 0531187487. 32 p. Grades 3–5.

Martin, Michael. *Spy Gear* (Edge Books). Capstone Press, 2008. ISBN 978-1429613040. 32 p. Grades 4–6.

Martin, Michael. *Spy Skills* (Edge Books). Capstone Press, 2008. ISBN 978-1429613088. 32 p. Grades 4–6.

Marx, Trish. *Elephants and Golden Thrones: Inside China's Forbidden City*. Abrams Books for Young Readers, 2008. ISBN 9780810994850. 48 p. Grades 4–6.

McCarty, Nick. *Troy: The Myth and Reality Behind the Epic Legend* (Prime Time History). Rosen, 2008. ISBN 9781404213654. 122 p. Grades 9–up.

McGee, Marni. *Ancient Greece: Archaeology Unlocks the Secrets of Ancient Greece* (National Geographic Investigates). National Geographic, 2006. ISBN 079 2278267. 64 p. Grades 4–8.

Meserole, Mike. *The Great Escape: Tunnel to Freedom* (Sterling, Point Books). Sterling, 2008. ISBN 9781402757051. 240 p. Grades 6–8.

Morris, Neil. *Pirates* (Amazing History). Smart Apple Media, 2008. ISBN 978-1599201047. 32 p. Grades 4–6.

Nobleman, Marc Tyler. *Gladiator* (Atomic Series). Raintree, 2007. ISBN 978-1410929761. 32 p. Grades 3–6.

Nobleman, Marc Tyler. *Knight* (Atomic Series). Raintree, 2007. ISBN 978-1410929716. 32 p. Grades 3–6.

Olson, Tod. *Leopold II: Butcher of the Congo* (A Wicked History). Franklin Watts, 2008. ISBN 9780531205013. 128 p. Grades 5–up.

Platt, Richard. *Pompeii* (Through Time). Kingfisher, 2007. ISBN 9780753460443. 48 p. Grades 3–6.

Rice, Earle, Jr. *Blitzkrieg! Hitler's Lightning War* (Monumental Milestones: Great Events of Modern Times). Mitchell Lane, 2007. ISBN 9781584155423. 48 p. Grades 5–8.

Roberts, Paul. *The Ancient Romans: Their Lives and Their World*. Getty, 2009. ISBN 9780892369867. 80 p. Grades 5–8.

Rubalcaba, Jill. *Ancient Egypt: Archaeology Unlocks the Secrets of Egypt's Past* (National Geographic Investigates). National Geographic, 2006. ISBN 0792278577. 64 p. Grades 5–up.

Shecter, Vicky Alvear. *Alexander the Great Rocks the World*. Darby Creek, 2006. ISBN 158196045X. 128 p. Grades 5–8.

Sherrow, Victoria. *Ancient Africa: Archaeology Unlocks the Secrets of Africa's Past* (National Geographic Investigates). National Geographic, 2007. ISBN 0792253841. 64 p. Grades 5–up.

Shirer, William L. *The Sinking of the* Bismarck*: The Deadly Hunt* (Sterling.Point Books). Sterling, 2006. ISBN 1402731833. 176 p. Grades 5–up.

Shuter, Jane. *Ancient China* (Time Travel Guide). Raintree, 2007. ISBN 978-1410930385. 64 p. Grades 4–6.

Sonneborn, Liz. *Pompeii* (Unearthing Ancient Worlds). Twenty-First Century Books, 2008. ISBN 9780822575054. 80 p. Grades 5–8.

Spengler, Kremena. *Hieroglyphs* (Ancient Egypt). Capstone Press, 2008. ISBN 9781429619172. 24 p. Grades K–3.

Spilsbury, Louise, and Richard Spilsbury. *History Detectives: Archaeologists* (Scientists at Work). Heinemann, 2007. ISBN 9781403499486. 32 p. Grades 4–6.

Steele, Philip. *Knights and Castles* (Navigators). Kingfisher, 2008. ISBN 978-0753462287. 48 p. Grades 4–7.

Stewart, David. *You Wouldn't Want to Be Tutankhamen! A Mummy Who Really Got Meddled With* (You Wouldn't Want to). Franklin Watts, 2007. ISBN 9780531187258. 32 p. Grades 3–6.

Temple, Bob. *The Golden Age of Pirates* (You Choose Books). Capstone Press, 2007. ISBN 9781429601627. 112 p. Grades 3–6.

Thompson, Gare. *Roald Amundsen and Robert Scott Race to the South Pole* (History Chapters). National Geographic, 2007. ISBN 1426301871. 48 p. Grades 2–4.

King Tut's Tomb **by Amanda Doering Tourville.**

Tourville, Amanda Doering. *King Tut's Tomb* (Ancient Egypt). Capstone Press, 2008. ISBN 9781429619189. 24 p. Grades K–3.

Van Vleet, Carmella. *Explore Ancient Egypt! 25 Great Projects, Activities, and Experiments* (Explore Your World). Nomad Press, 2008. ISBN 9780979226830. 89 p. Grades 1–5.

White, Steve. *The Battle of Midway: The Destruction of the Japanese Fleet* (Graphic Battles of World War II). Rosen, 2007. ISBN 140420783X. 48 p. Grades 5–8.

Whiting, Jim. *Medieval Castles* (First Facts). Capstone Press, 2009. ISBN 978-1429622677. 24 p. Grades K–2.

Woods, Michael. *Seven Wonders of Ancient Africa* (Seven Wonders). Twenty-First Century Books, 2008. ISBN 978-0822575719. 80 p. Grades 5–7.

Woods, Michael. *Seven Wonders of Ancient Asia* (Seven Wonders). Twenty-First Century Books, 2008. ISBN 978-0822575696. 80 p. Grades 5–7.

Woods, Michael. *Seven Wonders of Ancient Central and South America* (Seven Wonders). Twenty-First Century Books, 2008. ISBN 9780822575702. 80 p. Grades 5–7.

Medieval Castles **by Jim Whiting.**

Woods, Michael. *Seven Wonders of Ancient Greece* (Seven Wonders). Twenty-First Century Books, 2008. ISBN 9780822575740. 80 p. Grades 5–7.

Woods, Michael. *Seven Wonders of the Ancient World* (Seven Wonders). Twenty-First Century Books, 2008. ISBN 9780822575689. 80 p. Grades 5–7.

Woods, Michael, and Mary B Woods. *Seven Wonders of the Ancient Middle East* (Seven Wonders). Twenty-First Century Books, 2008. ISBN 9780822575733. 80 p. Grades 6–up.

Chapter ——— 11

Hot Topics: Magic, Riddles, Games, and Puzzles; Fascinating Facts and Reference Books; and Quirky Books of All Kinds

Kids love books that they can use, whether it's to learn a magic trick, solve a puzzle, tell a joke, or learn an amazing fact they can tell their friends. It's no wonder that *The Guinness Book of World Records* is one of the most popular "boy books" of all time. It's colorful, it's engaging, it's fun, and it's full of crazy facts for sharing with other kids. Many books provide a private experience, but the books in this chapter are perfect for social kids who want a shared experience. Encourage kids to read them together and talk about what they are learning.

BOOKTALKS

Carlson, Laurie M. *Houdini for Kids: His Life and Adventures with 21 Magic Tricks and Illusions.* Chicago Review Press, Inc., 2009. ISBN 9781556527821. 136 p. Grades 4–8.

Harry Houdini! What a great name! The man who used it wasn't born with it; he named himself after a famous magician from the early 1800s named Robert Houdin. Ehrich Weisz was his real name, and he was actually born in Hungary and came to America when he was four years old. Later he would claim that he was born in America, but it wasn't true.

His family was horribly poor. Ehrich was smart and worked hard, but neither of his parents learned to speak English. Ehrich did anything he could to help bring in money, from selling things on the street, working as an apprentice to a locksmith when he was 11 (where he likely learned a whole lot of useful things), and doing acrobatics, to doing card tricks and magic tricks on the sidewalk for donations. He even got a job cutting fabric in a necktie factory when the family moved to New York City.

It took many years and a lot of hard work before the guy who renamed himself Houdini made the big time—and the big bucks. He ran, he boxed, and he read and read and read and used libraries as much as he could. He read about the history of magic. He figured out how to do some great tricks. He met a pretty young woman, whom he married a few weeks later. He started realizing that doing a trick was not enough. The trick had to be presented well and leave the audience hungry for more. He had to bewilder and mystify ,and he had to be an absolutely dazzling performer. He worked in circuses and cheap "dime shows" in small towns.

When Harry was about 21 years old, he realized what trick might bring him fame and wealth. His experience working for a locksmith came in handy. He was able to break out of just about any handcuffs, and he became the handcuff king. When he got to a new town, he would ask police to bring in their best handcuffs, and he was almost always able to slip them off in less than a minute.

And then he got more and more daring. He started escaping from prison cells, from strait jackets, from freezing water, from milk cans, from all sorts of unlikely places. He became an escape artist who could get out of anything. And the people absolutely loved it and could hardly wait for more.

Some of his tricks were so good and so original that no one has figured out how on earth he pulled them off. Others were pretty simple. And one of the neat things about this book is that it shows you how to do 21 of Houdini's tricks! This is a fun, fun read.

Hillman, Ben. *How Big Is It?* Scholastic, 2007. ISBN 0439918081. 48 p. Grades 3–6.

This is a very cool book to look through. Sometimes we hear, for instance, that a snake is 33 feet long. What does that really mean? Can you picture 33 feet long? How about if you put a snake on an escalator? Now can you tell how huge it really is?

That is what this book does.

Maybe the most surprising picture is the very first one. It is a giant squid in front of a house. This giant squid is the same size as the biggest one ever found—55.2 feet—and no wonder sailors used to think there were monsters in the sea! Take a look!

Or how does a polar bear compare in size to a basketball player? How about a Goliath bird eating tarantula? How would that look on a dinner plate?

You will have a lot of fun when you look through this book!

Hillman, Ben. *How Weird Is It? A Freaky Book All about Strangeness*. Scholastic Press, 2009. ISBN 9780439918688. 48 p. Grades 3–7.

This book is just filled with freaky, weird information –and lots of equally weird photographs! Take a look at any of the chapters. It's easy! They're all only two pages long.

Here's some of the fun stuff you'll learn:

- Take a look at the photo on page 14. It's a half-Neanderthal, half-human basketball player. And it illustrates a mystifying topic. Exactly what were Neanderthals? Why did they disappear? How are they related to us human beings? Scientists everywhere argue about it all.

- Learn about the deep sea anglerfish on pages 18–19 and look at the photo. The females are big things that glow. The males are tiny little things that hunt around looking for a female to mate with. "If he finds the woman of his dreams, he bites her and doesn't let go—ever. He burrows in and gradually the front of him *dissolves,* and the two fish merge into one—literally sharing the same bloodstream. The only thing left is the back end of the male sticking out of the female's side. Anglerfish brides have been found with six or more half-grooms hanging off of them" (p. 19).

- Would you like to eat a plate of deep fried scorpions, complete with claws and stingers? It doesn't sound appetizing, does it? Well, Chinese kids think it is a great treat, but they think pizza is just disgusting? Why would that be? Learn on page 23.

This is a fun book!

Jackson, Donna M. *The Name Game: A Look behind the Labels*. Illustrated by Ted Stearn. Viking, 2009. ISBN 9780670011971. 64 p. Grades 3–5.

"The beginning of wisdom is to call things by their right names"—Chinese proverb quoted on page 1.

So what is your right name? Do people call you by your right name, or do you have a nickname? Do you like your name? Would you rather it was something else? And how did you get that name? How did your parents decide what your name should be?

Right at the beginning, we get some expert advice on how to pick names. One helpful suggestion is to pick a name that will not have embarrassing initials. Like Brian Albert Dahl.

Some parents don't care. They want a fun name. How would you like to be named Talula Does the Hula from Hawaii? And look at some of the celebrity baby names on page 14.

How did last names, or surnames, get started? Look at the list of ways starting on page 17 and then figure out which category your last name falls into. Mine is an occupational name. Baxter is the female version of Baker, or Bakester. So I know I had an ancestor somewhere who must have baked for a living.

You will learn about the differences in surnames in places like Iceland, which has a very confusing system to people who do not live there, and in China, where huge numbers of citizens share not very many last names. You will learn why dog and pet names should suit the animal. And how were the names of places and towns chosen?

Where did the name of the place you live in come from? How about nicknames, and names of hurricanes, and brand names?

You'll learn a lot of interesting things when you read this book.

Lankford, Mary D. *Mazes Around the World*. Illustrated by Karen Dugan. Collins, 2008. ISBN 0688165206. Unpaged. Grades 2–4.

Do you know what a maze is? Or a labyrinth? Sometimes those words mean the same thing. Sometimes they don't. They are described as patterns, sometimes puzzles, that take a path and get to a destination, sometimes confusingly. You probably enjoy doing mazes on paper with a pencil and probably getting lost along the way.

But most of the mazes in this book are 3-D mazes in real life—cut out bushes, or stones, or tracings in the ground. Would you like to walk in a maze—and not be able to see where on earth you were in it or how to get to the center?

There are mazes all over the world, and this interesting book describes several of them. There are wonderful pictures that will make you want to walk a maze soon!

WORTH READING

Nonfiction books with "boy appeal" that have received positive reviews in *Booklist*, *Horn Book Guide*, and/or *School Library Journal*.

Magic

Barnhart, Norm. *Amazing Magic Tricks, Apprentice Level* (Edge Books). Capstone Press, 2008. ISBN 9781429619431. 32 p. Grades 2–5.

Barnhart, Norm. *Amazing Magic Tricks, Beginner Level* (Edge Books). Capstone Press, 2008. ISBN 9781429619424. 32 p. Grades 2–5.

Barnhart, Norm. *Amazing Magic Tricks, Expert Level* (Edge Books). Capstone Press, 2008. ISBN 9781429619455. 32 p. Grades 2–5.

Barnhart, Norm. *Amazing Magic Tricks, Master Level* (Edge Books). Capstone Press, 2008. ISBN 9781429619448. 32 p. Grades 2–5.

Amazing Magic Tricks, Beginner Level **by Norm Barnhart.**

Fullman, Joe. *Card Tricks* (QEB Magic Handbook). QEB Publishing, 2008. ISBN 978-1595666048. 32 p. Grades 2–5.

Fullman, Joe. *Coin and Rope Tricks* (QEB Magic Handbook). QEB Publishing, 2008. ISBN 9781595666055. 32 p. Grades 2–5.

Fullman, Joe. *Mind Tricks* (QEB Magic Handbook). QEB Publishing, 2008. ISBN 9781595666079. 32 p. Grades 2–5.

Fullman, Joe. *Sleight of Hand* (QEB Magic Handbook). QEB Publishing, 2008. ISBN 9781595666062. 32 p. Grades 2–5.

MacLeod, Elizabeth. *Harry Houdini* (Kids Can Read). Illustrated by John Mantha. Kids Can, 2009. ISBN 9781554532988. 32 p. Grades 2–3.

Tremain, Jon. *Amazing Card Tricks*. Barron's Educational Series, 2007. ISBN 9780764160141. 128 p. Grades 7–up.

Zenon, Paul. *Amazing Magic, Cool Card Tricks: Techniques for the Advanced Magician* (Amazing Magic). Rosen, 2007. ISBN 9781404210851. 64 p. Grades 5–8.

Zenon, Paul. *Simple Sleight-of-Hand: Card and Coin Tricks for the Beginning Magician* (Amazing Magic). Rosen, 2007. ISBN 1404210709. 64 p. Grades 4–7.

Riddles, Games, and Puzzles

Acer, David. *Gotcha! 18 Amazing Ways to Freak Out Your Friends*. Kids Can, 2008. ISBN 9781554531943. 48 p. Grades 4–6.

Agee, Jon. *Orangutan Tongs*. Hyperion, 2008. ISBN 9781423103158. 32 p. Grades 1–5.

Aronson, Marc. *For Boys Only: The Biggest, Baddest Book Ever*. Feiwel & Friends, 2007. ISBN 0312377061. 160 p. Grades 5–8.

Blackwood, Gary. *Mysterious Messages: A History of Codes and Ciphers*. Dutton Children's Books, 2009. ISBN 9780525479604. 170 p. Grades 5–8.

Chmielewski, Gary. *The Classroom Zone: Jokes, Riddles, Tongue Twisters & "Daffynitions"* (Funny Zone). Norwood House, 2008. ISBN 9781599531458. 24 p. Grades 3–5.

Chmielewski, Gary. *Let's Eat in the Funny Zone: Jokes, Riddles, Tongue Twisters & "Daffynitions"* (Funny Zone). Norwood House, 2008. ISBN 9781599531816. 24 p. Grades 3–5.

Chmielewski, Gary. *The Science Zone: Jokes, Riddles, Tongue Twisters & "Daffynitions"* (Funny Zone). Norwood House, 2008. ISBN 9781599531830. 24 p. Grades 3–5.

Conner, Bobbi. *Unplugged Play: No Batteries. No Plugs. Pure Fun*. Workman, 2007. ISBN 9780761143901. 516 p. Grades 4–up.

Eisenberg, Lisa. *Silly School Riddles*. Illustrated by Elwood H. Smith. Dial, 2008. ISBN 9780803731653. 40 p. Grades 1–3.

Gilbert, Adrian. *Codes and Ciphers* (QEB Spy Files). QEB Publishing, 2008. ISBN 9781595665942. 32 p. Grades 3–6.

Goldstone, Bruce. *Greater Estimations*. Henry Holt, 2008. ISBN 9780805083156. 32 p. Grades 2–5.

Hall, Katy, and Lisa Eisenberg. *Simms Taback's Great Big Book of Spacey, Snakey, Buggy Riddles*. Viking, 2008. ISBN 9780670011216. 64 p. Grades 1–3.

KIDSLABEL. *Spot 7 Toys* (Spot 7). Chronicle Books, 2008. ISBN 9780811865630. 40 p. Grades K–2.

Munro, Roxie. *Mazeways: A to Z.* Sterling, 2007. ISBN 9781402737749. 48 p. Grades K–2.

Williams, Carol. *24 Games You Can Play on a Checker Board.* Gibbs Smith, 2007. ISBN 9781423600114. 64 p. Grades 3–6.

Fascinating Facts and Reference Books

Chancellor, Deborah. *Everything You Need to Know: An Encyclopedia for Inquiring Young Minds.* Kingfisher, 2007. ISBN 9780753460894. 320 p. Grades 2–5.

Chesire, Gerard. *Living World* (World of Wonder). Children's Press, 2008. ISBN 9780531238267. 32 p. Grades 1–4.

Chesire, Gerard. *People and Places* (World of Wonder). Children's Press, 2008. ISBN 9780531240281. 32 p. Grades 1–4.

DK Publishing. *One Million Things: A Visual Encyclopedia.* DK, 2008. ISBN 9780756638436. 304 p. Grades 5–up.

Kimmel, Eric A. *The McElderry Book of Greek Myths.* Margaret K. McElderry Books, 2008. ISBN 1416915346. 96 p. Grades K–6.

Laffon, Martine. *The Book of How* (Book Of . . .). Abrams Books for Young Readers, 2007. ISBN 9780810907164. 96 p. Grades 3–6.

Law, Stephen. *Really, Really Big Questions about Life, the Universe, and Everything Else.* Illustrated by Nishant Choksi. Kingfisher, 2009. ISBN 9780753463093. 64 p. Grades 5–8.

The Old Farmer's Almanac for Kids Volume 2 (Old Farmer's Almanac for Kids). The Old Farmer's Almanac, 2007. ISBN 9781571984340. 192 p. Grades 3–6.

Townsend, Michael. *Amazing Greek Myths of Wonder and Blunders.* Dial, 2010. ISBN 9780803733084. 160 p. Grades 2–4.

Woodford, Chris. *Cool Stuff 2.0: And How It Works.* DK, 2007. ISBN 978-0756632076 256 p. Grades 4–8.

Quirky Books of All Kinds

Bardhan-Quallen, Sudipta. *The Real Monsters.* Sterling, 2008. ISBN 978-1402737763. 88 p. Grades 5–8.

Brezina, Corona. *Treasure Hunters* (Extreme Careers). Rosen, 2008. ISBN 978-1404217881. 64 p. Grades 5–8.

Bull, Jane. *Make It!* DK, 2008. ISBN 9780756638375. 63 p. Grades 1–4.

Clark, Travis. *A Guys' Guide to Stress/A Girls' Guide to Stress* (Flip-It-Over Guides to Teen Emotions). Enslow, 2008. ISBN 9780766028579. 128 p. Grades 7–10.

Cleary, Brian P. *The Laugh Stand: Adventures in Humor* (Exceptional Reading & Language Arts Titles for Intermediate Grades). Millbrook Press, 2007. ISBN 9780822578499. 48 p. Grades 4–6.

Connelly, Elizabeth Russell. *Nicotine = Busted!* Enslow, 2006. ISBN 0766024733. 112 p. Grades 5–up.

Doeden, Matt. *Dragon Life* (Edge Books). Capstone Press, 2008. ISBN 978-1429612975. 32 p. Grades 4–6.

Doeden, Matt. *Dragonatomy* (Edge Books). Capstone Press, 2008. ISBN 978-1429612951. 32 p. Grades 4–6.

Dudley, William. *Unicorns* (The Mysterious & Unknown). Referencepoint Press, 2008. ISBN 9781601520289. 104 p. Grades 4–6.

Dunnington, Rose. *Sweet Eats: Mmmore Than Just Desserts*. Lark, 2008. ISBN 9781600592362. 112 p. Grades 4–6.

Enright, Dominique, and Guy Macdonald. *How To Be The Best At Everything* (The Boys' Book). Scholastic Press, 2007. ISBN 9780545016285. 128 p. Grades 4–7.

Family Fun Magazine. *What's Cooking? A Cookbook for Kids* (Ratatouille). Disney, 2007. ISBN 9781423105404. 64 p. Grades 3–6.

Fauchald, Nick, and Rick Peterson. *Indoor S'mores: And Other Tasty Treats for Special Occasions* (Kids Dish). Picture Window Books, 2008. ISBN 9781404840003. 32 p. Grades 2–4.

Fauchald, Nick, and Rick Peterson. *Keep on Rollin' Meatballs: And Other Delicious Dinners* (Kids Dish). Picture Window Books, 2008. ISBN 9781404839984. 32 p. Grades 2–4.

Fauchald, Nick, and Rick Peterson. *Walk-Around Tacos: And Other Likeable Lunches* (Kids Dish). Picture Window Books, 2008. ISBN 9781404839991. 32 p. Grades 2–4.

Frisch, Aaron. *The Story of Nike* (Built for Success). Creative Education, 2008. ISBN 9781583416082. 48 p. Grades 4–6.

Gallagher, Jim. *A Guys' Guide to Conflict/A Girls' Guide to Conflict* (Flip-It-Over Guides to Teen Emotions). Enslow, 2008. ISBN 9780766028524. 128 p. Grades 7–10.

Hess, Nina. *A Practical Guide to Monsters*. Mirrorstone, 2007. ISBN 978-0786948093. 80 p. Grades 4–7.

The Hilarious Adventures of Mish and Mash: The Story of How Two Monsters—and You—Make the Perfect Joke Book! Illustrated by Remie Geoffroi. OwlKids, 2009. ISBN 9782895792086. 160 p. Grades K–4.

Hinds, Maurene. *Witchcraft on Trial: From the Salem Witch Hunts to "The Crucible"* (Famous Court Cases That Became Movies). Enslow, 2009. ISBN 9780766030558. 104 p. Grades 8–12.

Hopkins, Lee Bennett. *Hamsters, Shells, and Spelling Bees: School Poems* (I Can Read Book 2). HarperCollins, 2008. ISBN 978-006074112. 48 p. Grades K–3.

Horn, Geoffrey M. *FBI Agent* (Cool Careers). Gareth Stevens, 2008. ISBN 9780836893267. 32 p. Grades 3–5.

Hosley, Maria. *Kidnapping File: The Graeme Thorne Case* (Crime Solvers). Bearport Publishing, 2007. ISBN 9781597165488. 32 p. Grades 3–6.

Witchcraft on Trial: From the Salem Witch Hunts to "The Crucible" **by Maurene Hinds.**

Robbery File: The Museum Heist **by Amanda Howard.**

Howard, Amanda. *Robbery File: The Museum Heist* (Crime Solvers). Bearport Publishing, 2007. ISBN 9781597165501. 32 p. Grades 3–6.

Hyland, Tony. *High-Rise Workers* (Extreme Jobs). Smart Apple Media, 2007. ISBN 9781583407424. 32 p. Grades 4–6.

Hyland, Tony. *Miners and Drillers* (Extreme Jobs). Smart Apple Media, 2007. ISBN 9781583407394. 32 p. Grades 4–6.

Janeczko, Paul B. *Hey, You! Poems to Skyscrapers, Mosquitoes, and Other Fun Things.* HarperCollins, 2007. ISBN 0060523476. 40 p. Grades 2–5.

Jeffrey, Laura S. *Marijuana = Busted!* Enslow, 2006. ISBN 0766027961. 104 p. Grades 5–up.

Johnson, Kristi. *Peanut Butter and Jelly Sushi and Other Party Recipes* (Snap Books). Capstone Press, 2008. ISBN 9781429613408. 32 p. Grades 4–6.

Kallen, Stuart A. *Alien Abductions* (The Mysterious & Unknown). Referencepoint Press, 2007. ISBN 9781601520234. 104 p. Grades 6–9.

Katz, Alan. *Oops!* Margaret K. McElderry Books, 2008. ISBN 9781416902041. 176 p. Grades 3–6.

Katz, Alan. *Uh-Oh* Illustrated by Edward Koren. Margaret K. McElderry Books, 2010. ISBN 9781416935186. 176 p. Grades 3–6.

Kerns, Ann. *Wizards and Witches* (Fantasy Chronicles). Lerner Publishing, 2009. ISBN 9780822599838. 48 p. Grades 5–8.

Kling, Andrew A. *Surveillance* (Crime Scene Investigations). Lucent Books, 2007. ISBN 9781590189917. 120 p. Grades 5–8.

Knock, Knock. Illustrated by Saxton Freymann et al. Dial, 2007. ISBN 978-0803731523. Unpaged. Grades 1–4.

Knudsen, Shannon. *Fairies and Elves* (Fantasy Chronicles). Lerner Publishing, 2009. ISBN 9780822599791. 48 p. Grades 5–8.

Knudsen, Shannon. *Fantastical Creatures and Magical Beasts* (Fantasy Chronicles). Lerner Publishing, 2009. ISBN 9780822599876. 48 p. Grades 5–8.

Krensky, Stephen. *The Bogeyman* (Monster Chronicles). Lerner Publishing, 2007. ISBN 9780822567608. 48 p. Grades 4–7.

Krensky, Stephen. *Creatures from the Deep* (Monster Chronicles). Lerner Publishing, 2007. ISBN 9780822567615. 48 p. Grades 4–7.

Krensky, Stephen. *Vampires* (Monster Chronicles). Lerner Publishing, 2007. ISBN 0822558912. 48 p. Grades 4–7.

Krensky, Stephen. *Zombies* (Monster Chronicles). Lerner Publishing, 2007. ISBN 9780822567592. 48 p. Grades 4–7.

La Bella, Laura. *Search-and-Rescue Swimmers* (Extreme Careers). Rosen, 2008. ISBN 9781404217867. 64 p. Grades 5–8.

Larios, Julie. *Imaginary Menagerie: A Book of Curious Creatures.* Harcourt, 2008. ISBN 9780152063252. 32 p. Grades 2–5.

Larrew, Brekka Hervey. *Wormy Apple Croissants and Other Halloween Recipes* (Snap). Capstone Press, 2008. ISBN 9781429613385. 32 p. Grades 4–6.

Lobster Press Staff. *Let's Clear the Air: 10 Reasons Not to Start Smoking.* Lobster Press, 2007. ISBN 9781897073667. 192 p. Grades 4–9.

Logan, John. *A Guys' Guide to Love/A Girls' Guide to Love* (Flip-It-Over Guides to Teen Emotions). Enslow Publishers, 2008. ISBN 9780766028555. 128 p. Grades 7–10.

Loy, Jessica. *When I Grow Up: A Young Person's Guide to Interesting and Unusual Occupations.* Henry Holt, 2008. ISBN 9780805077179. 40 p. Grades 4–6.

Marcovitz, Hal. *A Guys' Guide to Anger/A Girls' Guide to Anger* (Flip-It-Over Guides to Teen Emotions). Enslow, 2008. ISBN 9780766028531. 128 p. Grades 7–10.

Marcovitz, Hal. *A Guys' Guide to Jealousy/A Girls' Guide to Jealousy* (Flip-It-Over Guides to Teen Emotions). Enslow, 2008. ISBN 9780766028548. 128 p. Grades 7–10.

Marcovitz, Hal. *A Guys' Guide to Loneliness/A Girls' Guide to Loneliness* (Flip-It-Over Guides to Teen Emotions). Enslow, 2008. ISBN 9780766028562. 128 p. Grades 7–10.

A Guys' Guide to Anger/A Girls' Guide to Anger by Hal Marcovitz.

Mortensen, Lori. *Sphinx* (Monsters). KidHaven Press, 2007. ISBN 9780737736335. 48 p. Grades 4–7.

Nardo, Don. *Martians* (Monsters). KidHaven Press, 2007. ISBN 9780737736397. 48 p. Grades 4–7.

New, William. *The Year I Was Grounded* (Tradewind Books). Illus. by Robert Kakegamic. Tradewind Books, 2008. ISBN 9781896580357. 104 p. Grades 4–7.

O'Connor, George. *Zeus: King of the Gods*. First Second, 2010. ISBN 978-1596436251. 78 p. Grades 5–9.

O'Neill, Terry. *The Chupacabras* (Monsters). KidHaven Press, 2007. ISBN 9780737731620. 48 p. Grades 4–6.

Orndorff, Lt. Colonel John C. *Terrorists, Tornados, and Tsunamis: How to Prepare for Life's Danger Zones*. Abrams Books for Young Readers, 2007. ISBN 0810957671. 144 p. Grades 5–up.

Orr, Tamra. *Budgeting Tips for Kids* (Robbie Readers). Mitchell Lane, 2008. ISBN 9781584156444. 48 p. Grades 4–6.

Orr, Tamra. *Coins and Other Currency: A Kid's Guide to Coin Collecting* (Robbie Readers). Mitchell Lane, 2008. ISBN 9781584156406. 48 p. Grades 4–6.

Orr, Tamra. *A Kid's Guide to Earning Money* (Robbie Readers). Mitchell Lane, 2008. ISBN 9781584156437. 48 p. Grades 4–6.

Orr, Tamra. *A Kid's Guide to Stock Market Investing* (Robbie Readers). Mitchell Lane, 2008. ISBN 9781584156420. 48 p. Grades 4–6.

Orr, Tamra. *Savings Tips for Kids* (Robbie Readers). Mitchell Lane, 2008. ISBN 9781584156413. 48 p. Grades 4–6.

Creepy Castles **by Sarah Parvis.**

Parvis, Sarah. *Creepy Castles* (Scary Places). Bearport Publishing, 2008. ISBN 978-1597165761. 32 p. Grades 4–6.

Parvis, Sarah. *Ghost Towns* (Scary Places). Bearport Publishing, 2008. ISBN 978-1597165778. 32 p. Grades 4–6.

Parvis, Sarah. *Haunted Hotels* (Scary Places). Bearport Publishing, 2008. ISBN 978-1597165747. 32 p. Grades 4–6.

Perry, Andrea. *The Snack Smasher: And Other Reasons Why It's Not My Fault.* Atheneum, 2007. ISBN 0689854692. 40 p. Grades K–2.

Prelutsky, Jack. *Be Glad Your Nose Is on Your Face: And Other Poems: Some of the Best of Jack Prelutsky.* Greenwillow Books, 2008. ISBN 9780061576539 194 p. Grades K–3.

Prelutsky, Jack. *My Dog May Be a Genius.* Greenwillow Books, 2008. ISBN 9780068238630. 159 p. Grades 2–5.

Prentzas, Scott. *FBI Special Agent* (Cool Careers). Cherry Lake, 2008. ISBN 9781602793040. 32 p. Grades 4–7.

Price, Pamela S. *Cool Stamps: Creating Fun and Fascinating Collections* (Cool Collections). Checkerboard Library, 2006. ISBN 1596797746. 32 p. Grades 2–4.

Pringle, Laurence. *Imagine a Dragon.* Boyds Mills, 2008. ISBN 9781563973284. 30 p. Grades 2–4.

Regan, Sally. *The Vampire Book: The Legends, the Lore, the Allure.* DK, 2009. ISBN 9780756655518. Unpaged. Grades 5–up.

Rex, Adam. *Frankenstein Takes the Cake.* Harcourt, 2008. ISBN 9780152062354. 40 p. Grades 3–6.

Rumford, James. *Beowulf.* Houghton Mifflin, 2007. ISBN 9780618756377. 48 p. Grades 5–8.

Salzmann, Mary Elizabeth. *Cool Shells: Creating Fun and Fascinating Collections* (Cool Collections). Checkerboard Library, 2006. ISBN 159679772X. 32 p. Grades 2–4.

Scheunemann, Pam. *Cool Coins: Creating Fun and Fascinating Collections* (Cool Collections). Checkerboard Library, 2006. ISBN 1596797703. 32 p. Grades 1–4.

Schulte, Mary. *Sirens* (Monsters). KidHaven Press, 2007. ISBN 9780737734515. 48 p. Grades 4–7.

Seuling, Barbara. *There Are Millions of Millionaires: And Other Freaky Facts about Earning, Saving, and Spending.* Picture Window Books, 2008. ISBN 978-1404841154. 40 p. Grades 2–5.

Sierra, Judy. *Beastly Rhymes to Read After Dark.* Knopf Books, 2008. ISBN 978-0375837470. 32 p. Grades K–3.

Singer, Marilyn. *First Food Fight This Fall and Other School Poems.* Illustrated by Sachiko Yoshikawa. Sterling, 2008. ISBN 9781402741456. 40 p. Grades K–4.

Storrie, Paul D. *Beowulf: Monster Slayer* (Graphic Universe). Capstone Press, 2007. ISBN 9780822567578. 48 p. Grades 4–7.

Williams, Dinah. *Abandoned Insane Asylums* (Scary Places). Bearport Publishing, 2008. ISBN 9781597165754. 32 p. Grades 4–6.

Abandoned Insane Asylums by Dinah Williams.

Williams, Dinah. *Haunted Houses* (Scary Places). Bearport Publishing, 2008. ISBN 978-1597165730. 32 p. Grades 4–6.

Williams, Dinah. *Spooky Cemeteries* (Scary Places). Bearport Publishing, 2008. ISBN 9781597165624. 32 p. Grades 4–6.

Chapter 12

Creativity: Writing, Art and Drawing, and Entertainment

Creative kids want to read about creative people. This chapter includes books about writers, artists, and entertainers, and also books about how to become a writer, artist, entertainer, or even a video game designer. You can never have too many books about drawing and about current actors and musicians. Use these lists to make sure you spend your money on quality titles that kids will actually read and enjoy.

BOOKTALKS

Adkins, Jan. *Frank Lloyd Wright: A Twentieth Century Life* (Up Close). Viking, 2007. ISBN 9780670061389. 301 p. Grades 5–up.

He thought he was a genius, the most brilliant architect of all time. So did a lot of other people, probably more today than when he was alive. It did not matter that almost every single building he ever designed leaked, or that he always way underestimated the cost, that he never had any money himself, or that he drove almost everyone who worked with him crazy. Frank Lloyd Wright had the highest possible opinion of himself, and maybe he was right!

This book pulls you right in almost the minute you start reading it. Jan Adkins tells us that Wright wrote an autobiography. "[H]e tells us he was born on June 8, 1869. But the birth records . . . show he was born June 8, 1867. Wright gives us the wrong ages for his mother and father, mistakes his father's full name, and even lies about his own name. Why lie?" (p. 19).

Well, Frank Lloyd Wright, whose real name was Frank Lincoln Wright, liked a good story, and never minded making a good story even better. And his whole life was an amazing story.

He dropped out of college without even finishing the first year, and then somehow managed to get a good job with an architectural firm in Chicago. He kept moving up and up. He fell in love, he married a woman everyone adored, and he left her when he fell in love with a client's wife. Then, a (rightfully) unhappy employer killed that woman and several other people in his home. Wright kept designing fantastic buildings even when he was so old that hardly anyone could believe he was still capable of it. But he was!

You will want to know more about him, and, especially, to see at least some of his buildings when you finish reading. Thank heaven for Google!

Brighton, Catherine. *Keep Your Eye on the Kid: The Early Years of Buster Keaton.* Roaring Brook Press, 2008. ISBN 9781596431584. Unpaged. Grades 1–4.

Joe Keaton had parents in show business. He was born in a boarding house in Piqua, Kansas, and from that time on, he traveled—a lot!

When he was just a small boy, he fell down the stairs and Harry Houdini picked him up. Houdini said, "That was some buster the kid took!" And now Joe Keaton wasn't Joe Keaton anymore. He was *Buster* Keaton. His dad started throwing him across the stage and saying, "Keep your eye on the kid!" People just loved it!

And Buster found they liked it even better if he never smiled. So he didn't.

Read this and find out why Buster only went to school one day in his life and why he got expelled. Read about the first movie that he made and then see if you can watch a real movie with Buster Keaton in it. Check: did he *ever* start smiling?

Keep Your Eye on the Kid: The Early Years of Buster Keaton **by Catherine Brighton. Jacket shown with permission from Roaring Brook Press.**

Fleming, Candace. *The Great and Only Barnum: The Tremendous, Stupendous Life of Showman P.T. Barnum.* Schwartz & Wade, 2009. ISBN 9780375841972. 160 p. Grades 4–8.

Phineas Taylor Barnum wasn't born rich, and he did not always stay rich once he got there, but he died rich and he had an enormous amount of fun in the meantime. What did he do? "I am a showman," he said. He amused, delighted, bewildered, and intrigued people, who could hardly wait to see what he would come up with next. And this book tells his story with the zest it deserves.

He started out slowly, born in 1810 in the little town of Bethel, Connecticut. He had an uncle who was always playing jokes on people, and Phineas probably got some of those genes. He worked in a store for his uncle—read the story on page 17 of how he got rid of some worthless merchandise by selling lottery tickets and making a lot of people happy. But he knew he wanted more. When he was 24, he packed up his wife and daughter and moved to New York City. He had to work in a grocery store for a while, but he watched and he learned—and he realized that people loved a good story, even if it was a hoax—and when they found out they had been fooled, they usually were not angry. Instead, they were amused. Phineas waited for his chance.

And it came.

There was an unusual exhibit for sale. It was a slave named Joice Heath, who looked absolutely ancient, weighed only 46 pounds and could move only one hand and her mouth. Her owner said she was 161 years old and had been the nursemaid of none other than George Washington! Barnum even got proof of her age. He bought the rights to exhibit her in New York City, and she was a sensation. Everyone wanted to see George Washington's nursemaid. And when an autopsy was done when she died and the doctor said she could not have been older than in her eighties, it did not really matter. The newspapers told the world about the hoax, and, after that, P. T. Barnum became known as someone who exhibited things he knew were fake—which was sometimes true and sometimes not.

This is just a great read. You will be laughing and marveling as you read the story of this most unusual man.

Nobleman, Marc Tyler. *Boys of Steel: The Creators of Superman.* Alfred A. Knopf, 2008. ISBN 9780375838026. Unpaged. Grades 4–up.

During the Great Depression in the 1930s, two short, shy, sort of nerdy high school kids named Jerry Siegel and Joe Shuster lived in Cleveland, Ohio. Both wore glasses. Both were lousy at sports and not very good around girls.

Jerry loved to write science fiction and adventure stories. Joe loved to draw. Sometimes he illustrated Jerry's stories. They were lucky to be friends.

They decided they wanted to create and sell original stories together. One hot night Jerry had an idea: maybe he could create a nerdy guy just like himself—until that guy sort of morphed into someone else and started doing amazing things. This guy would be strong. He would be an alien. He would protect human beings. This guy lived on earth in a regular place. And maybe he would be able to talk easily with women—and could he fly? Jerry went to get Joe early in the morning to tell him his ideas.

Joe loved them, and he drew a picture right away. But he needed something on the front of the costume. They decided on an "s" for super (and also for Siegel and Schuster, their last names).

They made a bunch of comic strips, but no one really liked their idea. It took three years for someone to become interested, someone creating a new kind of magazine called a comic book. And he bought the lifetime rights to Superman for just $130. Jerry and Joe wouldn't get any more money than that, no matter what happened.

This is a super story—and it is true.

Parker, Robert Andrew. *Piano Starts Here: The Young Art Tatum.* Schwartz & Wade, 2008. ISBN 9780375839658. Unpaged. Grades 1–4.

In Art Tatum's home in Toledo, Ohio, a piano sat in the corner. When he was old enough to reach it, he started playing it—and he started playing it well.

Art had a terrible vision problem, so he needed to hear things and smell things well. And one thing he heard incredibly well was music.

By the time he was ten years old, he was playing in church. Then he started playing other places.

Art became famous. He was African American and he was almost blind, but boy could he play the piano. Robert Andrew Parker, who wrote and illustrated this beautiful book, tells us what he might have been thinking.

"When I am at the piano, I close my eyes. I play clouds of notes, rivers of notes, notes that sound like skylarks singing and leaves rustling, like rain on a rooftop I forget that my eyes aren't good. I have everything I need."

Parker-Rock, Michelle. *Jack Gantos: An Author Kids Love* (Authors Kids Love). Enslow, 2008. ISBN 9780766027565. 48 p. Grades 4–7.

Jack Gantos's first book was written over 30 years ago, and it is still pretty famous. You may even have read it.

"I wanted to write a book about a cat," he said. "I did not have one, so I thought I better get one" (p. 5). He and a friend of his at Emerson College in Boston named Nicole Rubel decided to work together. What did they write? *Rotten Ralph.* It is about a really rotten cat who drives his owner crazy, and it was so popular that a whole bunch of books about Rotten Ralph followed.

Jack Gantos: An Author Kids Love **by Michelle Parker-Rock.**

Some people think all writers grew up in a family of readers and writers and that their homes were full of books. This was certainly not true of Jack Gantos. He cannot even remember ever going to the public library when he was a kid.

One thing he did was move a lot. His dad kept the family moving, and Jack started keeping a diary, writing down what happened in his life. He still does. He keeps journals and plans his next books with them—and he tells you exactly how you can do it, too.

This is a neat book. It not only tells about his childhood and his life, but it is also loaded with photos and lots of how-to information.

If you enjoy Jack's books about Joey Pigza, or Rotten Ralph, or Jack Henry—or if you want to write yourself—you will have a good time with this book.

Scieszka, Jon. *Knucklehead: Tall Tales and Mostly True Stories about Growing Up Scieszka.* Viking, 2008. ISBN 9780670011063. 106 p. Grades 5–8.

If you know who Jon Scieszka is, you will also know that he is a pretty funny guy. He wrote books like *The True Story of the Three Little Pigs by A. Wolf* and *The Stinky Cheese Man.* You would probably guess that if he told the story of his own life, it would be funny. And you would be right.

Jon grew up in a family with six kids—and all of those kids were boys. They were always getting into trouble, frequently fighting, and caused their parents all sorts of grief. They would wrestle in the living room, and they would break things. They sometimes drove their parents crazy.

John had to protect himself from his older brothers. He had to be creative. Once his big brother tried to sell him his own shirt. He tells us he got really good at making oatmeal because he hated picking up dog poop. To find out how *that* happened, read Chapter 3.

Of course, he also had little brothers, and sometimes he got really good at taking advantage of them, too. Read about the time he bought 100 toy soldiers for $1.50 and what he did with them. (They weren't exactly what he thought they were going to be—and his dad had warned him!)

This is loaded with lots of old pictures of his family and of some of the things he talks about—like those toy soldiers. You'll laugh a lot!

WORTH READING

Nonfiction books with "boy appeal" that have received positive reviews in *Booklist, Horn Book Guide*, and/or *School Library Journal.*

Writing

Parker-Rock, Michelle. *Bruce Coville: An Author Kids Love* (Authors Kids Love). Enslow, 2008. ISBN 0766027554. 48 p. Grades 3–5.

Parker-Rock, Michelle. *Bruce Hale: An Author Kids Love* (Authors Kids Love). Enslow, 2008. ISBN 9780766027589. 48 p. Grades 3–5.

Parker-Rock, Michelle. *Sid Fleischman: An Author Kids Love* (Authors Kids Love). Enslow, 2008. ISBN 9780766027572. 48 p. Grades 3–5.

Rosinsky, Natalie. *Write Your Own Graphic Novel* (Write Your Own). Compass Point Books, 2008. ISBN 9780756538569. 64 p. Grades 4–8.

Art and Drawing

All About Drawing Dinosaurs & Reptiles. Walter Foster, 2008. ISBN 978-1600585791. 80 p. Grades 2–5.

All About Drawing Horses & Pets. Walter Foster, 2008. ISBN 9781600585807. 80 p. Grades 2–5.

All About Drawing Sea Creatures & Animals. Walter Foster, 2008. ISBN 978-1600585814. 80 p. Grades 2–5.

Baker, Kyle. *How to Draw Stupid and Other Essentials of Cartooning*. Watson-Guptill, 2008. ISBN 9780823001439. 112 p. Grades 6–up.

Barton, Christ. *The Day-Glo Brothers: The True Story of Bob and Joe Switzer's Bright Ideas and Brand-New Colors*. Illustrated by Tony Persiani. Charlesbridge, 2009. ISBN 9781570916731. Unpaged. Grades 4–6.

Bergin, Mark. *How to Draw Cars* (How to Draw). PowerKids Press, 2008. ISBN 9781435825208. 32 p. Grades 3–5.

Boos, Ben. *Swords: An Artist's Devotion*. Candlewick Press, 2008. ISBN 9780763631482. 96 p. Grades 6–up.

Boursin, Didier. *Folding for Fun: Origami for Ages 4 and Up*. Firefly Books, 2007. ISBN 1554072522. 64 p. Grades 3–6.

The Day-Glo Brothers: The True Story of Bob and Joe Switzer's Bright Ideas and Brand-New Colors **by Barton Christ.**

Demilly, Christian. *Pop Art* (Adventures in Art). Prestel USA, 2007. ISBN 9783791338941. 32 p. Grades 4–6.

Doble, Rick. *Career Building Through Digital Photography* (Digital Career Building). Rosen, 2007. ISBN 9781404219410. 64 p. Grades 7–up.

Dobrzycki, Michael. *The Art of Drawing Dragons, Mythological Beasts, and Fantasy Creatures: Discover Simple Step-by-Step Techniques for Drawing Fantastic Creatures of Folklore and Legend*. Walter Foster, 2007. ISBN 9781600580123. 144 p. Grades 7–up.

Hamilton, Sue L. *Jack Kirby* (Comic Book Creators). ABDO & Daughters, 2006. ISBN 978159928295. 32 p. Grades 3–5.

Hamilton, Sue L. *Joe Simon: Creator & Artist* (Comic Book Creators). ABDO & Daughters, 2006. ISBN 9781599283005. 32 p. Grades 3–5.

Hamilton, Sue L. *Joe Sinnott: Artist & Inker* (Comic Book Creators). ABDO & Daughters, 2006. ISBN 1599282992. 32 p. Grades 3–5.

Hamilton, Sue L. *John Buscema: Artist & Inker* (Comic Book Creators). ABDO & Daughters, 2006. ISBN 1599282976. 32 p. Grades 3–5.

Hamilton, Sue L. *John Romita, Sr.: Artist* (Comic Book Creators). ABDO & Daughters, 2006. ISBN 1599283026. 32 p. Grades 3–5.

Hanson, Anders. *Cool Drawing: The Art of Creativity for Kids* (Cool Art). Checkerboard Library, 2008. ISBN 9781604531428. 32 p. Grades 2–5.

Hanson, Anders. *Cool Sculpture: The Art of Creativity for Kids* (Cool Art). Checkerboard Library, 2008. ISBN 9781604531442. 32 p. Grades 2–5.

Hart, Christopher. *The Cartoonist's Big Book of Drawing Animals*. Watson-Guptill, 2008. ISBN 9780823014217. 224 p. Grades 2–6.

Hart, Christopher. *Drawing the New Adventure Cartoons: Cool Spies, Evil Guys and Action Heroes*. Chris Hart Books, 2008. ISBN 9781933027609. 128 p. Grades 4–up.

Hart, Christopher. *Manga Mania Romance: Drawing Shojo Girls and Bishie Boys*. Watson-Guptill, 2008. ISBN 9781933027432 147 p. Grades 5–8.

Henry, Sally. *Clay Modeling* (Make Your Own Art). PowerKids Press, 2008. ISBN 9781435825086. 32 p. Grades 3–6.

Hosley, Maria. *Airplanes* (First Drawings). ABDO & Daughters, 2007. ISBN 596797991. 24 p. Grades 1–4.

Hosley, Maria. *Cars* (First Drawings). ABDO & Daughters, 2007. ISBN 1596798009. 24 p. Grades 1–4.

Hosley, Maria. *Cats* (First Drawings). ABDO & Daughters, 2007. ISBN 1596798017. 24 p. Grades 1–4.

Hosley, Maria. *Dinosaurs* (First Drawings). ABDO & Daughters, 2007. ISBN 159-6798025. 24 p. Grades 1–4.

Hosley, Maria. *Dogs* (First Drawings). ABDO & Daughters, 2007. ISBN 159-6798033. 24 p. Grades 1–4.

Hosley, Maria. *People* (First Drawings). ABDO & Daughters, 2007. ISBN 159-6798122. 24 p. Grades 1–4.

Krensky, Stephen. *Comic Book Century: The History of American Comic Books* (People's History). Twenty-First Century Books, 2007. ISBN 9780822566540. 112 p. Grades 5–8.

Krier, Ann. *Totally Cool Origami Animals*. Sterling, 2007. ISBN 1402724489. 96 p. Grades 2–6.

Llimos, Anna. *Easy Bead Crafts in 5 Steps* (Easy Crafts in 5 Steps). Enslow, 2008. ISBN 9780766030824. 32 p. Grades K–3.

Llimos, Anna. *Easy Cardboard Crafts in 5 Steps* (Easy Crafts in 5 Steps). Enslow, 2008. ISBN 9780766030831. 32 p. Grades K–3.

Llimos, Anna. *Easy Clay Crafts in 5 Steps* (Easy Crafts in 5 Steps). Enslow, 2008. ISBN 9780766030855. 32 p. Grades K–3.

Llimos, Anna. *Easy Cloth Crafts in 5 Steps* (Easy Crafts in 5 Steps). Enslow, 2008. ISBN 9780766030848. 31 p. Grades K–3.

Llimos, Anna. *Easy Earth-Friendly Crafts in 5 Steps* (Easy Crafts in 5 Steps). Enslow, 2008. ISBN 9780766030862. 32 p. Grades K–3.

Llimos, Anna. *Easy Paper Crafts in 5 Steps* (Easy Crafts in 5 Steps). Enslow, 2008. ISBN 9780766030879. 32 p. Grades K–3.

Lunis, Natalie. *123 I Can Draw!* (Starting Art). Kids Can, 2008. ISBN 978-1554530397. 24 p. Grades 1–3.

Luxbacher, Irene. *123 I Can Make Prints!* (Starting Art). Kids Can, 2008. ISBN 9781554530403. 24 p. Grades 1–3.

Marcovitz, Hal. *Anime* (Eye on Art). Lucent Books. 2007. ISBN 1590189957. 104 p. Grades 6–9.

Masiello, Ralph. *Ralph Masiello's Ancient Egypt Drawing Book.* Charlesbridge, 2008. ISBN 9781570915338. 48 p. Grades 3–6.

McGee, Randal. *Paper Crafts for Chinese New Year* (Paper Craft Fun for Holidays). Enslow, 2008. ISBN 9780766029507. 48 p. Grades K–3.

McGee, Randal. *Paper Crafts for Kwanzaa* (Paper Craft Fun for Holidays). Enslow, 2008. ISBN 9780766029491. 48 p. Grades K–3.

Meinking, Mary. *Easy Origami* (Snap). Capstone Press, 2008. ISBN 9781429620208. 32 p. Grades 2–6.

Meinking, Mary. *Not-Quite-So-Easy Origami* (Snap). Capstone Press, 2008. ISBN 9781429620215. 32 p. Grades 2–6.

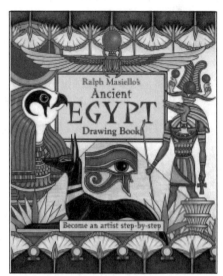

***Ralph Masiello's Ancient Egypt Drawing Book* by Ralph Masiello.**

Miller, Ron. *Digital Art: Painting with Pixels* (Exceptional Social Studies Titles for Upper Grades). Twenty-First Century Books, 2007. ISBN 9780822575160. 120 p. Grades 6–up.

Nguyen, Duy. *Monster Origami.* Sterling, 2007. ISBN 9781402740145. 96 p. Grades 5–7.

Nguyen, Duy. *Origami Birds.* Sterling, 2006. ISBN 1402719329. 96 p. Grades 6–9.

Nishida, Masaki. *Drawing Manga Dinosaurs* (How to Draw Manga). PowerKids Press, 2007. ISBN 9781404238459. 24 p. Grades 3–5.

Nishida, Masaki. *Drawing Manga Martial Arts Figures* (How to Draw Manga). PowerKids Press, 2007. ISBN 9781404238503. 24 p. Grades 3–5.

Nishida, Masaki. *Drawing Manga Medieval Castles and Knights* (How to Draw Manga). PowerKids Press, 2007. ISBN 9781404238497. 24 p. Grades 3–5.

Orr, Tamra. *Manga Artists* (Extreme Careers). Rosen, 2008. ISBN 9781404218543. 64 p. Grades 5–8.

Price, Pamela S. *Cool Comics: Creating Fun and Fascinating Collections* (Cool Collections). Checkerboard Library, 2006. ISBN 159679769X. 32 p. Grades 2–4.

Action Figures: Paintings of Fun, Daring and Adventure **by Bob Racza.**

Racza, Bob. *Action Figures: Paintings of Fun, Daring and Adventure*. Millbrook Press, 2009. ISBN 9780761341406. 32 p. Grades 1–6.

Ross, Kathy. *Crafts for Kids Who Are Learning about Dinosaurs* (Crafts for Kids Who Are Learning About). Millbrook Press, 2007. ISBN 978-0822568094. 48 p. Grades K–3.

Schwarz, Renee. *Wind Chimes and Whirligigs* (Kids Can Do It). Kids Can, 2007. ISBN 978-1553378686. 40 p. Grades 3–6.

Spilsbury, Richard. *Cartoons and Animation* (Art Off the Wall). Heinemann, 2006. ISBN 140348287X. 56 p. Grades 4–7.

Stephens, Jay. *Heroes! Draw Your Own Superheroes, Gadget Geeks & Other Do-Gooders*. Lark, 2007. ISBN 9781579909345. 64 p. Grades 4–6.

Stephens, Jay. *Monsters! Draw Your Own Mutants, Freaks & Creeps*. Lark, 2007. ISBN 9781579909352. 64 p. Grades 4–6.

Stephens, Jay. *Robots! Draw Your Own Androids, Cyborgs & Fighting Bots*. Lark, 2008. ISBN 157990937X. 64 p. Grades 3–6.

Svitil, Torene. *So You Want to Work in Animation & Special Effects?* (Careers in Film and Television). Enslow, 2007. ISBN 9780766027374. 128 p. Grades 5–10.

Svitil, Torene. *So You Want to Work in Set Design, Costuming, or Make-up?* (Careers in Film and Television). Enslow, 2008. ISBN 9780766027404. 28 p. Grades 4–6.

Entertainment

Abrams, Dennis. *Jay-Z* (Hip-Hop Stars). Chelsea House, 2007. ISBN 9780791095515. 112 p. Grades 6–12.

Abrams, Dennis. *Spike Lee*. Chelsea House, 2008. ISBN 9781604130430. 129 p. Grades 6–up.

Albert, Lisa Rondinelli. *So You Want to Be a Film or TV Actor?* (Careers in Film and Television). Enslow, 2008. ISBN 9780766027411. 128 p. Grades 4–6.

Andersen, Neil. *At the Controls: Questioning Video and Computer Games* (Fact Finders). Capstone Press, 2007. ISBN 9780736867689. 32 p. Grades 3–6.

So You Want to Be a Film or TV Actor? **by Lisa Rondinelli Albert.**

Brewer, Paul. *You Must Be Joking, Two! Even Cooler Jokes, Plus 11½ Tips for Laughing Yourself into Your Own Stand-up Comedy Routine.* Cricket, 2007. ISBN 9780812627527. 92 p. Grades 2–5.

Burlingame, Jeff. *Kurt Cobain: Oh Well, Whatever, Nevermind* (American Rebels). Enslow, 2006. ISBN 9780766024267. 160 p. Grades 8–11.

Cunningham, Kevin. *Video Game Designer* (Cool Careers). Cherry Lake, 2008. ISBN 9781602793057. 32 p. Grades 3–5.

Dougherty, Terri. *Tobey McGuire* (Modern Role Models). Mason Crest Publishers, 2008. ISBN 9781422205051. 64 p. Grades 6–up.

Dougherty, Terri. *Zac Efron* (People in the News). Lucent Books, 2007. ISBN 9781420500172. 104 p. Grades 6–10.

Duggleby, John. *Revolution: The Story of John Lennon* (Modern Music Masters). Morgan Reynolds, 2007. ISBN 1599350343. 176 p. Grades 6–up.

Dunkleberger, Amy. *So You Want to Be a Film or TV Director?* (Careers in Film and Television). Enslow, 2007. ISBN 0766027384. 128 p. Grades 6–9.

Dunkleberger, Amy. *So You Want to Be a Film or TV Screenwriter?* (Careers in Film and Television). Enslow, 2007. ISBN 0766026450. 128 p. Grades 6–9.

Edge, Laura B. *Steven Spielberg: Director of Blockbuster Films* (People to Know Today). Enslow, 2008. ISBN 9780766028883. 128 p. Grades 5–8.

Feinstein, Stephen. *Chris Rock* (African-American Heroes). Enslow, 2008. ISBN 9780766028944. 24 p. Grades 1–3.

Feinstein, Stephen. *Savion Glover* (African-American Heroes). Enslow, 2008. ISBN 9780766028975. 24 p. Grades 1–3.

**Hip-Hop and Street Dance
by Tamsin Fitzgerald.**

Fitzgerald, Tamsin. *Hip-Hop and Street Dance.* Heinemann, 2008. ISBN 9781432913786. 48 p. Grades 3–5.

Franks, Katie. *I Want to Be a Movie Star* (Dream Jobs). PowerKids Press, 2007. ISBN 9781404236196. 24 p. Grades 2–4.

Gorman, Jaqueline Laks. *Chris Rock* (Today's Superstars, Entertainment). Gareth Stevens, 2008. ISBN 9780836892352. 32 p. Grades 3–6.

Guzman, Lila. *George Lopez: Comedian and TV Star* (Famous Latinos). Enslow, 2006. ISBN 0766026442. 32 p. Grades 1–3.

Guzman, Lila, and Rick Guzman. *George Lopez: Latino King of Comedy* (Latino Biography Library). Enslow, 2008. ISBN 9780766029682. 128 p. Grades 6–up.

Hasday, Judy L. *Savion Glover: Entertainer: Legacy Edition* (Black Americans of Achievement). Chelsea House, 2006. ISBN 0791092232. 103 p. Grades 5–up.

Hirschmann, Kris. *Jonathan Ive: Designer of the iPod* (Innovators). KidHaven Press, 2007. ISBN 0737735333. 48 p. Grades 5–8.

Hirschmann, Kris. *LEGO Toys* (A Great Idea). Norwood House Press, 2008. ISBN 9781599531946. 48 p. Grades 4–6.

Hodge, Susie. *Latin and Ballroom Dance*. Heinemann, 2008. ISBN 9781432913779. 48 p. Grades 3–5.

Hyland, Tony. *Stunt Performers* (Extreme Jobs). Smart Apple Media, 2007. ISBN 9781583407394. 32 p. Grades 4–6.

Josephson, Judith Pinkerton. *Walt Disney: Genius of Entertainment* (People to Know Today). Enslow, 2006. ISBN 0766026248. 128 p. Grades 5–up.

Keedle, Jayne. *Zac Efron* (Today's Superstars, Entertainment). Gareth Stevens, 2008. ISBN 9780836892390. 32 p. Grades 3–6.

Lang, Lang, and Michael French. *Lang Lang: Playing with Flying Keys*. Delacorte, 2008. ISBN 9780385905640. 240 p. Grades 4–6.

Lee, Sally. *Freddie Prinze, Jr.: From Shy Guy to Movie Star* (Latino Biography Library). Enslow, 2008. ISBN 9780766029651. 128 p. Grades 6–up.

Lommel, Cookie. *Russell Simmons* (Hip-Hop Stars). Chelsea House, 2007. ISBN 9780791094679. 112 p. Grades 7–10.

Miller, Calvin Craig. *Reggae Poet: The Story of Bob Marley* (Modern Music Masters). Morgan Reynolds, 2007. ISBN 1599350718. 128 p. Grades 7–10.

Mitchell, Susan K. *Jack Black* (Today's Superstars, Entertainment). Gareth Stevens, 2008. ISBN 978-0836892376. 32 p. Grades 3–6.

Neimark, Anne. *Johnny Cash* (Up Close). Viking, 2007. ISBN 0670062154. 208 p. Grades 5–up.

Nichols, Travis. *Punk Rock Etiquette: The Ultimate How-to Guide for DIY, Punk, Indie, and Underground Bands*. Roaring Brook Press, 2008. ISBN 9781596434158. 144 p. Grades 8–up.

Rauf, Don. *Computer Game Designer* (Virtual Apprentice). Ferguson, 2008. ISBN 9780816067541. 64 p. Grades 6–9.

Schweitzer, Karen. *Soulja Boy, Tell 'Em* (Modern Role Models). Mason Crest Publishers, 2008. ISBN 9781422205099. 64 p. Grades 6–up.

Solway, Andrew. *African and Asian Dance*. Heinemann, 2008. ISBN 9781432913793. 48 p. Grades 3–5.

Punk Rock Etiquette: The Ultimate How-to Guide for DIY, Punk, Indie, and Underground Bands by Travis Nichols. Jacket shown with permission from Roaring Brook Press

Spitz, Bob. *Yeah! Yeah! Yeah! The Beatles, Beatlemania, and the Music That Changed the World.* Little, Brown, 2007. ISBN 031611555X. 24 p. Grades 7–10.

Swaine, Meg. *Career Building Through Interactive Online Games* (Digital Career Building). Rosen, 2007. ISBN 9781404219465. 64 p. Grades 7–up.

Tieck, Sarah. *Shia LaBeouf* (Big Buddy Biographies). Buddy Books, 2008. ISBN 9781604531237. 32 p. Grades K–3.

Todd, Anne M. *Jamie Foxx: Entertainer* (Black Americans of Achievement). Chelsea House Publications, 2008. ISBN 9781604130003. 106 p. Grades 6–up.

Trachtenberg, Martha P. *Bono: Rock Star Activist* (People to Know Today). Enslow, 2008. ISBN 9780766026957. 128 p. Grades 5–up.

Willett, Edward. *Jimi Hendrix: Kiss the Sky* (American Rebels). Enslow, 2006. ISBN 0766024490. 160 p. Grades 5–up.

Wimmer, Teresa. *The Beatles: Sgt. Pepper's Lonely Hearts Club Band* (What in the World?). Creative Education, 2008. ISBN 9781583416518. 48 p. Grades 4–6.

Woog, Adam. *YouTube* (Great Idea). Norwood House Press, 2008. ISBN 978-1599531984. 48 p. Grades 4–6.

Wyckoff, Edwin Brit. *Electric Guitar Man: The Genius of Les Paul* (Great Inventor Biographies). Enslow, 2008. ISBN 9780766028470. 32 p. Grades 5–8.

Acknowledgments

CHAPTER 1

Cover from *At Gleason's Gym* by Ted Lewin. Roaring Brook Press, 2007. Jacket shown with permission from Roaring Brook Press.

Cover from *Manny Ramirez and the Boston Red Sox: 2004 World Series* by Michael Sandler. Bearport Publishing, 2008. Reprinted with permission.

Cover from *Knockout! A Photobiography of Boxer Joe Louis* by George Sullivan. National Geographic, 2009. Reprinted with permission of the National Geographic Society.

Cover from *Football Skills: How to Play Like a Pro* by Marty Gitlin. Enslow, 2008. Copyright © Enslow Publishers, Inc.

Cover from *Hockey Skills: How to Play Like a Pro* by James MacDonald. Enslow, 2008. Copyright © Enslow Publishers, Inc.

Cover from *Matt Hasselbeck* by Michael Sandler. Bearport Publishing, 2009. Reprinted with permission.

Cover from *Swish: The Quest for Basketball's Perfect Shot* by Mark Stewart and Mike Kennedy. Copyright © Millbrook Press, 2009. Reprinted with permission.

CHAPTER 2

Cover from *All Stations! Distress! April 15, 1912: The Day the* Titanic *Sank* by Don Brown. Roaring Brook Press, 2008. Jacket shown with permission from Roaring Brook Press.

Cover from *Volcanoes* by Judy and Dennis Fradin. National Geographic, 2007. Reprinted with permission of the National Geographic Society.

Cover from *The Mysteries of Beethoven's Hair* by Russell Martin and Lydia Nibley. Charlesbridge, 2009. Used with permission by Charlesbridge Publishing, Inc.

Cover from *Written in Bone: Buried Lives in Jamestown and Colonial Maryland* by Sally Walker. Copyright © Carolrhoda Books, 2009. Reprinted with permission.

Cover from *Earthquakes* by Judy and Dennis Fradin. National Geographic, 2008. Reprinted with permission of the National Geographic Society.

Cover from *Into the Fire: Volcanologists* by Paul Mason. Heinemann, 2007. Reprinted with permission.

Cover from *The Mystery of Life on Other Planets* by Chris Oxlade. Heinemann, 2008. Reprinted with permission.

CHAPTER 3

Cover from *The Story Behind Toilets* by Elizabeth Raum. Heinemann, 2009. Reprinted with permission.

Cover from *Sewers and the Rats That Love Them: The Disgusting Story Behind Where It All Goes* by Kelly Regan Barnhill. Capstone Press, 2008. Reprinted with permission.

Cover from *Hawk & Drool: Gross Stuff in Your Mouth* by Sandy Donovan. Copyright © Millbrook Press, 2009. Reprinted with permission.

Cover from *Baby Bug Dishes* by Meish Goldish. Bearport Publishing, 2009. Reprinted with permission.

Cover from *Bug-a-licious* by Meish Goldish. Bearport Publishing, 2009. Reprinted with permission.

Cover from *Disgusting Hagfish* by Meish Goldish. Bearport Publishing, 2008. Reprinted with permission.

Cover from *Spider-tizers and Other Creepy Treats* by Meish Goldish. Bearport Publishing, 2009. Reprinted with permission.

Cover from *Getting to Know Your Toilet: the Disgusting Story Behind Your Home's Strangest Feature* by Connie Colwell Miller. Capstone Press, 2008. Reprinted with permission.

CHAPTER 4

Cover from *Smelly Stink Bugs* by Meish Goldish. Bearport Publishing, 2008. Reprinted with permission.

Cover from *Sneaky, Spinning Baby Spiders* by Sandra Markle.

Cover from *Poison Dart Frogs Up Close* by Carmen Bredeson. Enslow, 2008. Copyright © Enslow Publishers, Inc.

Cover from *Hairy Tarantulas* by Kathryn Camisa. Bearport Publishing, 2008. Reprinted with permission.

Cover from *Deadly Praying Mantises* by Meish Goldish. Bearport Publishing, 2008. Reprinted with permission.

Cover from *Anacondas* by Joanne Mattern. Capstone Press, 2008. Reprinted with permission.

Cover from *Cobras* by Van Wallach. Capstone Press, 2008. Reprinted with permission.

CHAPTER 5

Cover from *Dinosaurs in Your Backyard* by Hugh Brewster. Copyright © Abrams Books for Young Readers, 2009.

Cover from *The Search for Antarctic Dinosaurs* by Sally Walker. Copyright © Millbrook Press, 2007. Reprinted with permission.

Cover from *Reign of the Sea Dragons* by Sneed B. Collard III. Charlesbridge, 2008. Used with permission by Charlesbridge Publishing, Inc.

Cover from *Savage Slashers* by Natalie Lunis and Nancy White. Bearport Publishing, 2008. Reprinted with permission.

Cover from *Dinosaur Hunters: Paleontologists* by Louise Spilsbury and Richard Spilsbury. Heinemann, 2007. Reprinted with permission.

CHAPTER 6

Cover from *Remember Valley Forge: Patriots, Tories, and Redcoats Tell Their Stories* by Thomas B. Allen. National Geographic, 2007. Reprinted with permission of the National Geographic Society.

Cover from *Let it Begin Here! April 19, 1775: The Day the American Revolution Began* by Don Brown. Roaring Brook Press, 2008. Jacket shown with permission from Roaring Brook Press.

Cover from *A Boy Named Beckoning: The True Story of Dr. Carlos Montezuma, Native American Hero* by Gina Capaldi. Copyright © Carolrhoda Books, 2008. Reprinted with permission.

Cover from *Duel! Burr and Hamilton's Deadly War of Words* by Dennis Brindell Fradin. Walker Books, 2008. Reprinted with permission of Walker books for Young Readers.

Cover from *Ain't Nothing but a Man: My Quest to Find the Real John Henry* by Scott Reynolds Nelson. National Geographic, 2008. Reprinted with permission of the National Geographic Society.

Cover from *Bad News for Outlaws: The Remarkable Life of Bass Reeves, Deputy U.S. Marshal* by Vaunda Micheaux Nelson. Copyright © Carolrhoda Books, 2009. Reprinted with permission.

Cover from *Lincoln Through the Lens: How Photography Revealed and Shaped an Extraordinary Life* by Martin W. Sandler. Walker Books, 2008. Reprinted with permission of Walker Books for Young Readers.

Cover from *King George: What Was His Problem? Everything Your Schoolbooks Didn't Tell You About the American Revolution* by Steve Sheinkin. Roaring Brook Press, 2008. Jacket shown with permission from Roaring Brook Press.

Cover from *Daniel Boone's Great Escape* by Michael Spradlin. Walker Books, 2008. Reprinted with permission of Walker Books for Young Readers.

Cover from *Jesse James* by Carl R. Green. Enslow, 2008. Copyright © Enslow Publishers, Inc.

Cover from *The Revolutionary War Begins: Would You Join the Fight?* by Elaine Landau. Enslow, 2008. Copyright © Enslow Publishers, Inc.

Cover from *How to Get Rich on the Oregon Trail: My Adventures among Cows, Crooks & Heroes on the Road to Fame & Fortune by William Reed, Age 15* by Tod Olson. National Geographic, 2009. Reprinted with permission of the National Geographic Society.

CHAPTER 7

Cover from *Pocket Babies And Other Amazing Marsupials* by Sneed B. Collard III. Copyright © Darby Creek Publishing, 2007. Reprinted with permission.

Cover from *Teeth* by Sneed B. Collard III. Charlesbridge, 2008. Used with permission by Charlesbridge Publishing, Inc.

Cover from *African Critters* by Robert B. Haas. National Geographic, 2008. Reprinted with permission of the National Geographic Society.

Cover from *Being Caribou: Five Months on Foot with a Caribou Herd* by Karsten Heuer. Walker Books, 2007. Reprinted with permission of Walker Books for Young Readers.

Cover from *Tough, Toothy Baby Sharks* by Sandra Markle. Walker Books, 2007. Reprinted with permission of Walker Books for Young Readers.

Cover from *When the Wolves Returned: Restoring Nature's Balance in Yellowstone* by Dorothy Hinshaw Patent. Walker Books, 2008. Reprinted with permission of Walker Books for Young Readers.

Cover from *Bubble Homes and Fish Farts* by Fiona Bayrock. Charlesbridge, 2009. Used with permission by Charlesbridge Publishing, Inc.

Cover from *Top 10 Small Mammals for Kids* by Ann Gaines. Enslow, 2008. Copyright © Enslow Publishers, Inc.

Cover from *Face to Face with Lions* by Dereck Joubert and Beverly Joubert. National Geographic, 2008. Reprinted with permission of the National Geographic Society.

Cover from *Two Bobbies: A True Story of Hurricane Katrina, Friendship, and Survival* by Kirby Larson and Mary Nethery. Walker Books, 2008. Reprinted with permission of Walker Books for Young Readers.

Cover from *Finding Home* by Sandra Markle. Charlesbridge, 2008. Used with permission by Charlesbridge Publishing, Inc.

Cover from *How Many Baby Pandas?* by Sandra Markle. Walker Books, 2009. Reprinted with permission of Walker Books for Young Readers.

Cover from *Weddell Seal: Fat and Happy* by Joyce L. Markovics. Bearport Publishing, 2008. Reprinted with permission.

Cover from *Animals With Wicked Weapons: Stingers, Barbs, and Quills* by Susan K. Mitchell. Enslow, 2008. Copyright © Enslow Publishers, Inc.

Cover from *Face to Face With Gorillas* by Michael Nichols. National Geographic, 2009. Reprinted with permission of the National Geographic Society.

Cover from *Hammerhead Shark* by Deborah Nuzzolo. Capstone Press, 2008. Reprinted with permission.

Cover from *Secret of the Puking Penguins . . . and More!* by Ana María Rodriguez. Enslow, 2008. Copyright © Enslow Publishers, Inc.

CHAPTER 8

Cover from *Life on Earth—and Beyond: An Astrobiologist's Quest* by Pamela S. Turner. Charlesbridge, 2008. Used with permission by Charlesbridge Publishing, Inc.

Cover from *11 Planets: A New View of the Solar System* by David A. Aguilar. National Geographic, 2008. Reprinted with permission of the National Geographic Society.

Cover from *Your Skin Holds You In: A Book About Your Skin* by Becky Baines. National Geographic, 2008. Reprinted with permission of the National Geographic Society.

Cover from *Beyond: A Solar System Voyage* by Michael Benson. Copyright © Abrams Books for Young Readers, 2009.

Cover from *Sound Projects with a Music Lab You Can Build* by Robert Gardner. Enslow, 2008. Copyright © Enslow Publishers, Inc.

Cover from *Fighting Crime* by Ian Graham. Heinemann, 2008. Reprinted with permission.

Cover from *Magnets* by Charlotte Guillain. Heinemann, 2008. Reprinted with permission.

Cover from *The Human Brain: Inside Your Body's Control Room* by Kathleen Simpson. National Geographic, 2009. Reprinted with permission of the National Geographic Society.

Cover from *Secrets of the Deep: Marine Biologists* by Mike Unwin. Heinemann, 2007. Reprinted with permission.

CHAPTER 9

Cover from *Pararescuemen in Action* by Michael Sandler. Bearport Publishing, 2008. Reprinted with permission.

Cover from *Texas Rangers: Legendary Lawmen* by Michael Spradlin. Walker Books, 2008. Reprinted with permission of Walker Books for Young Readers.

Cover from *The U.S. Air Force* by Matt Doeden. Capstone Press, 2008. Reprinted with permission.

Cover from *Weapons of Ancient Times* by Matt Doeden. Capstone Press, 2008. Reprinted with permission.

Cover from *Off-Road Vehicles* by Ian Graham. Heinemann, 2008. Reprinted with permission.

Cover from *Green Berets in Action* by Marc Tyler Nobleman. Bearport Publishing, 2008. Reprinted with permission.

Cover from *Delta Force in Action* by Gail Blasser Riley. Bearport Publishing, 2008. Reprinted with permission.

Cover from *NASCAR Designed to Win* by Mark Stewart and Mike Kennedy. Copyright © Lerner Publications, 2007. Reprinted with permission.

CHAPTER 10

Cover from *Conquest! Can You Build a Roman City?* by Julia Bruce. Enslow, 2009. Copyright © Enslow Publishers, Inc.

Cover from *Siege! Can You Capture a Castle?* by Julia Bruce. Enslow, 2009. Copyright © Enslow Publishers, Inc.

Cover from *Real Pirates: The Untold Story of the Whydah from Slave Ship to Pirate Ship* by Barry Clifford. National Geographic, 2008. Reprinted with permission of the National Geographic Society.

Cover from *King Tut's Tomb* by Amanda Doering Tourville. Capstone Press, 2008. Reprinted with permission.

Cover from *Medieval Castles* by Jim Whiting. Capstone Press, 2009. Reprinted with permission.

CHAPTER 11

Cover from *Amazing Magic Tricks, Beginner Level* by Norm Barnhart. Capstone Press, 2008. Reprinted with permission.

Cover from *Witchcraft on Trial: From the Salem Witch Hunts to the Crucible* by Maurene Hinds. Enslow, 2009. Copyright © Enslow Publishers, Inc.

Cover from *Robbery File: The Museum Heist* by Amanda Howard. Bearport Publishing, 2007. Reprinted with permission.

Cover from *A Guys' Guide to Anger/A Girls' Guide to Anger* by Hal Marcovitz. Enslow, 2008. Copyright © Enslow Publishers, Inc.

Cover from *Creepy Castles* by Sarah Parvis. Bearport Publishing, 2008. Reprinted with permission.

Cover from *Abandoned Insane Asylums* by Dinah Williams. Bearport Publishing, 2008. Reprinted with permission.

CHAPTER 12

Cover from *Keep Your Eye on the Kid: The Early Years of Buster Keaton* by Catherine Brighton. Roaring Brook Press, 2008. Jacket shown with permission from Roaring Brook Press.

Cover from *Jack Gantos: An Author Kids Love* by Michelle Parker-Rock. Enslow, 2008. Copyright © Enslow Publishers, Inc.

Cover from *The Day-Glo Brothers: The True Story of Bob and Joe Switzer's Bright Ideas and Brand-New Colors* by Barton Christ. Charlesbridge, 2009. Used with permission by Charlesbridge Publishing, Inc.

Cover from *Ralph Masiello's Ancient Egypt Drawing Book* by Ralph Masiello. Charlesbridge, 2008. Used with permission by Charlesbridge Publishing, Inc.

Cover from *Action Figures: Paintings of Fun, Daring and Adventure* by Bob Racza. Copyright © Millbrook Press, 2009. Reprinted with permission.

Cover from *So You Want to Be a Film or TV Actor?* by Lisa Rondinelli Albert. Enslow, 2008. Copyright © Enslow Publishers, Inc.

Cover from *Hip-Hop and Street Dance* by Tamsin Fitzgerald. Heinemann, 2008. Reprinted with permission.

Cover from *Punk Rock Etiquette: The Ultimate How-to Guide for DIY, Punk, Indie, and Underground Bands* by Travis Nichols. Roaring Brook Press, 2008. Jacket shown with permission from Roaring Brook Press.

Author Index

Title Index

About the Authors

Kathleen A. Baxter served as the Coordinator of Children's Services in the Anoka County Library in suburban Minneapolis for over 25 years. In addition to five previous *Gotcha* books, she has written "The Nonfiction Booktalker" column for *School Library Journal* since 1996. She has presented at hundreds of national and state library and reading conferences all over the country. Kathleen has also taught classes in children's literature, served on the 2001 Newbery Committee, consults for publishers, and has presented all-day seminars on children's books for the Bureau of Education and Research. Visit her online at http://www.kathleenbaxter.com.

Marcia Agness Kochel has been a school media specialist in grades K–12 in North Carolina, Indiana, Minnesota, and Georgia. She reviews nonfiction books for *School Library Journal*, served on the 2006 Sibert Award Committee, was a judge for the 2006 Children's and YA Bloggers' Literary Awards (The Cybils) for middle grade and YA nonfiction, and blogs about middle school books at http://omsbookblog. blogspot.com/. She has an undergraduate degree from The College of William and Mary in Virginia and an MLS from The University of North Carolina at Chapel Hill. She is currently the head media specialist at The Galloway School in Atlanta.